MOST EVIL

MOST EVIL

AVENGER, ZODIAC, AND THE FURTHER SERIAL MURDERS OF DR. GEORGE HILL HODEL

STEVE HODEL

WITH RALPH PEZZULLO

DUTTON

DUTTON
Published by Penguin Group (USA) Inc.
375 Hudson Street, New York, New York 10014, U.S.A.
Penguin Group (Canada), 90 Eglinton Avenue East, Suite 700, Toronto, Ontario M4P 2Y3,
Canada (a division of Pearson Penguin Canada Inc.); Penguin Books Ltd, 80 Strand, London
WC2R 0RL, England; Penguin Ireland, 25 St Stephen's Green, Dublin 2, Ireland (a division of
Penguin Books Ltd); Penguin Group (Australia), 250 Camberwell Road, Camberwell, Victoria
3124, Australia (a division of Pearson Australia Group Pty Ltd); Penguin Books India Pvt Ltd, 11
Community Centre, Panchsheel Park, New Delhi—110 017, India; Penguin Group (NZ), 67
Apollo Drive, Rosedale, North Shore 0632, New Zealand (a division of Pearson New Zealand
Ltd); Penguin Books (South Africa) (Pty) Ltd, 24 Sturdee Avenue, Rosebank, Johannesburg
2196, South Africa

Penguin Books Ltd, Registered Offices: 80 Strand, London WC2R 0RL, England

Published by Dutton, a member of Penguin Group (USA) Inc.

First printing, September 2009
1   3   5   7   9   10   8   6   4   2

 REGISTERED TRADEMARK—MARCA REGISTRADA

LIBRARY OF CONGRESS CATALOGING-IN-PUBLICATION DATA
has been applied for.

ISBN 978-0-525-95132-2

Printed in the United States of America
Set in Minion

For the victims, living and dead

Contents

Introduction

My father, Dr. George Hill Hodel, was a monster.

While a handsome, successful doctor living the good life in 1940s Hollywood, surrounded by beautiful women and esteemed artists such as Man Ray, John Huston, Henry Miller, and others, he committed a series of heinous murders. One of his victims was a former girlfriend named Elizabeth Short—cast in infamy as the Black Dahlia.

The photos of her bisected, exsanguinated body lying in the weeds near Thirty-ninth and Norton have become a grisly centerpiece of Hollywood noir history. Sixty years later people are still shocked by the premeditated evil of the crime. To look at the photos is to realize that you're staring into the abyss. One can't help but ask (as I did): Who was the sicko who cut this poor woman in half? And what the hell was going on in his head?

I was just a kid. Five years old at the time of the murder. Eight when my father abruptly closed his business and fled the country for Asia. He'd been tipped off by friends in the LAPD.

Nobody told me that Dad was the chief suspect in a series of killings in a twenty-mile radius of our house on Franklin Street. Or that detectives from the Los Angeles District Attorney's Office had gone so far as to bug his bedroom and home office. Or that they were about to arrest him when he split.

I grew up innocent of my father's dark secrets. Then, irony of ironies: I chose to become a homicide detective. My first wife suggested it. I found out later she'd been my father's girlfriend.

Did she seduce me at nineteen as a form of revenge on Dad for dumping her? Probably. Did she want me to become a cop so I'd discover the horrific deeds committed by my father, ones that she only suspected? Maybe. I can't ask her now. She's dead.

I worked the Hollywood beat for twenty-four years, in the same neighborhood where I grew up—my father's killing ground in the 1940s. Over the decades, I had occasional, brief contact with Dad, who was living abroad and had remade himself into a very successful international marketing executive based in Manila. He was a sophisticated man of the world with a genius IQ—my mother claimed it was one point higher than Einstein's.

I retired in 1986. Dad died thirteen years later at the age of ninety-one.

I knew very little about my father when his ashes were scattered near the Golden Gate Bridge. Naturally, I was curious about the man he had been. I wanted to know more. Gentle inquiries started with a book of photographs he kept with him until his death. Two of them reminded me of a TV movie I'd seen about the Black Dahlia starring Lucie Arnaz.

My investigation widened and drew me into increasingly lurid and frightening territory. The result: my book *Black Dahlia Avenger: A Genius for Murder*.[1]

Then in 2003, Los Angeles head deputy district attorney Stephen Kay reviewed the evidence I'd collected and declared the Black Dahlia murder "solved." Old District Attorney files and forensics told the story. Only after delving into my father's dark mind was I able to explain why he posed Elizabeth Short's body the way he did and carved the ghastly smile into her face.

George Hodel did nothing by accident. He lived his life as a bizarre game that trumped even those of his hero, the Marquis de Sade, taunting and outwitting the police, seducing and brutally murdering innocent women.

He didn't stop in 1950. Nor did he begin in the '40s. Nor was Elizabeth Short just an ex-girlfriend.

---

1   Arcade, 2003; updated by HarperCollins in 2006.

I know now that my father was also responsible for a series of infamous murders in Chicago (where he was known for a time as the Lipstick Killer), Manila (where the local press dubbed him the Jigsaw Murderer), and the Bay Area of California (where he called himself Zodiac).

It's a bizarre, terrifying, and surreal story that will alter criminal history, exonerate the innocent, and change the way we think about the motives and signatures of serial killers. Hang on.

Steve Hodel

December 2008

PART ONE

DR. GEORGE HILL HODEL

Chapter One

The most fortunate of persons is he who has the most means to satisfy his vagaries.

Marquis de Sade

Who was George Hodel really? My half-sister, Tamar—who over the course of her fascinating, peripatetic life befriended many illustrious men, including Lenny Bruce, Jim Morrison, Harry Belafonte, Otis Redding, John Phillips, and others—describes him as the most powerful, intelligent, handsome man she's ever known. This despite the fact that he taught her how to perform oral sex at eleven, had sex with her at fourteen in the presence of three other adults, and branded her a liar the rest of her life.

Tamar's best friend, Michelle Phillips of the Mamas & the Papas, remembers opening a hotel room door in San Francisco in 1967 and seeing George for the first time. "I almost fainted," she said. "The aura of evil he gave off was so strong and palpable, it almost knocked me off my feet. That's the first and only time anything like that has ever happened to me."

As Tamar tells the story, George entered the Mamas & the Papas' suite at the St. Francis Hotel with two beautiful, young Asian women and immediately took over, ordering around the waiters and telling the band what they should and shouldn't eat before a concert. Tamar likens him to the charismatic ballet impresario Boris Lermontov in the movie *The Red Shoes*—impeccable clothes, sophisticated European manners, a deep, cultivated voice.

Later that evening a hash pipe was passed. Dad didn't partake. Tamar, who knew he'd smoked in the past, asked one of his Asian companions why. "Before when he smoked hash, he made me lock him in his bathroom," the young woman explained. "He always made me lock him in there and told me not to let him out. George said that when he smokes, sometimes he does terrible things. He would make me lock him in the bathroom and he would cry and stay there all night."

Dad left Los Angeles in 1950 after the very public incest trial involving his relationship with Tamar—he was declared innocent—and thereafter blew into town every six months or so unannounced. My brothers and I would be summoned to the lobby of some glamorous L.A. hotel and made to wait hours for the privilege of sharing a few minutes with the great man, who was on some important business and usually had to run to an urgent meeting. During one such visit he presented me with a Tinkertoy set for my birthday. I was sixteen years old.

In a drunken rage, my mother had once called him "a monster." She said, "He's a terrible man and he's done terrible things!" The next day she denied it.

After forty years of living the life of an expatriate in Asia, Dad retired to San Francisco and moved into a modern apartment overlooking the bay with his fourth wife, June. Once when I visited, I brought a loaf of bread but couldn't find a knife in the kitchen. When I asked June for one, she answered, "No. No. The great man doesn't allow any knives in the house."

Tamar wanted all her life to confront Dad with the painful truth of who he really was so he might begin to save his soul. But she never did. Why? "I was afraid of what he might do to me," she explained. "I knew he could kill me."

In 1969 when George was in town on business, he met a pregnant Tamar for lunch at a Beverly Hills hotel. As they passed through the lobby, Dad stopped and pointed to a pattern in the carpet. "What does that remind you of?" he asked.

"I don't know," Tamar answered. "Some kind of flower or something. Maybe rhododendrons."

"Look again," George said, tracing the outlines with the toe of his shoe. "It's a vagina and lips."

He then stomped hard in the middle of the design and asked, "Did that hurt?"

Tamar learned later that while she was in bed resting, days before the birth of her third child, George took her thirteen-year-old daughter, Deborah, out to dinner. Years later, Deborah confessed that while they were eating, she became groggy and passed out. She came to on a bed in a hotel room, completely nude with her legs spread open. Looking up, she saw her grandfather snapping pictures.

Joe Barrett, who knew Dad in the 1940s when Joe was a young artist renting a room in our house on Franklin Avenue, said he liked my father and described him as "surrounded by people, but close to no one." They spent hours shooting the breeze in my dad's office. "George was brilliant," Joe remembered, "but not original. I think that bothered him."

Dad's last instructions: "I do not wish to have funeral services of any kind. There is to be no meeting or speeches or music and no gravestone or tablet. I direct that my physical remains be cremated and that my ashes be scattered over the ocean."

Naïve about much of his terrible history and about many of these family legends, I spent a good deal of time with Dad toward the end of his life. We became friends, to a point, but he never really opened up, and I know now that I didn't really know him.

Most of what I've learned about my father came after his death in 1999. Up until then, except for a couple of shadows, he seemed to have lived a full, privileged, and highly productive life. But in order to fully understand this complicated man and the activities he'd kept hidden for so long, I have to start again at the beginning, with the official narrative of his life.

George Hill Hodel entered this world in Los Angeles on October 10, 1907, the only son of well-educated, Russian-born parents. His mother, Esther, a smart, no-nonsense woman, had worked as a dentist in Paris before emigrating to the United States in 1905. His father, George, was a banker who had escaped from mandatory military conscription in Russia by changing his last name from Goldgefter to Hodel and posing as a wealthy traveler on a temporary visit to see his ailing grandmother. With expensive luggage and his first-class train ticket in hand, he managed to cross the Polish border, then on to Paris and freedom.

Despite the fact that they settled in South Pasadena, French was the primary language spoken at home. The house built in 1920 was a hand-some estate designed by Russian architect Alexander Zelenko in the style of a Swiss chalet. It included a detached guesthouse, where George Jr. pursued his intellectual and musical studies without distraction.

His parents had reason to believe their son was special. At an early age, tests showed that little George had a genius IQ of 186. At age six, he was identified as a musical prodigy. By age nine "Georgie" was playing solo piano concerts at Los Angeles's Shrine Auditorium, and even the great Russian composer Sergei Rachmaninoff traveled to my grandparents' house in Pasadena, accompanied by the Russian minister of culture, to hear him play.

LOS ANGELES EVENIN(

BOY OF NINE CHIEF SOLOIST AT SHRINE HOLIDAY EXERCISES

George Hodel, young musician who will perform at Fall of Bastile celebration

1.1 **George Hodel, 1917**

In 1921, at age thirteen, the boy genius's scholastic test scores were the highest ever recorded in California's public school history. Following his graduation from South Pasadena High School at fourteen, he entered the California Institute of Technology to pursue studies in chemical engineering. George Hodel wasn't your average kid.

A year into his studies at Caltech, another precocious tendency reared its head. The sixteen-year-old had an affair with a faculty member's wife and got her pregnant. The woman left her husband and moved east, where she had the baby—a girl aptly named Folly. It's here that my father's life seemed to take a rebellious left. Though Caltech administrators were able to keep the sex scandal from becoming public, they quickly and quietly demanded my father's withdrawal from the university. Father complied, and after drifting for a year or two, at age seventeen, was able to obtain fake ID showing him to be twenty-one. After obtaining a chauffeur's license, he immediately got a job hacking for the Los Angeles Yellow Cab Company at night.

But his real interest seemed to be the crime reporting he did for the *Los Angeles Record*, which in the 1920s was one of Los Angeles's major newspapers.

Prohibition was in full swing, and Dad would ride along with the LAPD vice squad officers and follow them in at midnight as they kicked down the doors to South Central speakeasies. He was there to record the lurid details as pimps, prostitutes, and johns—including the occasional "slumming" Beverly Hills couple and maybe the odd Superior Court judge—were hauled off. The precocious kid from Pasadena was now L.A.'s youngest crime reporter, rubbing shoulders with hoods, murderers, and corrupt officials.

The latter, like oranges, seemed to grow on trees.

Among my dad's cohorts was a lawyer named Kent Kane Parrot, who reputedly owned most of the officers on the Los Angeles Police Department.

This murky moral setting served as fodder for his best friend and future film director John Huston. One of their pals was a brooding artist named Fred Sexton, who later sculpted the bird that was fought over by Sydney Greenstreet, Humphrey Bogart, and Peter Lorre in *The Maltese Falcon*.

They acted like young existential bohemians in the '20s, smoking hashish and frequenting opium dens in Chinatown. It was a perfect set of conditions in which to launch a literary magazine. George's avant-garde rag was called *Fantasia*.

In a December 9, 1925, article in the *Los Angeles Evening Herald*, drama critic Ted Le Berthon provided his readers with an up-close-and-personal look at George Hodel. In his article "The Clouded Past of a Poet," he described the young writer/editor as "tall, olive-skinned, with wavy black hair and a strong, bold nose. His eyes are large, brown, somnolent." According to Le Berthon, "George drowned himself at times in an ocean of deep dreams. Only part of him seemed present. He would muse, standing before one in a black, flowered dressing gown lined with scarlet silk, oblivious to one's presence. Suddenly, though, his eyes would flare up like signal lights and he would say, 'The formless fastidiousness of perfumes in a seventeenth century boudoir is comparable to my mind in the presence of twilight.'"

Heady stuff. George dated an attractive fellow bohemian by the name of Emilia Lawson. His buddy John Huston squired a slim, petite intellectual named Dorothy Harvey. When John and Dorothy ran off to Greenwich Village, New York, to get married, George and Emilia opened a bookstore in downtown L.A.

Then for reasons unexplained (maybe it's because he'd just turned twenty), George veered more mainstream. First, he took a job as a radio host for the *Southern California Gas Company's Music Hour*, introducing classical music listeners to everything from Beethoven to Gilbert and Sullivan. Then, he and Emilia and their newborn son (named Duncan) moved to San Francisco, where George enrolled at the University of California, Berkeley, and pursued a course of study in pre-med.

Berkeley led to medical school at nearby University of California, San Francisco. He supported his young family by driving a cab until he and Emilia landed something far better: They were hired by the *San Francisco Chronicle* to write a weekly column called "Abroad in San Francisco."

It would seem as though George had a full plate. But somehow he found the time to get involved with another woman: Dorothy Anthony, a young art student/model who bore him a third child, a daughter named Tamar.

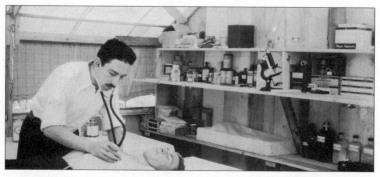

1.2 **Young Dr. Hodel, circa 1937, Santa Fe, New Mexico**

Medical school led to an internship at San Francisco General Hospital, then his first doctoring gig with the New Mexico State Department of Public Health attending to the medical needs of the Hopi and Navajo reservations and serving as a surgeon at the Civilian Conservation Corps (CCC) logging camp.

1.3 Me (far left) and my brothers Mike and Kelvin at the Franklin House, 1946

By the early '40s, he'd returned to L.A., reunited with Dorothy Harvey Huston, recently divorced from John, married her, and quickly had four sons: Michael, John, me, and Kelvin.[2] He was now the senior VD control officer for Los Angeles County and also operated his own private practice specializing in the treatment of venereal diseases in downtown L.A.

An esteemed, well-heeled physician with a wide range of interests,

2 John, my older twin brother, entered the world twenty minutes ahead of me. We were both premature, with exceptionally low birth weights (three pounds) and remained in incubators under twenty-four-hour observation. John died two weeks after delivery, due to "failure to thrive."

my father cultivated friendships with surrealist artist Man Ray, author Henry Miller, Beat poet Kenneth Rexroth, and others. I remember the mid-1940s as a fun time as a young boy, playing with my brothers and meeting my parents' glamorous friends at the architecturally distinctive John Sowden House on Franklin Avenue in Hollywood.

1.4 **Dr. George Hodel purchased the Lloyd Wright–designed "Franklin House" in 1945**

It wasn't until 1999 that I discovered my mom and dad had actually divorced in 1944. Nor did I have the slightest inkling that the LAPD was investigating my father in connection with the death of his twenty-seven-year-old girlfriend and secretary, Ruth Spaulding, who died from an overdose of barbiturates on May 9, 1945.

I knew from family lore that Dad had joined the United Nations Relief and Rehabilitation Agency (UNRRA) and had become a military officer assigned to a billet in China at the end of World War II, but did not know of the details.

I have since discovered that in August 1945, while the LAPD was actively investigating George Hodel as a possible murder suspect in the death of Ruth Spaulding, George made the application to UNRRA. In his application he requested to be stationed "anywhere overseas, but would prefer Asia." He was accepted and after conducting some research at the "home office" in Washington, D.C., during the fall and winter of 1945, he was assigned as "chief regional medical officer" to Hankow, China. He arrived in early February 1946 and was given the honorary rank of lieutenant general and assigned a military jeep, complete with a three-star flag, a driver, his own personal cook, and two administrative aides. Just seven months later, in September 1946, Father unexpectedly resigned his commission and resumed his medical practice in Los Angeles.

From my seven-year-old perspective, my dad, who had recently returned from China, was extremely cool. He sometimes drove a military jeep; was tall, suave, and good-looking; and had an endless stream of beautiful young women lined up outside his home-office waiting to see him. Sure, every once in a while he took me down to the basement to whale on my backside with his belt. But I knew I had it coming. He'd caught me smoking a cigarette on the front steps.

There were multiple compensations, such as spying on my fourteen-year-old half-sister, Tamar, and other young ladies sunning themselves nude in the courtyard. Life with Dad was good.

1.5 **Tamar Hodel, age sixteen**

Then suddenly, in 1950, just before my ninth birthday, the curtain came down. Mom packed my brothers and me into a friend's pickup and drove us away from Hollywood. I didn't learn the reason until ten years later, when I found out that my father had been accused of committing incest with Tamar.

The details were incredibly lurid, especially for the 1940s. Dad had sexual intercourse with his fourteen-year-old daughter in front of his friend Fred Sexton and two other adult women. After an abortion, Tamar ran away and was found by the police. During her detention and follow-up interview with LAPD Juvenile detectives, Tamar disclosed the details of the 1949 sex acts with her father, as well as the fact that he taught her how to perform oral sex several years prior, when she was just eleven.

Due to his high position as L.A. County's chief VD control officer, Father's 1949 arrest by the LAPD for child molestation and incest obviously made for front-page news.

At a preliminary hearing, witnesses, including Dad's lifelong friend Fred Sexton and the two women who had been present, testified to the facts surrounding the charges and testified to observing the sex acts. Father was "held to answer," and a full jury trial was scheduled for December 1949.

Father immediately hired L.A.'s two top-gun criminal defense attorneys, Jerry Giesler and Robert Neeb, to prepare his criminal defense. "Get Me" Giesler was legendary for his ability to obtain acquittals. His client list was a Who's Who of Hollywood luminaries that included Alexander Pantages (rape), Errol Flynn (sex crimes with juveniles), Charles Chaplin, Bugsy Siegel, Greta Garbo, Edward G. Robinson Jr.,

1.6 George Hodel booking photo for incest, October 1949

Robert Mitchum, Busby Berkeley, and even the "Scopes Monkey Trial" attorney, Clarence Darrow. Now it was my father's turn.

The three-week jury trial was held at the Los Angeles Hall of Justice, in December 1949. The People's case was overwhelming. The witnesses testified to actually observing the sex acts between father and daughter. And the case was bolstered by the introduction of admissions made by George Hodel to the arresting detectives, in which he told them that he and his daughter "have been studying the mysteries of sex" and that "these things must have happened. I need to talk to my psychiatrist, but I am afraid he will find something wrong with me." Incredibly, even with the prosecution's airtight, slam-dunk case—the jury found him not guilty.

The defense team of Giesler and Neeb had worked their magic. Later police reports discovered in 2004 would document and suggest a possible $10,000 payoff may have been made during the trial, along with a separate police interview that established cash payoffs by Father to his abortionist accomplice, made just four days after the jury's verdict. Regardless, Dad was acquitted. He and his attorneys were able to convince a jury that "the teenager had fantasized the whole thing."

Tamar, branded forever in our family as "Tamar the liar," was shipped back to San Francisco.

As summarized in my 2003 book, *Black Dahlia Avenger: A Genius for Murder*, and supported by electronic surveillance stakeouts and tape-recorded admissions found in the secret 1950 Hodel-DA Files, we now know that my father *by his own admission* was "The Black Dahlia Avenger" and murdered both Ruth Spaulding and Elizabeth Short. In the spring of 1950, tipped by his friends in law enforcement of his imminent arrest for the Dahlia murder, Father quickly slipped out of the country and moved to Hawaii, where he obtained a degree in psychiatry.

My brothers and I were left to fend for ourselves and help prop up our mother, who had become an alcoholic and was barely able to cope. We moved from one cheap rental in the Valley to another, trying to avoid the bill collectors, hoping our mother would stay sober enough to land a scriptwriting job with one of the film studios.

When I caught up with my father a decade later, in 1960, I had become a hospital corpsman in the U.S. Navy assigned to Subic Bay, Philippines, and he was as fabulous as ever. I'll never forget our first reunion at Dad's office/residence in Manila. Appropriately, he had leased Gen. Douglas MacArthur's old World War II headquarters on Manila Bay. There he stood in front of his huge mahogany desk, larger than life, wearing his white sharkskin suit and chain-smoking Havana cigars. At age fifty-two, he'd exchanged his life in L.A., doctoring to the rich and famous, for that of an international marketing executive based in Manila. And he'd replaced Mom and my brothers and me with a high-society Filipina wife and four handsome new children.

I tried not to judge him. I told him I still loved him. Despite his stiff formality, I found myself captivated by his personal charm and charisma. A true man of the world. Listening to his beautiful speaking voice reciting one adventure after the next was spellbinding. With each weekend visit I became more enamored with my father's lifestyle. During my two-year billet in the Philippines we wined, dined, and visited his favorite brothels on a regular basis. I learned that he and his Filipina wife, Hortensia, were living apart.

He eventually divorced her, too, after she sought an annulment from the Pope, and moved on to a succession of young Asian beauties that ended with him marrying his fourth wife, June, who at twenty-three was in charge of his Tokyo office.

1.7 **June and George Hodel, Bush Street residence, San Francisco, circa 1997**

The next thirty years of my life were focused on my career as an LAPD homicide detective, while during this same period my father continued to build his company and reputation. By the 1970s the protean Dr. George Hill Hodel had reinvented himself as the most respected market research expert in Asia.

In 1990, just three years after my retirement from the LAPD, my father and June (who by then had been married to him for twenty years) decided to relocate their lives and business to the United States. They chose downtown San Francisco and moved into an office/penthouse residence on Bush Street, in the heart of San Francisco's financial district. For the next nine years I would be a regular visitor to their home and became very close to both my father and his most loving wife, June. My father died there of congestive heart failure in May 1999 at the age of ninety-one.

1.8 **George Hodel, circa 1997**

Chapter Two

There is nothing in itself which is wrong or evil, not even murder.

Henry Miller, *The World of Sex*

On the morning of June 2, 1999, as my father's widow scattered his ashes over San Francisco Bay, I quietly bid farewell to the parent I barely knew. I believed he'd been a highly intelligent, accomplished man who'd lived an extraordinary life.

Hungry to learn more about this man I loved and admired, I started asking questions. One of the first people I reconnected with was my half-sister, Tamar. Minutes into our initial conversation she dropped a bomb: "Steve, did you know our father was a suspect in the Black Dahlia murder?"

Say that again?

"Steve, did you know our father was a suspect in the Black Dahlia murder?"

How did she know? Where had this come from?

Tamar claimed that LAPD detectives told her this as they transported her as a witness to and from court during the incest trial in 1949.

Even though I'd been a Hollywood homicide detective for twenty-four years, this was news to me. Given my professional background and the fact that my father might have been a suspect in one of the most infamous murders in California history, I probed further. And as I did, I found myself looking deeper and deeper into something I didn't want to see.

Three years of investigation yielded my first book, *Black Dahlia Avenger*, and its horrible conclusion: My father wasn't just flawed; he was evil. He was a serial killer, responsible for the death of Elizabeth Short and at least six other women.

I was more stunned than anyone else. Mystery writer James Ellroy, in his moving foreword, wrote:

> Steve Hodel convinced me. His knowledge is conclusively cataloged in this book. I began the book unimpressed, and came away converted. *Black Dahlia Avenger* is a densely packed evidence exhibit and a treatise on the aesthetic of evil.

In the months immediately following *Black Dahlia Avenger*'s publication, my life turned upside down. My father's widow was horrified. Other family members objected to the way they'd been portrayed. Some felt vindicated and cheered me on. Strangers came forward with bits of information that added to the bitter legacy of George Hodel—one that I carried with sadness and guilt.

He was my father, after all. He'd passed on genes, blood, personality imprints, God knows what else. I carried his painful legacy like a load of rocks.

I had two choices: Crawl into a hole and hide, or continue to pursue the truth. I chose the latter. Call it a natural impulse. It's the thing I'd been trained to do: follow leads wherever they take me, present the evidence. I'd been a professional investigator all my adult life.

But was I also pulled by forces that operated on a deeper psychic level, somewhere beyond my comfort zone? My mother and father had named me after my mother's favorite fictional character, Stephen Dedalus from *Portrait of the Artist as a Young Man* by James Joyce.

Dedalus, too, was a seeker of truth and one who sought to fly away from constraints. According to Greek mythology the original Daedalus constructed a pair of wings for himself and his son, Icarus, to escape the island of Crete, where they were imprisoned by King Minos. Earlier, he'd been ordered by King Minos to build a labyrinth to hold the Minotaur.

I wasn't the only one of my dad's children auspiciously named. He told my half-sister Tamar that he'd named her after a poem by Robinson Jeffers about an incest victim, then slept with her when she was fourteen.

Is it possible that I'd been preordained to play the role of truth-seeker? Had I been cast by my father (the Minotaur) to capture him in infamy by revealing his dark deeds?

Weird. But not as far-out as it sounds. My father, a self-described surrealist and devotee of the Marquis de Sade, identified with the Minotaur. He even posed Elizabeth Short's dead body as a tribute to a photographic representation, *The Minotaur* (1936), by his friend Man Ray.

According to Greek mythology, the Minotaur possessed the head and tail of a bull and the body of a man. He was kept trapped in a labyrinth on the Isle of Crete and fed young virgins.

It all played perfectly into my father's fantasies. Dad viewed himself in grandiose terms as psychopaths often do. He cast a wide, very powerful spell. You'll see.

I consider myself a somewhat shy, self-effacing man, one who used to spend a good deal of his time hiding behind a shot glass. Suddenly, with the publication of my first book about the Black Dahlia murder, I was thrust into the spotlight's glare.

But Dad's story had to be told. It was too important. And I felt I owed it to the victims and their families, to my half-sister Tamar, to my brothers, to myself.

Opportunists and crackpots who carefully guarded their own Black Dahlia theories took their shots. I was called a liar, a fantasist, and even a serial killer myself. The lesson: don't tread on other people's myths.

Meanwhile, *Black Dahlia Avenger* had sprung to the top of national bestseller lists, climbing to number two in Southern California. The story of my family became national news, with print articles in *Newsweek*, *People*, and the Associated Press as well as radio and television coverage, including segments on *Dateline NBC*, CNN, CBS's *The Early Show*, and ABC's *The View*.

It was a thick tome, heavy with evidence. By page 600 I'd presented evidence connecting either George Hodel or his accomplice, Fred Sexton, to thirty-one separate crimes committed in the 1940s. Those thirty-one fell into three categories: (1) Definites, (2) Probables, and (3) Possibles.

The data linking my father to the eight crimes in the Definites category was especially compelling. Los Angeles head deputy district attorney Stephen Kay agreed. After reviewing my entire Black Dahlia Avenger investigation and all related photos and exhibits, he sent me a ten-page written opinion. Here are two brief extracts:

September 30, 2001

To Whom It May Concern:

The most haunting murder mystery in Los Angeles County during the twentieth century has finally been solved in the twenty-first century. . . .

I have personally read all of Steve's written account of his father's life and crimes and I have no doubt that his father not only murdered Elizabeth Short (the Black Dahlia) but also murdered Jeanne French less than one month after the Black Dahlia murder.

But there was more. Much more. You see, my father didn't stop killing when he left L.A. in 1950. He left a gruesome trail of more horror, more blood spilled, and more young lives ended in shockingly brutal ways.

But before we talk about the murders that continued in this country and abroad into the late 1960s, we need to examine the MOs for the crimes my father committed in the '40s. Because even the cleverest of criminals leaves behind clues, which when analyzed carefully yield a unique signature. My father, who was devious enough to never be caught, took this a step further—sending notes and evidence and deliberately taunting the police.

Understanding the details of the Dahlia murder and the other, similar murders of young women in L.A. in the 1940s, all of which I am convinced are the work of George Hodel, will lay the foundation for the emerging portrait of an international serial killer who didn't stop killing until late in his life.

Mrs. Ora Murray—"The White Gardenia Murder"

On the night of July 26, 1943, a man who said his name was Paul introduced himself to the forty-two-year-old victim at a downtown L.A. dance hall. Ora Murray, who was married to an Army sergeant stationed in Mississippi, was in L.A. visiting her sister. Witnesses described Paul as "in his thirties, tall, thin, black hair, wearing a dark double-breasted suit, dark fedora, exceptionally suave and a good dancer."

Paul told the victim that he "lives in San Francisco, and is just down to L.A. for a few days," gave Ora a Navajo or Hopi Indian bracelet, and offered to "show her Hollywood." He then drove her to an isolated golf-course parking lot, a few miles southwest of Hollywood, where he pummeled her face and body with a blunt instrument.

Investigators determined that the primary cause of death was "ligature strangulation" with the secondary cause being "concussion of the brain and subdural hemorrhage." Postmortem, the killer wrapped Ora's dress around her body "like a sarong" and delicately placed a white gardenia flower under her right shoulder.

Miss Georgette Bauerdorf

Georgette Bauerdorf was the attractive, twenty-year-old daughter of an oil magnate. As a means of helping boost the morale of World War II soldiers, she worked as a volunteer junior hostess at the popular Hollywood Canteen, where she and many Hollywood film stars danced and socialized with uniformed GIs on leave.

On the morning of October 12, 1944, a janitor entered her prestigious West Hollywood apartment to investigate the sound of "running water." He found Miss Bauderdorf's dead body submerged in the bathtub. Police speculated that she was followed home from the USO club.

The suspect had assaulted her and forced a nine-inch rolled medical Ace bandage into her mouth. The coroner determined that the cause of death was from asphyxiation, which meant she was dead when the suspect placed her in the bathtub and filled it with water. Bruises, scratches, and finger marks on her neck and body indicated that she had tried to fight back.

On September 21, 1945, approaching the one-year anniversary of the crime, the suspect left a typed note for police, which was published in the *Los Angeles Examiner.*

To the Los Angeles police—

Almost a year ago Georgette Bauerdorf, age 20, Hollywood Canteen hostess was murdered in her apartment in West Hollywood—

Between now and Oct. 11—a year after her death—the one who murdered her will appear at the Hollywood Canteen. The murderer will be in uniform. He has since he committed the murder been in action at Okinawa. The murderxx of Georgette Bauerdorf was Divine Retribution—

Let the Los Angeles police arrest the murderer if they can—

Figure 2.1 shows how the original note appeared in the September 21, 1945, *Examiner* along with Georgette's photograph. A separate *Los Angeles Times* piece on the same day informed readers that LAPD crime-lab analysis of red smudges, visible on the typed paper (shown right) proved to be *iodine*, and was placed there by the suspect to represent blood.

2.1 *Los Angeles Examiner,* September 21, 1945

Elizabeth Short—"The Black Dahlia"

On the morning of January 15, 1947, twenty-two-year-old Elizabeth Short's nude and surgically bisected body was found posed in the vacant lot of a residential neighborhood five miles south of Hollywood. Medical examiners determined that prior to her death she had been cut with a scalpel-like instrument on the face, breasts, and left thigh. The bisection was between the second and third intervertebral lumbar disks—an operation known as a hemicorpectomy, a procedure taught in U.S. medical schools in the 1930s. The torture continued with a vertical incision, consistent with a hysterectomy, in the suprapubic region. Also, pubic hair was cut from her labia and inserted into her rectum, and a large piece of flesh cut from the left thigh was stuffed into her vagina.

The crime's shocking sadism and the victim's beauty quickly made the murder national news. The first major clue arrived eight days later, when a man who identified himself as the Black Dahlia Avenger placed a taunting telephone call to *Los Angeles Examiner* city editor James Richardson and promised to send Richardson "a few of her belongings." Richardson informed the police about this phone call immediately but kept it secret from the public for seven years, hoping the Avenger would call again. He never did.

The caller kept his promise the next day when he dispatched a package containing Elizabeth Short's photographs, Social Security card, birth certificate, and personal address book. Included was a cut and pasted note which read:

2.2 "Los Angeles Examiner and Other Los Angeles Papers / Here! Is 'Dahlia's Belongings Letter to Follow"

Three days later, the promised "letter to follow" arrived, this time hand-printed.[3]

2.3 "Here it is. Turning in Wed Jan. 29 10 A.M. Had my fun at police. Black Dahlia Avenger"

In the weeks that followed, the Black Dahlia Avenger played bait-and-switch with investigators through additional communications often signed with the initials "B.D.À." or "B.D."

3   This, the only undisguised handwritten note sent in by the "Black Dahlia Avenger," was identified by me in 2001 as being written by my father, Dr. George Hill Hodel. Subsequently, Ms. Hannah McFarland, a court-certified Questioned Document expert, independently comparing known samples, identified this and three additional Avenger notes as being written by George Hodel.

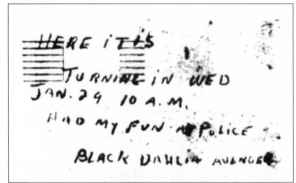

2.4 January 28, 1947: Avenger note enlarged

2.5 "Dahlia's Killer Cracking, Wants Terms"

2.6 "To Los Angeles Herald Express I will give up in Dahlia killing if I get 10 years. Don't try to find me"

2.7 "Have changed my mind, you would not give me a square deal. Dahlia killing was justified."

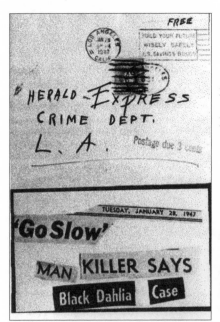

2.8 The *Herald Express*, January 28, 1947: "'Go Slow' Man Killer Says Black Dahlia Case"

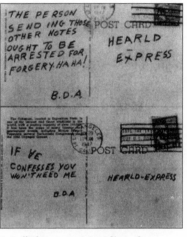

2.9 "The person sending those other notes ought to be arrested for forgery. Ha Ha! B.D.A." "If he confesses you won't need me. B.D.A."

2.10 "Ask news man at 5 & Hill for clue. Why not let that nut go I spoke to said man B.D.A." "To Herald Expess/Building 1243/Trenton St./Zone is Los Angeles Calif."

2.11 January 27, 1947: Avenger envelope

2.12 January 29, 1947: *Los Angeles Evening Herald Express* **envelope**

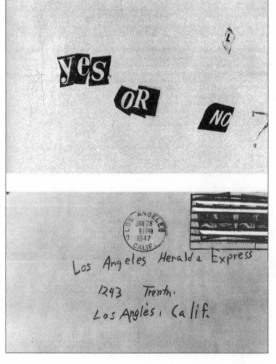

2.13 January 29, 1947: Avenger note

In 1947, two nationally recognized handwriting experts were tasked with analyzing the Avenger's handwriting. Questioned document examiner Clark Sellers found that "the writer took great pains to disguise his or her personality by printing instead of writing the message and by endeavoring to appear illiterate. But the style and formation of the printed letters betrayed the writer as an educated person."

Expert Henry Silver concluded that the Avenger was "an egomaniac, and the handwriting's fine sense of rhythm could indicate he was possibly a musician and or a dancer."[4]

By the spring of 1950, Los Angeles investigations had zeroed in on Dr. George Hodel as their prime suspect. They had him under active surveillance and were close to making an arrest. Although they were aware of his imminent plans to leave the country, District Attorney investigators waited too long to make their move and George Hodel fled the country sometime in late March 1950.

Soon thereafter, DA investigator Lt. Frank Jemison was ordered to close down his investigation and turn over all evidence, recordings, and interviews to the LAPD. DA documents verify that a minimum of fifteen Hodel acquaintance interviews were conducted by investigators. Thirteen of those interviews have "disappeared" from both LAPD and the District Attorney's Office files. The two surviving interviews implicate him in crimes, establish a relationship with Elizabeth Short, and place her at his Franklin residence prior to the murder.

Jemison was further instructed to include a written agreement "that the case would never be assumed by the District Attorney's Office, and that all the files and evidence would remain with the Los Angeles Police Department Homicide Division."

In what I know from my years in law enforcement to be a classic CYA—Cover Your Ass—move, Lieutenant Jemison complied with the orders but also secreted copies of the George Hodel investigation files in the DA's vault, creating a second set of books. Had he not done this, it

---

4 While I tend to be somewhat skeptical about graphology (analyzing handwriting to determine personality traits) due to its subjective nature, I must acknowledge that the two experts were correct on four out of four. George Hodel was highly educated, a musician, a highly skilled ballroom dancer, and an egomaniac.

is doubtful the identity of the prime suspect would have ever been revealed.

It wasn't until after the publication of my book in 2003 that L.A.
County district attorney Stephen Cooley finally opened the DA vaults
and made public the secret files, revealing a fifty-year-old secret: Dr.
George Hill Hodel was not only the prime suspect in the Elizabeth Short
murder, he was also under active investigation in connection with three
additional murders from 1947 to 1949: Jeanne French, Gladys Kern, and
Jean Spangler.

Mr. Armand Robles

Although not a murder, a bizarre and seemingly senseless robbery occurred in downtown Los Angeles four days before the Black Dahlia was
killed, which bears scrutiny.

As seventeen-year-old Armand Robles was walking down the sidewalk, a man knocked him to the ground, stole his wallet, and drove
away. Robles later described the assailant as "tall and well dressed, driving a newer model car."

At the time, Robles didn't report the assault. But two weeks after the
murder of Elizabeth Short, two separate photographs of Robles were
mailed to the press in messages from the killer.

As soon as the photos were printed in connection with the Dahlia
story, the teenager and his mother informed the press that the

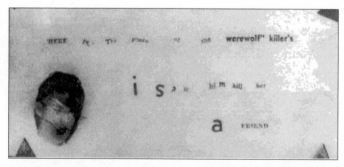

2.14 "Here is the photo of the werewolf killer's I saw him kill
her a friend"

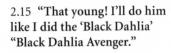

2.15 "That young! I'll do him like I did the 'Black Dahlia'" "Black Dahlia Avenger."

photographs were in Robles's wallet that had been taken in the assault that occurred on January 10.

Mrs. Jeanne French—"The Red Lipstick Murder"

On February 10, 1947, the *Herald Express* printed a special edition with this sensational headline:

WEREWOLF STRIKES AGAIN!
KILLS L.A. WOMAN, WRITES "B.D." ON BODY

Earlier that day, construction workers had discovered the nude body of forty-year-old registered nurse and former actress Jeanne French in a vacant lot seven miles west of the Dahlia site.

2.16 "Red Lipstick Murder" crime scene, February 10, 1947

The victim had been brutally bludgeoned with a tire iron and stomped to death. The suspect then wrote a taunting note on the victim's nude torso with lipstick from her purse:

FUCK YOU
B D

Even though the victim's stockings and underclothing were missing, the killer had ceremoniously draped her fox-fur coat and red dress over her body and carefully arranged her shoes on either side of her head. A white handkerchief was found nearby.

Witnesses established that Jeanne French had dined the night before at the Piccadilly Drive-in with "a dark-haired man with a small mustache." The waitress recalled that although both customers addressed her in English, they conversed with each other in French. Mrs. French was last seen in the restaurant parking lot getting into the man's "1936–7 dark-colored vehicle." George Hodel spoke fluent French and drove a black 1936 Packard sedan.

LAPD homicide captain Jack Donahoe publicly acknowledged in the *Los Angeles Examiner* the Department's belief that the Black Dahlia and Red Lipstick murders were connected, under the headline DAHLIA CASE SIMILARITIES CHECKED IN FOURTH BRUTAL DEATH MYSTERY. In that article, the LAPD provided "11 Points of Similarity" linking the murders. According to the LAPD, the crime remains unsolved.

Mrs. Gladys Eugenia Kern

The *Los Angeles Times* headline of February 17, 1948, alerted readers to the latest in a string of mysterious murders:

**WOMAN SLAIN IN HOLLYWOOD MYSTERY;
POLICE SEEK ANONYMOUS NOTE WRITER**

The victim this time was fifty-year-old real estate agent Gladys Kern, who was stabbed to death while showing a vacant house on Cromwell

Avenue in Hollywood to a potential buyer.[5] Her body was found two days later by a fellow agent.

The cause of death: multiple stab wounds to the back. The murder weapon: an eight-inch jungle knife that was found wrapped in a bloody handkerchief in the kitchen sink.

Witnesses helped investigators piece together a composite drawing of the suspect, who was seen leaving with Mrs. Kern from her office the day of her murder. They described him as:

Male, approximately 50 years of age, 6 feet tall, long full face, graying hair, wearing a business suit with a moderate cut, well dressed and neat, with a New York appearance in his dress and manner. [A second, separate witness described him as having dark curly hair and wearing a dark blue suit.][6]

2.17 Kern murder suspect composite compared to George Hodel

---

5   The crime scene is less than two miles from George Hodel's Franklin residence, and the victim's real estate office was one mile away.

6   Since the composite was prepared without a moustache, I have airbrushed out my father's. While I suspect my father did have a moustache in 1948, I cannot say with any degree of certainty. Also, witnesses cannot be relied on for accuracy. Normally, with six witnesses, you will get three or four widely varying descriptions.

The strongest lead in the investigation was a bizarre handwritten note that had been left in a downtown mailbox at Fifth and Olive (two blocks from my father's medical office) the day after Gladys Kern's murder and a day before her body was discovered. The mailbox turned out to be the same one used by the Black Dahlia Avenger a year earlier.

Figure 2.18 is a copy of the note that I obtained from the Los Angeles DA files in 2003.

2.18 Copy of Kern murder note as found in DA files in 2003

After examining the letter and comparing it to known samples of my father's handwriting, questioned document examiner Hannah McFarland concluded that it's "probable" that Dr. George Hill Hodel was the author.[7]

7 A questioned document examiner (QDE) is a forensic handwriting analyst. In handwriting terminology a "probable" means "The evidence contained in the

The long and rambling note is peppered with what I believe to be intentional misspellings, mangled syntax, and missing words and punctuation to mislead investigators:[8]

I made **aquaintance** of man three weeks ago while in Griffith Park he seemed a great sport we got friendly **friday** night asked me if I wanted to make about $300. He said he wanted to buy a home for his family but he was a **racketter** and no **real estater** would do business with him he suggested I buy a home for him in my name then he would go with person to look at property to make sure he liked and I was to tell **real estater** that he was lending me the cash so he had to inspect the property after looking at house she drove me to pick him up and he **followe** in his car then went in house alone to inspect and I waited outside after while I went up to **investigaate**, there I found her lying on floor, him trying to take ring off fingers he pulled gun on me and told me he just knocked her out he knew I carried money so he took my wallet with all my money tied my hands with my belt let lay down on sink and attached belt to faucet. after he left I got free and tried to revive her when I turned her over, I was covered with blood pulled knife out then suddenly I came to I washed my hands and knife then I looked in her bag for her home phone and address then left and ran out while outside I found he put small pocket book in my coat pocket and threw it away, also in my pocket was an old leather strap.

I knew this man as **Leuis** Frazier he has 36 or 37 Pontiac **fordor** very dark number plates look like 46 plates but with 48 stickers about 5 ft.-10, Jet black curly hair wears blue or tan **garbardine** suit told me he was a fighter and looks it I won't rest till I find him I know

handwriting points rather strongly toward the questioned and known writings having been written by the same individual; however, it falls short of the 'virtually certain' degree of confidence." [*Journal of Forensic Sciences*, Letters to the Editor, March 1991]

8   I have bolded the unusual words and misspellings.

every place we went **to gether** I know that man is my only **aliby** and without him I feel equally guilty.

P. [or possibly "rp."?]

Mrs. Mimi Boomhower—"The Merry Widow Murder"

On the night of August 18, 1949, LAPD detectives were summoned to the home of Bel-Air socialite and heiress Mimi Boomhower. They found the lights on, her car in the garage, and her refrigerator filled with fresh food and produce. But Mrs. Boomhower was nowhere to be found.

Investigators learned from her business manager, Carl Manaugh, that Mrs. Boomhower told him "she was meeting a gentleman at seven p.m. at her home," whom he believed was a prospective buyer for her residence.

No crime scene was ever established, and no witnesses ever came forward. However, the victim's leather purse was found in a telephone booth at a supermarket located at 9331 Wilshire Boulevard in Beverly Hills. A message was written in large hand-printed letters on the purse.

2.19 **Boomhower purse**

Again, document expert Hannah McFarland compared the handwriting on the Boomhower purse to known samples of Dr. George Hodel's handwriting. This time she concluded that it was "highly probable" that the writing on the purse was that of George Hodel.

Mimi Boomhower's body was never found, and sixty years later the case remains in LAPD files labeled "unsolved."

2.20 "Police Dept—We found this at beach Thursday night"

Miss Jean Spangler

The October 11, 1949, issue of the *Los Angeles Daily News* sounded another alarm:

FEAR NEW DAHLIA DEATH
200 IN ACTRESS HUNT

Beautiful twenty-seven-year-old actress Jean Elizabeth Spangler had disappeared. She was last seen seated in a Hollywood restaurant, engaged in a heated argument with two men—one of whom closely fit the description of Dr. George Hodel.

As in the Boomhower investigation, Jean Spangler's body was never found. Again, the only evidence was her purse, found lying in the grass in Hollywood's Fern Dell Park, which happened to be located half a mile from George Hodel's Franklin Avenue house. A note written by the victim was found inside the purse, which read:

Kirk,
    Can't wait any longer. Going to see Dr. Scott.
    Will work best this way while Mother is away.

Detectives theorized that Miss Spangler may have been pregnant and was considering getting an abortion.

The following is a map of the seven crimes, all of which were committed within a short distance of my father's house. In five of these seven crimes, as part of his signature, the killer included a taunting note to the police or press.

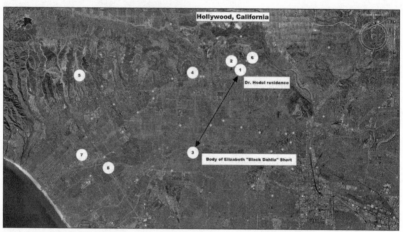

2.21 1940s Hollywood crimes in relationship to Hodel residence

1. George Hodel's "Franklin Avenue house"
2. Jean Spangler's purse found in Fern Dell Park—0.5 miles
3. Elizabeth Short—7.3 miles
4. Georgette Bauerdorf—4.2 miles
5. Mimi Boomhower—7.1 miles
6. Gladys Kern—1.1 miles
7. Jeanne French—9.4 miles
8. Ora Murray—7.7 miles

Before we move on to the next series of crimes I believe my father committed, let's take a minute to identify the primary MOs of the killer known as the Black Dahlia Avenger, who operated in 1940s Los Angeles:

• The crimes all occurred within a ten-mile radius of Hollywood.
• The killer targeted solitary women.

- In the cases of Ora Murray, Elizabeth Short, Jeanne French, Gladys Kern, and Jean Spangler, the suspect was seen in public with the victim prior to her murder.
- The suspect was described as in his thirties, tall, thin, sophisticated, dapper; "a dark-haired man with a small mustache."
- After a vicious assault on the victims, the killer covered their nude bodies with items of the victims' personal clothing. (Murray, Bauerdorf, and French)
- On two separate occasions he killed his victims by means of ligature strangulation and or asphyxiation. (Murray, Bauerdorf)
- A white handkerchief was left at the crime scene. (French, Kern)
- In the cases of Elizabeth Short and Jeanne French, the victims' nude bodies were carefully posed in vacant lots.
- The killer taunted the police and press by personally telephoning them and by repeatedly mailing in handwritten, typed, and cut-and-pasted notes and clues after the crime.
- He chose the name "Black Dahlia Avenger" and used the press to identify, promote, and market himself to the public.

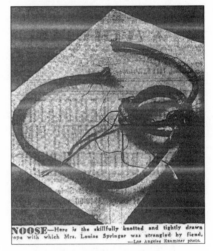

NOOSE—Here is the skillfully knotted and tightly drawn rope with which Mrs. Louise Springer was strangled by fiend.
—Los Angeles Examiner photo.

2.22 *Los Angeles Examiner,* June 18, 1949, showing precut clothesline ligature used in Louise Springer murder

- The killer was a highly intelligent man with an overdeveloped ego, who enjoyed publicly humiliating and outwitting authority.

All eight of the crimes examined in this chapter occurred well within a ten-mile radius of the Franklin house. The crime scenes, the details left behind by the killer, and the characteristics of the victims were similar enough to firmly link four of them in the minds of the investigators at the time. Knowing what we now know about serial killers, I am certain that any competent investigator would conclude at the very least that these eight crimes must be considered possibly linked to the same man. With the preponderance of similarities in MO, witness descriptions of the suspect, crime-scene locations, victim profiles, and especially the highly unusual contact made by the at-large suspect with authorities via letter and telephone, my own homicide training would have certainly led me to believe that a serial killer was operating in 1940s Los Angeles.

There may well be other crimes attributable to George Hodel during this period that have been mostly lost to history. I have identified at least three possible victims in whose cases simply not enough evidence currently exists to make a positive connection. However, the connections that do exist are fascinating: Marian Newton (San Diego, murdered 7/17/47), Louise Springer (Los Angeles, murdered 6/13/49) and Geneva Ellroy (El Monte, murdered 6/22/58) were all strangled using a precut length of clothesline cord that the killer brought with him. In the Marian Newton homicide the dapper, well-dressed suspect met the victim at a downtown dance hall, invited her for a drive, took her to an isolated location, and strangled her. As in the Kern and French homicides, he also left two white handkerchiefs at the scene, near the body.

I believe the eight crimes enumerated above to be the work of my father, George Hodel. I also believe we will never know the complete extent of his murderous activities in L.A. What we do know is that DA investigators considered him a prime suspect in the dismemberment of Elizabeth Short, and were actively investigating his possible involvement in the murders of Jeanne French, Gladys Kern, and Jean Spangler.

As the following chapters will confirm, the signatures and MOs of the crimes in L.A. will link my father to further crimes in California, elsewhere in the United States, and abroad. Finally, the Avenger's crimes will be revealed as one part of the incredible, intricate puzzle Dr. George Hodel created during his long career as a serial killer.

Chapter Three

Repudiating the virtues of your world, criminals hopelessly agree to organize a forbidden universe. They agree to live in it. The air there is nauseating: they can breathe it.

Jean Genet, The Thief's Journal

Of all the murders linked to my father, certainly the most sensational was that of Elizabeth Short. Why had he singled her out? Was she simply a girlfriend who provided a convenient target for his disturbed fantasy? Or was there a more practical reason for my father to kill her?

The pasted note sent to Captain Donahoe on January 30, 1947, had read "Dahlia killing justified." What did that mean?

I knew that my father and Elizabeth Short were acquainted and that they had dated, possibly as early as 1944. Several separate witnesses saw them together at the Franklin house and other Hollywood locations in the months leading up to her murder.

As District Attorney Detective Lt. Frank Jemison stated during his March 22, 1950, interview with my mother:

(Jemison-Hodel transcript, page 5)

Lt. Jemison: "Let me advise you that we do have information that he [George Hodel] did associate with Beth Short and as you know . . ."

Two days after this interview with my mother, DA/LAPD audio surveillance transcripts record George Hodel talking to a friend "in a low voice" at the Franklin house. The transcripts show him whispering about "the Black Dahlia." Transcripts read, "Hodel talks about leaving the country, mentions the FBI. Hodel mentions being afraid about something." On March 26, 1950, just hours before my father fled the country, the final page of the transcript entered by LAPD detective Meyer, reads, "Hodel talking about picture police have of him and some girl—thought he had destroyed them all."

I'd learned that George was extremely jealous of Elizabeth showing affection to other men, especially those in military uniform. According to witnesses and her own letters, Elizabeth did flirt with military men during the war years, and afterward, in 1946, while George was in China serving as an officer with the United Nations.

In September of that same year, my father was unexpectedly discharged "for personal reasons." He returned to Los Angeles and spent several weeks in a local hospital. During that same time Elizabeth, who was also living in Los Angeles, informed friends that she was "going to marry George, a lieutenant, when he got out of the hospital on November 1."

What happened? What caused Elizabeth to change her mind? In the final stages of my Dahlia investigation, I came to believe that George killed Elizabeth out of jealousy. FBI files contained an in-depth interview with a military man (his name was redacted) who had a one-night stand with Elizabeth. Their date was on September 20, 1946, at the Figueroa Hotel in downtown Los Angeles. In their conversation, she informed him that she was attempting to break up with an older man she had been seeing, but didn't quite know how to, as he was very jealous and she "didn't want to hurt his feelings." My theory was that, spurned and rejected, George turned his fury against Elizabeth. Nobody said no to George Hodel!

But then information came to light that provided a chilling new twist. In 2001, while putting together the first pieces of the Elizabeth Short "Black Dahlia" and Jeanne French "Red Lipstick" murder puzzles, I came across a headline in a Los Angeles newspaper from 1946 referring to a man named William Heirens as "The Lipstick Murderer." Thinking the names an interesting coincidence, I briefly looked into the Heirens case.

Bill Heirens had been arrested for the horrific murders of two adult women and a six-year-old girl in Chicago. After killing one of the women, he'd allegedly used lipstick to write a message to police on the living-room wall of her apartment.

Knowing that my father, Dr. George Hodel, had scrawled FUCK YOU. B. D. in red lipstick on the nude body of one his victims (Jeanne French) a year later (1947), I wondered if the murders were connected. But a cursory review of the evidence the police claimed to have against Heirens, especially his confession, seemed to indicate the Chicago case had been solved. I didn't investigate further.

Then in 2003 I came across documents in Lt. Frank Jemison's investigative summary of Elizabeth Short's murder that had been locked away in the Los Angeles District Attorney's vault for almost sixty years. In a report dated 2/20/51, Lieutenant Jemison stated that Elizabeth Short had spent three weeks in Chicago in 1946 during July, sleeping with reporters and befriending detectives because "she was keenly interested in the famous Heirens Chicago murder case."

Copied below is a verbatim extract from Lieutenant Jemison's investigative report:

R301248Lt. Frank B. Jemison2-20-51
Elizabeth Short Murder
pg: 4
8.Unknown Chicago Police Officer

. . .

Further that the following named persons knew victim while she was in Chicago enroute to Long Beach, California in July 1946: Jack Chernau, residence, 7107 Grand Avenue, Chicago, he registered at the Blackstone Hotel with Short and saw her approximately fifteen times in three weeks. He had intercourse with her; he was in the upholstery business. Slig Diamond, a newspaperman whose residence is Park Row Hotel, Chicago, he saw Short over a ten-day period and has stated that he had intercourse with her and says that she was always talking about murder cases. Lou Paris, feature writer for the *Chicago Daily Times*, Chicago, knew Short and talked with her at which time she was keenly interested in the famous Heirens Chicago murder case. John Giampa, 3421 West Lexington, was a mailer for Chicago Herald American; he knew her and said that Short knew a Chicago detective who worked on the Heirens case. Jan Jansen, a reporter on the *Chicago Daily News*, has stated that he knew victim in Chicago. All of these named persons knew Short in the month of July, 1946, approximately six months before the murder and any one of these men could have had honorary special Chicago police badges. . . .

Why would Elizabeth Short, a naïve waitress and cashier, travel to Chicago in the summer of 1946 in an effort to obtain inside information about a series of murders?

Six months later, and just three months after my father's return from China, her tortured, bisected body was found in a vacant L.A. lot.

When I dug deeper into the Los Angeles District Attorney's files, I came across another interesting fact: In January 1947, just a few days before her murder, Short was seen in front of Columbia Broadcasting Studios on Sunset Boulevard, waiting to get into the Jack Carson radio show. On her arm was a tall, dapper man in his late thirties who escorted her to the front of the line. There he flashed a badge at the usher, who opened the velvet rope and let them in.

In the lobby the head usher, John "Jack" Egger, reexamined the badge, which read CHICAGO POLICE DEPARTMENT, before admitting the couple to Studio A.

Egger knew the beautiful young Elizabeth well. In a February 7, 1950, transcribed interview with Lt. Frank Jemison and LAPD Sgt. F. A. Brown, he remembered seeing her "at least twenty times before, at CBS, but always alone."

Here are excerpts from that interview:

Egger: The man pulled out a badge and showed it to me, which I examined, and it was a Chicago police badge, at least it stated Chicago Police Department on the badge. . . .

I let them both in without waiting in line and without a ticket.

Sgt. Brown: Did Neemo [junior usher] recognize her as knowing her when he brought this Chicago policeman to you, was there any conversation about that, did he know her?

Egger: The thing sir, we always notice a girl like that, she was a striking girl, with that raven hair, blue sweater or pink sweater, she more or less became a legend and when we saw her with a man we paid more attention, so Neemo brought the two of them up to me and then transpired what I told Mr. Jemison.

John Egger went on to describe Elizabeth's companion as "male, early forties, five foot ten, one-eighty, with penetrating eyes." Egger felt he could recognize the man from a photograph if he ever saw him again.

As a result of this information, and the fact that Lieutenant Jemison knew that Elizabeth Short had traveled to Chicago and become intimate with both reporters and a detective working on another investigation, he contacted the Chicago Police Department and requested a list of names of all retired Chicago detectives living in the Los Angeles area. Printed below is part of Chicago Police Department Chief of Detectives Andrew W. Aitken's response:

March 20, 1950

Dear Sir: -Att. H. I. [sic] Stanley, Chief B of I.

Replying to your letter of March 14th, in further reference to Elizabeth Short murder, . . . you mention a star-shaped badge similar to the badge of the Chicago Police Department, which was displayed by a man who accompanied the deceased shortly before the murder on January 15th, 1947.

Please be advised that consideration must be given to the fact that the Chicago police badge is easily and frequently copied, particularly in this vicinity and usually by private watch services who outfit and equip their employees in similar uniforms. . . .

In an interesting twist of fate, Jack Egger became an investigator for the L.A. County District Attorney's office after he left CBS. Subsequent to the DA's Office, he joined the Beverly Hills Police Department, where he rose to the rank of captain of detectives. Later he became chief of security for a major film studio in Hollywood.

On December 12, 2003, I met with Chief Egger, whom I found to be cordial and cooperative. After reviewing the circumstances of his meeting with Elizabeth Short fifty-three years earlier, I showed him photo-

3.1 Dr. George Hodel, circa 1950

graphs of my father circa 1949. After slowly and deliberately studying the face and features, Chief Egger said he was "ninety-nine percent certain" this was the same man who was with Elizabeth Short in early January 1947 at the CBS studio.

Egger remembered him as "very dapper, very stern, and never cracked a smile." Anyone who knew my father can confirm that Egger's description fits him to a tee.

By mid-February, 1950, Lieutenant Jemison had identified my father as the prime suspect in the Elizabeth Short murder and had gone so far as to surreptitiously install microphones in my father's house. Simultaneously, he had his detectives looking at two other possible suspects who were listed as "Elizabeth's unidentified Los Angeles doctor" and an "unknown Chicago police officer."

3.2 Elizabeth Short, circa 1946

Based on what I found in the DA file and Chief Egger's 2003 positive identification, I'm now convinced that the three suspects were in fact the same man, Dr. George Hodel. In January 1947 my father was Elizabeth Short's suitor, her "unidentified doctor" and, as we now know, a man with a badge, passing himself off as the "unknown Chicago police officer."

What was behind this new Elizabeth Short/Chicago connection? I couldn't get it out of my head. I knew I'd have to dig into the case of the

"Lipstick Killer" in Chicago to get to the bottom of her bizarre obsession with the crime. That investigation would prove as shocking to me as that of the Black Dahlia Avenger.

I now believe that Elizabeth Short must have known something disturbing about my father, perhaps something he let slip during an intimate moment or while under the influence. Her search for the truth, coupled with perhaps a misguided confession of those suspicions to George Hodel, may well have sealed her fate and caused her to become one of the most infamous murder victims in history. She died because of what she'd learned about my father's savage activities in Chicago.

As we'll see, in the act of dumping Elizabeth Short's body, he left a hidden message that links both crimes and underscores his motivation: revenge. But before we get to George Hodel's hidden message, we have to examine Chicago's crime of the century in detail.

PART TWO

CHICAGO

Chapter Four

For heaven's sake catch me before I kill more I cannot
control myself.

Note written in lipstick on a wall at the
Frances Brown crime scene, December 1945

At the start of June 1945, with the U.S. air and ground assault starting
to break through the Japanese defenses in Okinawa, Chicagoans clung
to the hope that the war would soon be over and their sons and hus-
bands would return home.

They awoke the chilly morning of June 6 to discomforting news. A
day earlier, an eighteen-year-old girl named Jacqueline Ross returned to
the apartment she shared with her older sister and divorced mother to
discover her mother Josephine's nude, dead body lying in bed.

Police investigators found bloodstains and blood splatter on the
bedroom's northeast wall, the radiator cover, and curtains. A violent
struggle between the forty-three-year-old victim and her assailant had
produced multiple bruises to the victim's body and a deep laceration to
her right hand. She'd also been struck five times in the head with a blunt
instrument, which may have rendered her unconscious before the suspect finished her off by severing the jugular vein in her neck. Detectives
found two strands of black hair, believed to be the suspect's, clutched in
the victim's hand.[9]

Rather than simply leaving Josephine Ross on the floor and fleeing
the scene, the suspect left certain unique postmortem signatures that
distinguished this from other burglary-rape-murders. He dragged
Ross's body to the bathroom, placed it in the bathtub and, using a
douche bag, washed the blood from her wounds. Then he toweled the

---

9 If they have not been destroyed, this hair evidence could potentially contain
usable DNA.

body dry, carried it to the bed, and placed white medical adhesive tape (3 by ¼-inch strips) over several of the facial lacerations. Finally, he covered the victim's head with a red skirt and tied a silk stocking tightly around her throat in a form of "posing." This extremely rare practice is found in less than 1 percent of all homicides. In my three hundred separate homicide investigations, I only had *one* case where the suspect posed the victim.

Police found a woman's housecoat, two towels, a roll of adhesive tape, a douche bag with the hose and nozzle attached, and a brassiere with the straps torn from the cups floating in the bathtub in five inches of bloody water. The victim's white pajamas had been left at the foot of the bed.

Two tenant witnesses came forward with descriptions of the likely suspect. Mrs. Bernice Folkman said she saw a man in the fifth-floor corridor at approximately ten thirty a.m., whom she described as male, twenty to thirty years old, black wavy hair, wearing a light-colored sweater. Witness Elmer Nelson provided a similar description and observed the man leaving the building via the fire escape.

For a full year following the murder, the police were unable to produce a likely suspect. Six months later, as Chicagoans prepared for the Christmas holidays, they were confronted with more horror:

4.1 Josephine Alice Ross

On the morning of December 10, 1945, the nude, dead body of Miss Frances Brown, a thirty-three-year-old member of the WAVES (Women Appointed for Voluntary Emergency Service) who had just been discharged from the Navy, was found in the apartment she shared with a female friend on Chicago's north side, a quarter mile southwest of the Josephine Ross murder site. Miss Brown's body was posed in a kneeling position on the side of the bathtub with her head resting on the bottom of the tub.

Chicago detectives determined that the victim had been accosted in her bedroom, where she, much like Josephine Ross, had tried to fight off her knife-wielding assailant. As in the Ross case, they found defensive-wound lacerations near the web of Miss Brown's right thumb.

The struggle continued on Miss Brown's bed, where she was stabbed through the neck with her own eight-inch bread knife. The suspect then finished her off with two shots from a .38 caliber handgun—one through the right arm and the second into the right side of her forehead.

Her attacker then dragged the body through the living room and into the bathroom, where he removed her blood-soaked pajama bottoms, wrapped her pajama top around the knife that was still embedded in her neck, and used a douche bag and nozzle to wash her body clean.

After posing the body in the bathtub, Frances Brown's killer walked to the south living-room wall, removed a large framed picture and, using a lipstick taken from her purse, wrote in three- to six-inch letters:

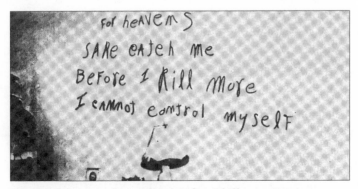

4.2 "**For heavens sake catch me Before I kill more I cannot control myself.**"

All fingerprints were wiped away except for a badly smudged partial print that was found on the bathroom doorjamb. Detectives speculated that the suspect entered the apartment by climbing an exterior fire escape and coming in through a window.

The building's night manager John Dedrick saw a suspicious man leave the elevator and nervously try to exit the front door at approximately four a.m. He described the person as a male Caucasian, thirty-five to forty years old, dark-complexioned, wearing a dark overcoat and dark fedora. Two tenants claimed that they had heard what sounded like gunshots between two and four a.m.

Several days after the murder, the tenant directly below Miss Brown's apartment reported a threatening phone call from an unidentified man who said, "I'm the lipstick killer. You'll get it next if you don't keep your mouth shut."

This sadistic murder, like the Josephine Ross crime, remained a disturbing puzzle with few prospects for being solved. Then four weeks later, an even greater act of evil shook the city of Chicago and the nation, grabbing headlines like the terrible Lindbergh kidnap-murder of 1932.

Shortly after midnight, on Monday, January 7, 1946, blond, blue-eyed, six-year-old Suzanne Degnan was tucked into bed and kissed good night by her father. James Degnan, an executive with the Office of Price Administration, had recently moved his wife and two daughters from Baltimore to the top floor of a house in the Edgewater neighborhood on Chicago's north side.

When James went to awaken young Suzanne at around seven thirty a.m., he found an empty bed. And he noticed that the bedroom window that had been left nearly closed was now wide open. He and his wife, Helen, searched the house. Finding no sign of their daughter, they called the police.

Within an hour, a hundred uniformed police officers and detectives began a house-to-house search of the neighborhood. In Suzanne's bedroom, detectives found a ransom note written in pencil on a dirty piece of paper. The note, which had been freshly smeared with oil (possibly to cover any fingerprints), read:

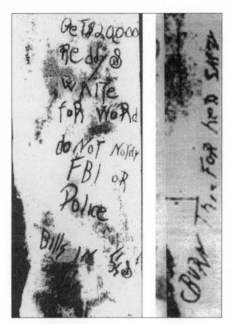

4.3 (Front) "Get $20,000 reddy & waite
for word do not notify FBI or Police
Bills in 5's & 10's." (Back) "Burn this for
her safty."

Between seven thirty and eleven a.m., the suspect phoned the Degnan
residence four times and attempted to make arrangements for delivery of
the ransom money. Chicago detectives at the time were confident this was
the actual suspect because in his conversation he claimed to "have a lock
of her blond hair and a piece of her blue pajamas." The pajamas had not
yet been found nor any description of them released to the public. Here
is how James Degnan described one of the calls:

> Shortly after ten o'clock the police had the telephone fixed so that
> calls could be recorded and they instructed me to answer it and
> try to deal with the kidnapper from then on. In a short while a
> man called and asked if Suzanne was there. Before I could answer
> he was disconnected or had hung up. That call was traced to a
> drugstore in Rogers Park.

In their search of the immediate area, officers found a seven-foot makeshift ladder with a broken rung that they speculated may have been used by the suspect(s) to climb through the bedroom window and abduct the child.

Throughout the afternoon hours of January 7, Chicago radio station WGN broadcast a plea from James Degnan to the kidnapper not to harm his child. He assured the suspect that he would raise the $20,000 ransom and deliver the money.

Late in the afternoon an anonymous tip arrived, most likely from the suspect, suggesting that "police search the storm drains in the neighborhood." They did. At seven p.m. Suzanne's decapitated head was found in a storm drain a half block south of the residence.

In the macabre scene that followed, hundreds of Chicagoans followed police officers from alley to alley, sewer to sewer, as patrolmen called out "nothing here" or "we found a leg." The left leg still attached to a partial torso was discovered in a sewer just south of the residence. The right leg lay in an alley catch basin two blocks farther west. The main torso had been dumped in a sewer two blocks south on Ardmore Avenue.

Police eventually located the dismemberment site in a basement on Winthrop Avenue, two hundred yards from the Degnan residence. They speculated that the suspect or suspects had broken in during the early morning hours and used the laundry tub to wash and dismember the body. Body parts had been wrapped in shopping bags and rags taken from some of the basement lockers. An examination of the basin revealed pieces of flesh and blond hair.

Mrs. Joseph Hradek, who lived directly above the basement, said she was awakened at approximately two forty-five a.m. by the sound of a window being slammed and running water. Police confirmed that all the body parts were "washed clean." Another resident reported that she heard footsteps and noises in the basement, followed by the sound of someone walking by her room, through the corridor, and out into the alley. She claimed that the person repeated these actions at least four times.

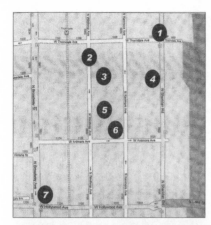

4.4 Location of Degnan body parts

1. Degnan home
2. Murder room
3. Head found
4. Left leg found in sewer
5. Right leg found in catch basin
6. Torso found in sewer
7. Arms found in sewer

4.5 The basement "murder room" and basins where the suspect performed the dismemberment.

The brutal horror of Suzanne Degnan's murder was first reported in the *Chicago Daily Tribune*'s final January 8, 1946, edition:

4.6

Los Angeles and the rest of the nation quickly picked up the story:

4.7

News commentators referred to another "Jack the Ripper" loose in Chicago, while police dubbed the suspect "The Mad Butcher of Kenmore Avenue."

Teams of investigators acted quickly, locating important eyewitnesses and recovering valuable evidence. Here are the highlights of their early findings:

- A witness going to work at three a.m. observed a man alight from a slate-colored car parked south on Kenmore. The man removed a bundle and transferred it from the front to the rear of the vehicle.
- A milk wagon driver identified the seven-foot ladder as the same one he saw on the top of a car parked near the Degnan home on

January 6, at six a.m. (some eighteen hours before the kidnapping). Inside the car was a lone male, thirty-five years old, dark complexion.

- Police confirmed that they believed more than one suspect was involved in the abduction because "it would be impossible for a single suspect to carry the seventy-four-pound child down the rickety ladder without help."
- Police described this possible scenario: (1) Automobile used to carry victim from her home to basement on Winthrop Avenue, where body was dismembered. (2) Victim strangled, and an attempted rape occurred in the suspect's automobile. (3) Kidnapper(s) used a sharp knife, and was highly skilled in cutting. Possible doctor or butcher? (4) Based on undisclosed secret analysis from the police crime lab, the ransom note was written one week before the crime occurred.
- Police Chief Walter Storms told reporters that "the girl's murderer was either a physician, a medical student, a very good butcher, an embalmer, or perhaps a livestock handler." Dr. Jerry Kearns, the coroner's expert, declared that "the killer had to be an expert in cutting meat, because the body was separated at the joints. Not even the average doctor could be so skillful."
- Soil particles found on the bottoms of the victim's feet indicated she walked after being taken down the ladder. This indicated Suzanne was not slain in the bedroom.
- Two men's white handkerchiefs, twelve inches square (one bloodstained and twisted like a gag), were found near 6035 Winthrop Avenue.
- Two black curly hair strands were found on the child's torso when recovered from the storm sewer. According to police, "the hairs were found on the body inside the cloth bag and have to belong to the suspect."
- Police now believed that the killer may have taken the child out the front door when the neighbor's boxer dogs first started barking at 12:25 a.m.
- Mary and Thomas Keegan, third-floor tenants at the Degnan

house, were awakened between one thirty and two a.m. when the neighbors' dogs barked a second time. They heard two men arguing on the sidewalk. Fifteen minutes later, they heard a man and a woman talking. The woman said, "This is the best-looking building in the neighborhood, and the best looking couple."

• According to a *Los Angeles Times* article on January 12, 1946, under the headline KIDNAP VICTIM BURIED; AREA COMBED FOR CLUE, on January 11 as mourners attended the funeral of little Suzanne Degnan, police found a clue that possibly connected the Degnan crime to the "Lipstick Killer" of Frances Brown. A note handwritten in lipstick was found on a lamppost near the basement where Suzanne's body was dismembered. It read "stop me before i kill more."

• On January 12 at ten thirty a.m., a witness, David Decker, saw a suspicious-looking man loitering in the vestibule at 1023 Thorndale Avenue, near the Degnan residence. The man dropped a yellow piece of paper on the floor and left. Decker recovered the note, which read "i did it. please get me." He described the man as male, twenty-five to thirty years old, tall and thin, dark complexion, dark suit coat, light-colored slacks, wearing a dark cap.

4.8 "stop me before i kill more"

• Another note, with what appeared to be deliberate misspellings, was mailed to the Chicago police by a person claiming to be the killer:

"Why don't you catch me. If you don't **ketch** me soon, I will **cummit** suicide. There is a reward out for me. How much do I get if I give myself up. When do I get that 20,000 dollars they wanted from that Degnan girl at 5901 Kenmore Avenue. You may find me at the Club

Tavern at 738 E. 63rd St. known as Charlie the Greeks. Or at Con-
way's Tavern at 6247 Cottage Grove Av. Please hurry now."

- On January 30, 1946, a severed human ear was mailed to Mrs.
Degnan. The handwritten message that accompanied it read "WILL
CUT YOUR EAR NEXT." It was later determined that the ear had been
stolen from a medical laboratory. The package was double-
stamped, and if the evidence still exists, the saliva under the two
stamps could be a potential source for DNA.
- On February 20, 1946, some six weeks after the murder, city util-
ity workers found the child's severed arms inside a sewer three
blocks from the Degnan home. Both arms were found palms
downward next to a four-foot section of broom handle, which
authorities believed was used to pry open the sixty-pound manhole.
- Cause of death was found to be manual strangulation. Both finger
and ligature marks were found on the victim's neck. In an alley-
way nearby the "murder room," police recovered two white, knotted, precut lengths of clothesline cord, which appeared to show
bloodstains.
- The coroner estimated the time of death at between twelve thirty
and one a.m.

The weight, value, and interpretation of much of this evidence would
change and modify itself, depending on what suspect was taken into
custody. By the time Chicago investigators focused on William Heirens,
some six months later, many of these original facts would vanish and be
forgotten, especially those that directly contradicted law enforcement's
new theory of the case.

Chapter Five

I can't tell you if she suffered, Sheriff Mulcahy. I didn't kill her.

Bill Heirens to Sheriff Michael Mulcahy, September 6, 1946

Throughout 1946 Chicago police investigators tracked down evidence and pursued every lead in the Suzanne Degnan murder case with zeal. "We're leaving nothing undone," Captain Joseph Goldberg told reporters. Thousands of people were questioned, including busboys, bartenders, postal clerks, cab drivers, ex-convicts, and anyone with a past record of sexual misconduct. Police went so far as to wiretap the phone lines of neighboring butcher shops and tree surgeons. Several suspects were arrested and cleared.

5.1 January 9, 1946

The most notorious of these was Hector Verburgh, the sixty-five-year-old janitor in charge of maintenance at the Winthrop Avenue building where the dismemberment took place. Despite an alibi from his wife of thirty years and a reputation for being "as harmless as a fly," the stocky native of Belgium was grilled by State's Attorney William Tuohy, Police Commissioner John C. Prendergast, Chief of Detectives Walter G. Storms, and Mayor Edward Kelly. Also, Verburgh's wife, Mary, was hauled to the police station and badgered by detectives who tried to get her to implicate her husband.

After two days of torture the elderly janitor was released and hospitalized with a separated shoulder and other ailments. From his hospital bed, Verburgh described his ordeal.

> Oh, they hanged me up, they blindfolded me. . . . They had handcuffs on me for hours and hours. They threw me in a cell and blindfolded me. They handcuffed my hands behind my back and pulled me up on bars until only my toes touched the floor. I no sleep, I no eat, I go to the hospital. Oh, I am so sick. Any more and I would have confessed anything.

Two years later, in 1948, the city of Chicago would agree to settle Hector Verburgh's claim for wrongful arrest and police brutality for a sum of $20,000—a considerable amount in 1948 dollars.

The police didn't stop looking for suspects. A young man named James Freutel, who lived two doors down from the Degnans, said that he was afraid to go outside. "I felt that if I looked to the right or the left, a cop would jump from behind a tree and grab me. They were taking everyone in."

By the end of June, Chicago detectives were frustrated and angry. They'd arrested four separate suspects and forced them to confess under physical and emotional duress, only to have to release them when their alibis checked out. Then a hapless, seventeen-year-old burglar named William Heirens fell into their net.

Heirens was a mixed-up kid. At the age of thirteen he'd confessed to a series of eleven burglaries. Detectives found two .38 revolvers hidden behind his mother's refrigerator and an army rifle on the roof, along with a cache of furs and men's and women's clothing.

A quiet, pensive boy, raised in a troubled household, Bill Heirens was shipped off to a series of reform schools, where he seemed to blossom. Upon graduation he was admitted to the University of Chicago. He did well at first, but during his sophomore year he became disappointed with himself. "I was not making the grades I wanted," he later explained. "I was allowing my love relationships to affect my life too much."

Unhappy and feeling financially pressured, Heirens returned to burglary. His methodology was simple. He'd knock on the front door of an apartment in a high-rise building and, if no one answered, enter through the front door and grab everything of value—cash, jewelry, guns, whatever small objects he could lay his hands on. He never committed physical or sexual assault.

On the muggy afternoon of June 26, 1946, more than six months after the Degnan murder, Bill Heirens walked into the Wayne Manor Apartments on the north side and took an elevator to the third floor. In his pocket was a small pistol he'd nabbed during a previous burglary. Seeing an open apartment door, he entered and removed a single dollar bill from a wallet he saw in the living room. As he exited, a neighbor yelled out.

A call was quickly made to police. Detective Tiffin Constant and his partner, who were in the area, cornered Heirens in the rear stairway of a nearby building. According to Detective Constant, Heirens pointed the handgun at him and pulled the trigger. When the gun didn't go off, Constant responded with three quick shots that missed. Bill Heirens threw his gun at Constant, then leaped down the steps onto the detective.

An off-duty policeman named Abner Cunningham was returning from the beach in his bathing suit when he heard the commotion. He subdued the teenager by breaking three empty flowerpots over his head.

Suffering from a possible skull fracture, Bill Heirens was taken to nearby Edgewater Emergency Hospital, then to the Bridewell Jail Hospital where he was booked.

Chicago detectives wondered why a hot prowl burglar like Bill would attempt an escape after having three shots fired at him. They suspected he was running away from something else. Their speculation quickly turned to the crime that had most frustrated them that year: Maybe Heirens was the sex maniac who broke into little Suzanne Degnan's room six months before and knew he'd get the chair if he were caught.

In days following his booking, the terrified teenager was grilled around the clock, deprived of sleep and food, prevented from seeing his parents, had ether poured onto his testicles, and was injected with Sodium Pentothal. When these failed to elicit a confession, he was subjected to very painful spinal taps without anesthesia and given a polygraph exam without consent.

The analysis of Bill Heirens's 1946 polygraph exam was kept secret until 1953, when it was obtained by polygraph experts. In their opinion, Heirens showed a truthful response about not killing Suzanne Degnan. This was a great puzzlement to the experts, since they had been told "his guilt had been established with absolute certainty."

Determined to make their case, investigators resorted to another dirty tactic: releasing information to Chicago's five newspapers that they said "proved Heirens guilty." Among the evidence cited by police were "hidden indentations" on the Degnan ransom note that they claimed connected it to Heirens. The FBI later dismissed this conclusion and determined that the "indentations" did not exist.

Fingerprints on the Degnan note, which were initially unreadable smudges, mysteriously developed into readable prints, and identified as Heirens's. On June 30, 1946, Chicago PD captain Emmett Evans had told reporters, "Heirens has been cleared of suspicion on the Brown murder because the fingerprint left in the apartment was not his." Twelve days later, the police found twenty-two points of similarity, and the previously eliminated print became Heirens's.

Decades later, a reexamination of the fingerprint on the note by a court-qualified expert found that it is "a rolled fingerprint" of the type created during the booking of a prisoner. The expert indicated that in the thousands of crime-scene prints he had examined, he had never seen one like it. The state's reward money was split between two individuals, both police officers. Half went to Sgt. Thomas Laffey, Chicago PD's fingerprint expert who, in July, 1946, after personally fingerprinting Heirens, found a new fingerprint on the Degnan note, which he subsequently identified as Heirens's. The other half of the reward money went to the arresting officer, Cunningham.

Eyewitness George Subgrunski, who claimed he had seen a thirty-five-year old male with a dark overcoat and fedora near the Degnan residence, said it wasn't Heirens when he was shown a photo of the suspect on July 11. Five days later, Subgrunski changed his mind.

On July 16, 1946, George Wright of the *Chicago Tribune* breached all journalistic ethics by concocting a confession and publishing it as if it were real. The headline read THE HEIRENS STORY! HOW HE KILLED SU-ZANNE DEGNAN AND 2 WOMEN. Quoting "unimpeachable sources," Wright's story claimed that Heirens killed Degnan for ransom; shot Frances Brown, waited on her fire escape, and then returned to stab her; and stabbed Josephine Ross when she awoke during an attempted burglary. The so-called confession was picked up by the other Chicago papers and across the nation.

In the face of this very public assault, seventeen-year-old Bill

5.2 July 30, 1946: Heirens in white shirt (center ring) about to give his "confession."

Heirens's own defense attorneys convinced him that the only way he could save himself from the electric chair was to plead guilty and "take a deal." The terrified youth agreed and confessed to the Ross, Brown, and Degnan murders. The confession was accepted as truth despite the fact that all three statements contained glaring errors and factual impossibilities about the murders.

At the September 1946 sentencing hearing, State's Attorney William J. Tuohy in his closing arguments to the judge, made what in my opinion, has to be one of the most shocking and bizarre judicial statements I've ever heard. Recognizing Heirens's defense attorneys, the lead prosecutor said to the court:

> Without the aid of the defense, we would to this day have no answer for the death of Josephine Ross. Without their aid, to this day a great and sincere public doubt might remain as to the guilt of William Heirens in the killing of Suzanne Degnan and Frances Brown.

In his closing comments, Heirens's lead defense attorney, John Coghlan, thanked the prosecutor for his kind words and concluded:

> When we became convinced that the State had a prima facie case . . . our duty at that time required that we in no manner assist him in defeating justice . . .

On September 6, 1946, the day after Bill was sentenced to three consecutive terms of life in prison, he was visited by Sheriff Michael Mulcahy, who said, "You probably didn't realize this, Bill, but I'm a personal friend of Jim Degnan. He wants to know, did his daughter suffer?"

"I can't tell you if she suffered, Sheriff Mulcahy," Bill Heirens answered. "I didn't kill her. Tell Mr. Degnan to please look after his older daughter, because whoever killed Suzanne is still out there."

While Chicago authorities and a majority of its residents were relieved by Heirens's conviction, doubts about his guilt began to surface immediately. One skeptic was popular mystery writer/researcher Georgiana Craig, who wrote under the name Craig Rice and who'd been hired by the *Chicago Herald-American* to produce a series of analytical articles about the murders. After poring over police records and interviewing Heirens and others, she concluded, "Let's think about Billy Heirens. I've seen him. I've talked to him [and] I believe him innocent."

Another early doubter was the chaplain at Statesville Prison. William Heirens, for his part, started telling anyone who would listen that he was innocent. According to a prison psychological profile filed in 1951, "He [Heirens] denies the alleged murders although he frankly admits the numerous robberies. He states: 'I confessed because there was a chance of being condemned to death.'"

In 1953 Heirens petitioned the Illinois Supreme Court for a retrial. In denying his request, the Court admitted that "the search of the petitioner's living quarters, the incessant and prolonged questioning of petitioner while he was confined to a hospital bed, and the unauthorized use of Sodium Pentothal and a lie detector were flagrant violations of his rights." But the Court concluded that since the case was settled on a plea bargain, the violations were not the mitigating factor in the conviction.

In the decades since, numerous appeals for retrial, clemency, and parole have been turned down. Meanwhile, Bill Heirens developed into a model prisoner, overseeing production in the prison garment factory, running a television and radio repair shop, and counseling other inmates. On February 6, 1972, after taking courses offered by visiting professors and through television from nearby Lewis College, Heirens became the first inmate in Illinois to receive a college degree.

In 2007, Columbia University forensic psychiatrist Dr. Michael H. Stone examined the Degnan murder evidence and interviewed William Heirens. His conclusion: "I feel his profile simply does not match that of a murderer."

In early June 2003, I flew to Chicago and met with author Dolores Kennedy, Clinical Professor of Law Steven A. Drizin, and members of William Heirens's defense team at the Northwestern University School of Law. Later that day, Dolores and I drove to the Dixon Correctional Center in northwestern Illinois. As we approached the lockup, I reflected back to the photos of the strong, handsome young man I'd seen as he was arrested fifty-six years earlier in 1946.

As the prison guards walked inmate number C-06103 toward us, I saw an old man broken in body and spirit. Bill Heirens was so frail and diabetic, it was difficult for him to speak.

At that moment I experienced a special kind of pain that comes from witnessing a great injustice. After returning to California, I felt compelled to write an appeal to the Illinois Prisoner Review Board stating my professional belief that Heirens is innocent and asking them to "at long last free Bill and allow him to live his final few years in dignity and respect."

So far my request and thousands of others have been denied. My hope is that this book will open a new examination of the Ross-Brown-Degnan murders by pointing to a much more likely suspect.

5.3 William Heirens, 2003

Chapter Six

Stop me before I kill more.

Note written in lipstick near the Degnan
murder scene, January 1946

Knowing what I did about Elizabeth Short's interest in the Degnan murder, I shifted my investigative compass to 1946 Chicago shortly after the publication of the *Black Dahlia Avenger*. Almost immediately I found a number of remarkable matches between my father's MOs as BDA and the murders of Josephine Alice Ross, Frances Brown, and Suzanne Degnan.

In the case of Josephine Alice Ross:

- The victim was assaulted in her residence and strangled. Her body was then placed in a partially filled bathtub. (Bauerdorf)
- After cutting and slashing the nude body, the suspect used a douche bag and nozzle to wash the body clean. (Short)
- The victim's nude body was posed. (Short, French)
- After a brutal overkill assault, the attacker covered the nude body with the victim's personal items of clothing and tightly tied the woman's own silk stocking around her throat. (French, Springer, Ellroy)
- Two witnesses described the suspect as male, age twenty to thirty, with black wavy hair.

In the case of Frances Brown:

- Her body was stripped nude and posed in the bathroom. (Short, French)
- The suspect used a douche bag and nozzle to wash the body clean. (Short)

- The suspect stabbed the victim with a knife that was then wrapped in cloth. (Kern)
- Night manager John Dedrick saw the killer exit the elevator and described him as male, Caucasian, thirty-five to forty years old, dark complexioned, wearing a dark overcoat and dark fedora hat.

6.1 **George Hodel, Franklin House, circa 1949**

George Hodel, who would have been thirty-eight in 1946, was Caucasian, six feet tall, and dark complexioned. This photograph shows him sitting on his desk in our Franklin Avenue house circa 1949. His physical appearance three years earlier would have been virtually the same.

The most critical piece of evidence left by the suspect at the Brown crime scene was the note written on the wall in bright red lipstick.

6.2 **"For heaven's sake catch me before I kill more I cannot control myself"**

A month after the Brown murder, the Degnan murder suspect left a similarly worded message, also handwritten in lipstick, adjacent to the murder room basement where Suzanne Degnan was slain. It read:

Stop me before I kill more.

And when witness David Decker observed the suspicious-looking man you may recall he described as "male, Caucasian, twenty-five to thirty, tall and thin, dark complexion, dark suit coat, light-colored slacks, dark cap" in the vestibule across from the Degnan residence, the description was consistent with how George Hodel appeared in 1946, when he was thirty-eight.[10] Although George Hodel was slightly older than the estimate, eyewitnesses' estimates frequently vary as much as five to ten years. The suspect had dropped a note, which Decker retrieved and gave to police.

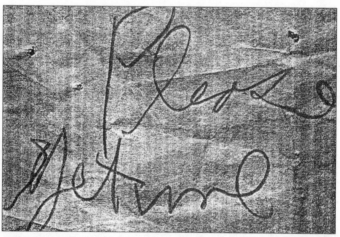

6.3 "Please get me"

A handwriting expert who examined the note at the time concluded, "It was written using the left hand, possibly to disguise the handwriting."

10 This overall description is consistent with how George Hodel appeared in 1946. Though thirty-eight, he could easily pass for a man many years younger.

In January 1947, a year later, my father—calling himself the Black Dahlia Avenger—mailed a postcard that was intercepted by Federal Postal Inspectors. It read:

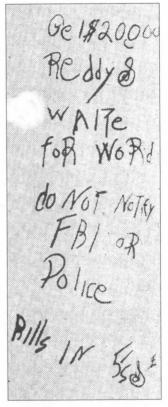

6.4

> We're going to Mexico City—catch us if you can.
>   2K's

In all three instances—the Lipstick Killer, the Degnan kidnapper, and the Black Dahlia Avenger—we find the same Jekyll-and-Hyde dynamic. Dr. Jekyll (the good half) asks desperately to be caught. While Mr. Hyde (the murderous monster within) taunts the police, demanding ransom money, and promising more victims, more murders, more blood.

The suspect in the Suzanne Degnan murder also left a ransom note in the victim's bedroom.

It contained what seem to be deliberate misspellings—"Reddy," "waite," and "safty." My father in his Black Dahlia Avenger mailings misspelled common words like Herald as "Hearld" and "Herld," and Los Angeles spelled "Los Angels." To repeat what nationally recognized handwriting expert Clark Sellers concluded from his analysis of the Avenger mailings:

6.5

It was evident the writer took great pains to disguise his or her personality by printing instead of writing the message and by endeavoring to appear illiterate. But the style and formation of the printed letters betrayed the writer as an educated person.

Also of special interest in the Degnan ransom note was the symbol that appears to represent an ampersand sign. Closer examination shows it to the musical notation known as a treble clef (also called a G clef) written backward.

During William Heirens's confession, Chicago police ordered him to rewrite the note. Heirens, who had no musical training, didn't know what the treble clef was and was unable to reproduce it. This comes through clearly in the confession transcript of Bill Heirens being questioned by State's Attorney William Tuohy and his assistant Wilbert Crowley, which reveals the suspect clumsily responding to questions about the symbol despite the questioner's attempt to lead him through this difficult spot.

> Q: Do you remember discussing with Mr. Tuohy the fact that you did not know how to make the character "&"?
> A: That is right.
> Q: You do know how to make that character, don't you?
> A: Made an "S" but I did not know how to make that. I never made that character before in my life.
> Q: Before you did make that character on that ransom note?
> A: Yes.
> Q: That is a photostat. No, that is a photograph of the ransom note that was written, that is exactly how you wrote it, isn't it?
> A: Yes.
> Q: Can you see that?
> A: Yes.
> Q: That is how you made it, isn't it?
> A: Yes.

George Hodel, on the other hand, had been a musical prodigy since age seven. Not only had he seen the treble clef symbol on a daily basis throughout his childhood, he would have handwritten the symbol hundreds of times while scoring his own compositions.

In the *Chicago Tribune* of January 10, 1946, handwriting expert Vernon Faxton concluded that "the ransom note, while attempting illiteracy, indicates a more educated person."

The author of the article also pointed out that "Musicians pointed to the backward ampersands, similar to treble clefs, as indicating the author of the ransom note was a musician."

Figure 6.6 is a sample of Bill Heirens's handwriting from a letter he wrote to a friend in December 1945, some three weeks *before* the Suzanne Degnan kidnapmurder occurred. As numerous experts have pointed out, it bears no resemblance to the handwriting found on the ransom note.

Suspecting that my father might have been the author of the Brown and Degnan murder notes, I contacted questioned document examiner Hannah McFarland and asked her to compare the handwriting in those notes to known samples of George Hodel's

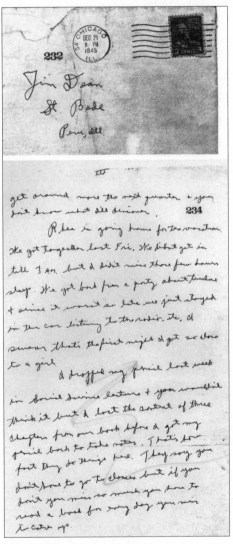

6.6 **William Heirens's handwriting, December 21, 1945**

handwriting. QDEs stress the importance of trying to obtain known samples, written as close in time to the questioned documents to which they are being compared. Our handwriting generally changes, sometimes quite dramatically, over the years. I included samples that spanned seventy-five years.

In addition, I asked her to examine handwriting samples that appeared on four snapshots that had been removed by newspaper reporters from Elizabeth Short's personal photo albums back in 1947. These four original Elizabeth Short snapshots were eventually sold as part of a *Los Angeles Examiner*'s archive collection and put up for auction years later in February 2003, when I acquired them.

These four snapshots were all originally owned by Elizabeth Short. All four were pasted into one of several of her personal photo albums that were recovered by police during the early stages of the 1947 investigation. Black album paper can be seen sticking to the back of each photograph, indicating they were ripped from one or more of her private albums.

Some Dahlia researchers have speculated that the handwriting on these photos was that of either Elizabeth Short or possibly news reporters who initially took possession of the albums and were allowed by LAPD detectives to keep them. Based on new information from my own investigation and supported by documentation found in the DA files, it is my opinion that the words seen on the snapshots were written by George Hodel. I believe that my father somehow came into temporary possession of the albums, possibly during Elizabeth's stay with him at either the Franklin house or a hotel. During their time together, perhaps he happened upon the photos of her with former boyfriends and asked her to name her old boyfriends as he wrote each name on the photograph.

Having recognized the handwriting on the four photos as my father's, and knowing that he would have had opportunity to label the photos while in possession of Elizabeth Short's album, I was interested to see if the QDE would establish a link between the Black Dahlia Avenger, the Lipstick Murderer, and my father.

6.7   6.8

Figures 6.7–6.10 were part of a set of five seperate photos mentioned in the DA
secret files that were mailed in by "The Avenger" to the *Los Angeles Herald
Examiner* a week after Elizabeth Short's murder. They establish that the suspect had access to her photos and/or photo album.

6.9

6.10

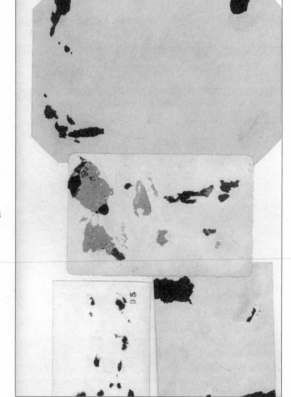

6.11 Back of
photographs showing
they were ripped from
her photo album(s)

On May 7, 2003, I received Questioned document examiner Hannah McFarland's report.[11] It read, in part:

Dear Mr. Hodel:

I have examined the following questioned documents (digitally reproduced) in an attempt to identify the author.

- Hand printing on four snapshot photographs from the mid-1940s
- Brown Note, printed using lipstick, December 1945
- Ransom Note, January 1946
- Gladys Kern Note, 1948

I compared these questioned documents to known (genuine) documents (digitally reproduced) that you have represented to me as having been authored by Dr. George Hill Hodel. Following are these known documents:

- K-1 Reverse side of self-portrait photograph, "Merlin gazes at cracked mirror," 1924
- K-2 Reverse side of self-portrait photograph, "Portrait of a chap suddenly aware of the words of Sigmund Freud," 1924
- K-3 Medical calendar book, "Genius and Disease," 1944
- K-4 "Chinese Chicken" drawing, April 1949
- K-6 "Love and Aloha to Father and Alice, Honolulu, 9/25/53"
- K-7 "Love to Dorero, December, 1974"
- K-8 "Dad," printed signature mailed to you, 1997
- K-9 Notes prepared for conference with wife, 10/15/98

Based upon the available evidence it is my professional opinion that the following four questioned documents were probably hand printed by the author of K-1 to K-9:

11 I am including excerpts rather than the entire report because at the time of my original 2003 request, I included additional documents to be examined that had no bearing on the Elizabeth Short investigation but were highly relevant to relating him to later crimes.

- Three of the four snapshots (see below for the remaining snap-shot)
- Ransom note
- Gladys Kern note

The *probable* opinion allows me to incorporate these four documents as additional comparison material against other questioned documents, which provides additional evidence of common authorship.

Note that the above expressed opinion is not conclusive because I examined non-original questioned documents and because there is less agreement between the questioned and known documents. And it appears the author deliberately altered their hand printing, except for the snapshots, to avoid identification. This disguise prevents a higher degree of agreement between the questioned and known documents. Although the snapshots do not appear disguised, the printing on them shows differences that could be due to natural variation.

In the world of handwriting terminology, a "probable" finding points "strongly toward the questioned and known documents having been written by the same individual," but falls short of "virtually certain." QD experts define six degrees of confidence that are less than "probable." They are: "indications," "no conclusion," "indications did not," "probably did not," "strong probability did not," and "elimination." (Source: *Journal of Forensic Sciences*, Letters to the Editor, March 1991)

In her report, QDE Hannah McFarland describes certain characteristics that led to her conclusion that George Hodel was the "probable" author of the Suzanne Degnan ransom note. I quote:

Ransom Note

- The letter "O" slants to the left while the other letters are primarily vertical or slant to the right;

- Variable letter size with the letter "O" repeatedly being much smaller than the other letters;
- Terminal downstrokes that are extra long;
- Terminal upstrokes that are extra high;
- Wide word spacing;
- The portion of the capital "R," "B," and "P" that resemble a capital "D" has extra-long horizontal initial and terminal strokes;
- The letter "U" does not have a downstroke on the right;
- The capital "I" is simplified by being devoid of cross-bars;
- Use of upper- and lowercase letters;
- Ascending cross-bars

Ms. McFarland based her conclusion that George Hodel "probably" wrote the Frances Brown "Lipstick Killer" message on the following:

Brown Note
- The letter "O" is much smaller than the other letters;
- The terminal downstroke of the letter "S" is extra long;
- Wide word spacing;
- Slant is primarily vertical;
- The letter "C" has a loop at the top

I declare under penalty of perjury under the laws of the State of Washington that the foregoing is true and correct to the best of my knowledge.

EXECUTED this seventh day of May, 2003, in Seattle, Washington

HANNAH McFARLAND

The similar handwriting is certainly a compelling link between George Hodel and the Chicago crime scenes, but it remains just one piece of the puzzle. As mentioned earlier, Chicago detectives had established that Suzanne Degnan had been strangled before her body was expertly dissected with a sharp knife. According to the Associated Press two lengths of clothesline were found in the basement where the dismemberment took place. This conflicts with other reports that they were found in the alley just outside "the murder room."

Figure 6.12, below, is a comparison of the Degnan noose to one used by the Black Dahlia Avenger to strangle Louise Springer in Los Angeles in June 1949.

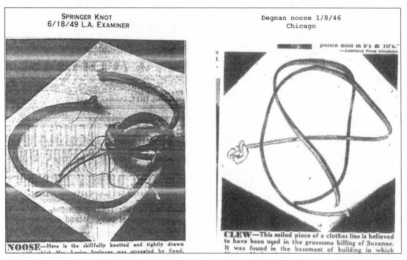

6.12

Also found near the Degnan crime scene were the two handkerchiefs. According to police, one of these was "wrapped like a gag."

In at least three of the Black Dahlia killings, a white handkerchief was left at the scene. This is so unusual a signature that I have always suspected it may have been an important part of the killer's MO. George Hodel, a medical doctor, would have easy access to chloroform and probably carried it in his black bag. Poured onto a handkerchief, it would be the perfect way to quickly silence his victims and prevent them from calling out. To my knowledge, none of the handkerchiefs were ever examined for traces of this chemical substance.

Interestingly, neither the handkerchief nor precut lengths of clothesline were mentioned in Bill Heirens's "confession." Instead, he claimed that he "just used [his] hands" to strangle the child inside her bedroom.

After the Chicago coroner examined the assembled pieces of Suzanne Degnan's body, he concluded: "It was a very clean job with absolutely no signs of hacking as would be evident if a dull tool was used." Dr. Jerry Kearns, the coroner's expert, added: "The killer had to be an expert. . . . Not even the average doctor could be so skillful."

In the coroner's report, the cause of death was listed as asphyxiation by strangulation. There were some visible marks to the neck. However, due to the decapitation, the coroner was unable to determine if it was caused by the ligatures found near the crime scene. In reviewing the 1946 coroner's protocol, I noticed a description of the actual bisection.

> The head has been removed at the level of the 4th cervical vertebra. . . . The trunk has been divided at the level of the umbilicus anteriorly and the 2nd lumbar vertebra posteriorly.

I found this highly significant. Why? Because in my Black Dahlia investigation the medical experts and surgeons who reviewed the Elizabeth Short coroner's reports and autopsy photos all came to the conclusion that the person who performed the bisection was a trained physician and surgeon—like my father.

In their opinion, Elizabeth Short's killer knew how to bisect a human body without having to cut through bone. As mentioned earlier, the procedure is known as a hemicorpectomy. It requires the physician to divide at the level of the umbilicus anteriorly and the second lumbar vertebra posteriorly. The hemicorpectomy on little Suzanne Degnan in January 1946 was the same one performed on Elizabeth "Black Dahlia" Short in January 1947.

Subsequent to the bisections, both victims were washed clean and sadistically posed in their respective city's streets so that the killer could create maximum horror. Suzanne Degnan's killer wanted the parts found, since he telephoned the police shortly after his crime and told them where to look. In the Elizabeth Short murder only about a year later, the killer would make certain they would be found with no need for a phone call by simply posing the body in plain view of a quiet suburban street.

And the brazen taunting didn't stop there. In the Elizabeth Short case, Dr. George Hodel, calling himself the Black Dahlia Avenger, mailed a wrapped package to the *Los Angeles Examiner* containing some of the victim's personal belongings: her address book, photographs, and identification. Suzanne Degnan's killer addressed and mailed a similar package, not to the press, but to the child's parents. In an act of pure evil, the monster sent the grieving mother a small cardboard box containing a human ear and the message: "will cut your ear next."

We know now that the bisection of Suzanne Degnan, her strangulation with a precut piece of clothesline, the handwriting in notes and at the crime scenes, the contacting of newspapers and investigators via handwritten notes, and the posing of Josephine Ross and Frances Brown all closely matched the crime signatures of the Black Dahlia Avenger's activities in L.A. While the evidence fell short of a smoking gun, I had not yet uncovered anything to rule my father out, and the circumstantial and forensic evidence was getting stronger as the investigation progressed.

My thoughts turned to the matter of opportunity: Could George Hodel have even been in Chicago to commit the crimes? Although it has so far been impossible to pinpoint where Dr. George Hodel was on a particular day some sixty years ago, I have been able to establish that he traveled often between 1944 and 1946. I know for a fact that my father made multiple trips east for business purposes and to study Chinese in preparation for his UN assignment to Hankow, China. In researching the subject, I learned that during the war years, the military's top language training school, known as the Army Specialized Training Program (ASTP), was located in Chicago, Illinois. The program offered a course in accelerated Chinese and was taught at the University of Chicago. If in fact this was the crash course my father took in preparation for China, he would have walked the grounds and shared the campus with a then-unknown young student by the name of William Heirens.

My father's letters confirm that he was in Washington, D.C., in January 1946, and in February 1946 he left for China. His UN assignment ended abruptly in August 1946 when he was discharged for unspecified "personal reasons" and returned to Los Angeles.

Therefore, it is possible that George Hodel visited Chicago in 1945 and again in 1946 either on business or as part of his training for his upcoming assignment with the United Nations Relief and Rehabilitation Administration. He could also have stopped in Chicago on his way to Washington, D.C., as very few direct flights existed at the time and many would have stopped in Chicago.

I found all of this deeply disturbing. As a veteran homicide detective it was clear to me that the Josephine Ross, Frances Brown, and Suzanne Degnan murders were not the acts of an opportunist teenage burglar with no previous history of violence. Instead, the murders were likely committed by a sophisticated and experienced sadist like my father— someone who felt compelled to kill. And I could not ignore the multiple coincidences between the Chicago and Los Angeles murders. But we are still missing a final piece of the puzzle, one that has convinced me that the bisections of Elizabeth Short and Suzanne Degnan were committed by the same person.

Chapter Seven

'Tis strange but true; for truth is always strange—
stranger than fiction.

Byron, *Don Juan*

There's another very tantalizing piece of evidence that my father left
deliberately to link himself to the murder of Suzanne Degnan. I discovered it by chance as I was retracing the likely route he would have driven
to dump Elizabeth Short's body at the location where she was discovered.

In nearly all of the historical references to the Black Dahlia crime
scene, the cross street has been identified as Thirty-ninth and Norton,
in the Leimert Park section of Los Angeles. That's wrong. The actual
location was nearly a full city block north.

Many have asked: Why this location? In *Black Dahlia Avenger* I detailed and substantiated the reasons why Elizabeth Short's body was
posed the way it was: as George Hodel's surreal homage to his friend
Man Ray's most famous works, *The Minotaur* and *The Lover's Lips*. But
why was the body *placed* where it was? For such a deliberate killer, there
must have been a specific reason.

The answer from LAPD detectives in 1947: "It was a quiet residential
neighborhood, and a lover's lane, where he wouldn't be seen."

But the real reason has nothing to do with it being a lover's lane, and
everything to do with George Hodel's word games and an eerie link to
Chicago and the Suzanne Degnan murder the year before.

George Hodel had been a cabdriver for the Los Angeles Yellow Cab
Company in the 1920s. He knew the city's streets. Name any address,
and the young genius, renowned for his perfect photographic memory,
could take you there.

On the chilly winter morning of January 15, 1947, Dr. George Hodel
was alone at the Franklin house. His ex-wife and three sons were

temporarily away, staying at their uncle's home nearly two miles away. He began to prepare his masterpiece.

The extended torture and sadistic sexual abuse of his victim/girlfriend, Elizabeth Short, had ended. She lay dead. Like the operation performed on little Suzanne Degnan just a year before, he skillfully bisected the body. He knew exactly how and where to go with his scalpel. As with the Degnan body, the bisection was made between the second and third lumbar vertebrae. Using a coconut fiber brush, he then washed the two sections clean in the master bathtub, drying them with a towel. He walked downstairs and retrieved two large empty paper cement sacks from the basement, left behind by day laborers who'd been working for a week to reinforce the structural pillars beneath the house.

The doctor returned to the master bath, lifted one-half of his victim's body onto one of the cement sacks, carried it out to the rear garage, and placed it on the backseat of his car. He returned and did the same with the second half of the body, likely covering both with paper bags (later found near the body) for concealment.

The dapper physician backed his 1936 black Packard sedan out of the garage and into the alley that paralleled Franklin Avenue, then drove east the short 100 feet to Normandie Avenue. Hollywood's Los Feliz neighborhood was still asleep.

After a right turn from the alley, he headed south to Santa Barbara Boulevard. There he made another right and drove west two short miles, smiling to himself as the street sign came into view—DEGNAN BLVD.

He turned right onto Degnan and drove north, looking for just the right spot. Too many houses. He continued north, edging off to the left as he approached the division ahead. The Packard crept north another block. Perfect! A large vacant lot, with the nearest house a block away.

Still facing north, he pulled the car to the west curb, quickly exited, and removed the body parts, one at a time. Carrying each piece on its separate paper sack he set them in the open field, just inches from the sidewalk. Working quickly, he would have posed the upper torso, placing the hands overhead, to mimic Man Ray's famous photograph *The Minotaur*. Then the lower section, juxtaposed and offset a little to the east.

He pulled the empty cement sacks away from the body, throwing them to the north, away from his sculpture. Now, the final touches. Removing one of her earrings from his pocket he placed it loose inside her left ear. Finally, he took a man's black-faced military wristwatch from his jacket pocket, ripped the wristband away from the body of the watch, and used his handkerchief to carefully wipe the face and band of telltale fingerprints.

Again, his sardonic grin appeared as he positioned the watch inside the gaping upper torso. Finished, and in such a short time.

7.1 Elizabeth Short's posed body compared to Man Ray's *The Minotaur* (1936)

Glancing west from Degnan across the empty lot, George thought he caught the profile of a man standing in the field, half a block away. Back in the car, he drove north on Degnan to Coliseum, then west one block to Crenshaw Boulevard. Back to the Franklin house. Halfway home he pulled to the east curb just south of Olympic Boulevard, where he removed Elizabeth's empty purse and shoes from the floorboard and set them on top of a garbage can, outside a restaurant, which was just opening for the breakfast crowd. Thanks to an alert witness these items would later be recovered by LAPD and positively identified as belonging to the victim, Elizabeth Short.

Now all the Avenger had to do was wait for his evening newspaper and the headlines that were sure to come. He didn't have to wait long.

The *Los Angeles Examiner* printed a special "Extra" afternoon edition with the front-page story that would consume Los Angelenos for the next full month:

WOMAN'S NUDE BODY FOUND IN LOVER'S LANE
FIEND TORTURES, KILLS GIRL; LEAVES BODY IN L.A. LOT

George Hodel was pleased, but also disappointed. Reporters, as usual, had gotten it wrong. According to their accounts the body had been found at Thirty-ninth and Norton. No! It was Thirty-ninth and Degnan. Incompetent fools had messed up his subtle message.

As it turns out, it was George Hodel who had gotten it wrong, not the press. George zigged when he should have zagged.

The Franklin house, at Franklin and Normandie (5121 Franklin Avenue), was just seven miles north of where Elizabeth Short's body was posed. The most direct route was as I've previously described: south on Normandie, west on Santa Barbara (now renamed Martin Luther King Jr. Boulevard), then right on Degnan. Even sixty years later, maps show what was apparent at the time: Deg-

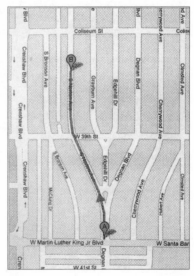

nan divides in two a block north of what was then called Santa Barbara, becoming in effect two different streets altogether. One continues as Degnan, the other is called Norton Avenue.

Leimert Park residents found it so confusing that the city was eventually forced to post signs and arrows to clarify directions. If you want to stay on Degnan, *bear to the right*. Even Google Maps has placed arrowed instructions showing Degnan breaking off to the right.

But in 1947 there were no posted 7.2 signs or warnings—just the divided street. Unmarked, it was a fifty-fifty guess. George Hodel guessed wrong and bore left, thinking he was still on Degnan. He had rolled onto Norton Avenue instead.

7.3

As he set aside the evening paper, George might have thought to himself, "No matter. Perhaps it's better to play my cards closer to my vest."

Elizabeth had gone to Chicago and discovered aspects of his secret. She had to die, but not without honor. A part of him respected her ingenuity. He'd wanted to reward and memorialize her in death.

Something very special, fitting, another clue—in plain sight, yet fiendishly hidden. He searched his sick, brilliant mind. Then it came to him. The perfect grave marker:

7.4

As we'll see, my father's street name messages didn't begin or end with Degnan Boulevard.

On Tuesday, February 19, 1946, six weeks after six-year-old Suzanne Degnan was murdered, Chicago electrical workers made a ghastly discovery. Opening a manhole cover three blocks from the Degnan residence, they found the last parts of Suzanne's body—her arms—eerily preserved with little or no decomposition, as if stored in underground refrigeration, due to Chicago's cold winter weather.

As I read the 1946 *Chicago Tribune*'s gruesome description of the discovery, I saw it. The paper had even unwittingly capitalized the message making it impossible to miss. It read:

> The arms were found bent at the elbows in an alley just off HOLLYWOOD St.

Another diabolical signpost—the killer's "message" confirming for me his special signature. I believe George Hodel, the Hollywood physician, after placing little Suzanne Degnan's body parts in underground storm drains throughout Chicago's north side, then deliberately selected a street name as his grave marker and compass. He set it to secretly point westward to "Hollywood." A year later, as the Black Dahlia Avenger, he

7.5 **Position of Degnan's arms as posed in sewer**

would repeat his surgical crime, only this time with louder taunts and longer headlines. As before, he would use his victim's body parts as his directional compass, this time pointing eastward, back to Chicago, back to—Degnan.

As our investigation continues we shall soon see how all of this was an intrinsic part of my father's plan.

For me, the answer came when I found more murders; or more murders found me. And then the pieces of the ghastly, psychopathic game my father had played his entire adult life started to fit together. It gets stranger and darker still.

PART THREE

MANILA

Chapter Eight

The truth will come to light; murder cannot be hid long.

William Shakespeare, *The Merchant of Venice*

Following the publication of *Black Dahlia Avenger* in 2003 I received hundreds of e-mails and letters. Some called me a nutjob, others commended my courage. Several readers in the Philippines alerted me to the fact that the murder-bisection of Elizabeth Short bore a very strong resemblance to a high-profile murder-dismemberment that occurred in Manila in 1967.

From the mid-1950s until 1988 George Hodel based his home and business in the Philippine capital of Manila. He moved there after fleeing Los Angeles, married a young woman from a prominent Filipino family, reinvented himself as an international market research expert, and quickly sired four more children.

An American contact in Manila helped me assemble the details of the case. On Tuesday, May 30, 1967, residents of Manila awoke to shocking front-page news in the *Manila Times*:

PAIR OF GIRL'S LEGS FOUND ON TRASH PILE

Was anybody—probably an 18-year-old girl—murdered in Manila these past few days? This question is bothering Manila police homicide investigators after a garbage collector found a pair of legs, severed neatly into four parts at the knees and hip joints and wrapped in old newspapers, on a trash pile on Malabon St., and Rizal Ave., Sta. Cruz, at 11:25 last night.

A day later, the nude, dissected torso of the young woman was found in a vacant lot, not far from the Guadalupe Bridge, in Manila's Makati

Rizal business district. Like little Suzanne Degnan, the woman's head and legs had been removed. Her head was never found.

For a few hours, the woman remained a Jane Doe. Then, just as had occurred in the Black Dahlia murder police identified her from finger-prints. In this case, the prints were on an application she'd filled out to be a restaurant waitress.

The horrific crime was quickly named Manila's "crime of the century" and was described by police as "the most brutal murder in our department's history." Like the murder of Chicago's Suzanne Degnan and L.A.'s Black Dahlia, the murder of Lucila Lalu y Tolentino commanded page-one headlines for months. Because of the bisection and scattered body parts, press dubbed the crime "The Jigsaw Murder."

8.1 and 8.2 **Lucila Lalu y Tolentino**

The victim—Lucila Lalu y Tolentino—was an attractive twenty-nine-year-old Filipina born in the fishing and farming community of Candaba in Central Luzon's Pampanga province. Lucila, or Lucy as her friends called her, had recently started two businesses at the same location—Lucy's Beauty Shop and the Pagoda Cocktail Lounge at 1616 Mayhalique Street in Manila.

She was last seen in the beauty shop by her brother, Cesar, at about ten p.m. on May 28, 1967. Peering through the locked glass window, he saw her sleeping on a couch. Police later speculated that she might have already been dead at the time.

Investigators determined that Lucila Lalu's hands had been tightly tied behind her back with rope before she was severely beaten, then strangled. The suspect used newspapers, some of which were two weeks old, to wrap pieces of her body.

The police follow-up investigation provided little new information. One witness came forward who'd heard Lucila arguing with a man at her beauty shop on the night of her murder. She'd heard Lucy yell out, "*Bakit! Bakit!*" ("Why? Why?") Then ten minutes later, "*Ayoko! Ayoko!*" ("I don't want to! I don't want to!")

Another witness claimed she saw Lucila dragged from her place of business and forced into a car and driven away. No description of her abductor was ever publicly released. But Manila police did tell the press they thought "a possible suspect is a wealthy man who is an expert in the use of knives." Driving one's own car in Manila in 1967 would have been a sign of some wealth. They also suspected the motive was "jealousy" and revealed that the victim had a number of different boyfriends.

The most telling evidence came from the report by the coroner and medical experts, which stated:

> The dismemberment was surgical in nature—the bones were not cut but were "disarticulated," i.e., "the bone ligaments were cut thus loosening the bones from their sockets (hip and knee joints). . . ."
>
> The skin incision on the points of amputation were surgical in nature and expertly done with the use of a very sharp bladed instrument.

According to the autopsy, the victim was also "one month pregnant."

Lucila Lalu had previously given birth to a son, fathered by her boyfriend, Pat Vera, a veteran police officer with the Manila Police Department. Vera was arrested along with four or five other men, who were all eventually released.

Then the Manila police zeroed in on a first-year dental student named Jose Luis Santiano, who rented a room above Lucila's shop. After extensive grilling, the suspect "confessed." But as soon as he was transferred from police custody, he retracted his confession, claiming it had been given under duress.

Despite the public outrage, Santiano was prosecuted and convicted. The case then went to the Court of Appeals, which found that the young man's confession was inconsistent with the known facts of the crime. Furthermore, the judges didn't believe that Santiano had the skill to perform the dismemberment. The evidence, in their opinion, pointed to a trained physician rather than a first-year dental student with no experience in surgical procedures.

Santiano was acquitted of the charges and set free. Forty years later, the murder remains unsolved.

The facts show that the Lucila Lalu murder was strikingly consistent in MO to both the Black Dahlia and Degnan crimes—a forcible abduction of a female, the binding of the victim's hands and feet with rope, followed by ligature strangulation. Then came the skilled bisection of the body by what law enforcement officers in all three crimes opined was "performed by a highly trained surgeon" who, after his "operation," then washed clean and towel-dried the body parts. Finally, we see the killer's deliberate placement of his victims' bodies on the public streets of three major cities: Chicago, Los Angeles, and Manila. His acts revealed his clear intent— which was to so shock and outrage the public that his killings would generate the maximum publicity and sensationalism. It worked!

According to police reports, the victim's arms and legs had been wrapped in newspapers and placed atop a trash can at Malabon Avenue and Rizal Boulevard, six blocks north of Lucila's beauty salon and the Pagoda Club bar. A current map shows that the trash can was located directly across the street from Manila's Department of Health.

Like the Black Dahlia murderer in 1947, Lucila Lalu's killer had performed the operation elsewhere, though Manila police never discovered the murder site, then drove a few miles away and placed the torso in a vacant lot, posing it just off a roadway. The *Manila Times* described the location as being "in Makati District, on Epifanio de los Santos Avenue, approaching the Guadalupe Bridge."

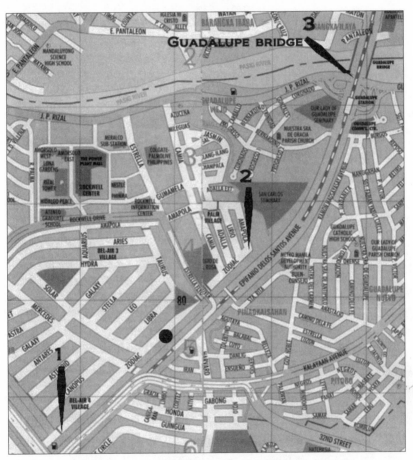

8.3 **Map showing the Makati District of Manila, Philippines**

I haven't been able to ascertain the exact spot where the dissected torso was placed, but the general vicinity was easy to locate on a map. The above map shows the Makati District. The vacant lot was on "Epifanio de los Santos Avenue approaching Guadalupe Bridge."

I've marked the bridge as number 3. The body was placed some-where between markers 1 and 2 just off a highway named Epifanio de los Santos, immediately south of the bridge and abutting and running parallel to a street named Zodiac. Interestingly, the street immediately above Zodiac is Libra, which was George Hodel's astrological Zodiac sign.

In the 1950s, before his papal annulment from his third wife, Hortensia, my father's family residence was in Makati, in Forbes Park, less than a mile away from Zodiac and Epifanio de los Santos Avenue. He traversed these streets many times. He would have known their names.

8.4

1. Dr. Hodel's INRA-ASIA Office/Penthouse residence on Manila Bay, 1967
2. Hodel family residence in Forbes Park, Makati District
3. Location Lucila Lalu's body parts found in Makati District
4. Guadalupe Bridge, Makati District
   Distances: Hodel office (1) to Hodel residence (2) = 3 miles; Hodel residence to victim's body = 1/2 mile

In 1967, my father, now more than ten years single, was living as a bachelor in the Admiral Apartment on Manila Bay. His ex-wife and their four children, my half-brothers and half-sisters, continued to reside in the Makati District in the ultrawealthy Forbes Park neighborhood, the Beverly Hills of Manila. I visited them occasionally on weekend liberty, during 1960–1961, when I was stationed at nearby Subic Bay Naval Base.

During my frequent weekend liberties to Manila, Father and I would regularly go drinking at the casinos and nightclubs scattered along Dewey Boulevard on Manila Bay. These clubs featured dancing girls and young prostitutes. It is possible that some of these same "working girls" would have frequented Lucila Lalu's nearby Pagoda Club. In the mid-1960s, did George Hodel have a relationship, amorous or otherwise, with Lucila Lalu? Did he know her, perhaps as a patron at her Pagoda Club or as a financial supporter of her business? Did Lucy at one point approach the wealthy American doctor with a disturbing announcement: "I am pregnant with your child!"?

Little direct evidence of George Hodel's involvement in Lucila Lalu's death has yet to come to light. But once again we have tantalizing circumstantial evidence: As in the Dahlia and Degnan cases, a beautiful, disarticulated victim is found scattered around a city for maximum impact and horror. Living nearby is George Hodel.

And what was the significance of his placing Lucila Lalu's torso on or near Zodiac Street? I would soon find out. As with Degnan and Dahlia, the answer would come from yet another series of crimes, a connection so preposterous as to be unbelievable—until I became convinced it was true.

PART FOUR

ZODIAC

Chapter Nine

Bates had to die. There will be more.

Z

Up until three years ago, my sole contact with anything having to do with Zodiac occurred back around 1972, while I was still working as a detective at Hollywood Homicide. Inspector William "Bill" Armstrong—one of the two San Francisco homicide detectives assigned to the Zodiac case—blew into town to try to locate a witness related to his investigation. I helped him find some source information and check a few addresses. Then the two of us went out for drinks.

As we shared whisky at VJ's, a cop bar on Sunset, Bill sounded optimistic that the Zodiac case would be solved.

Little did I know.

My next brush with Zodiac came thirty-three years later when a webmaster named Tom Voigt approached me about making my black dahliaavenger.com Web site more accessible. Intrigued, I went to my computer and called up another site Tom had designed—Zodiackiller.com. The volume of documentation on the famously still-unsolved Zodiac murders was astounding.

Casually, I clicked on a Special Bulletin believed to have been originally prepared by the San Francisco Police Department, which featured a composite drawing of the suspect from verbal descriptions provided by eyewitnesses. I nearly fell out of my chair. The original police source of this composite drawing (one of several) is still in question. To my knowledge, it first appeared *publicly* on the 1974 paperback cover of *Great Crimes of San Francisco*. The book was an anthology of San Francisco area true-crime essays written by various authors and edited by Dean W. Dickensheet. The crimes spanned eight decades. The essay on Zodiac was entitled "This is the Zodiac Speaking..." and was written by then *San Francisco Chronicle* reporter Duffy Jennings, who had replaced

Paul Avery. In January 2007, a confidential source of mine contacted Duffy Jennings, who verified that the composite originated from law enforcement. Jennings could not recall which agency; however SFPD would be the most likely, as their name is shown on the bulletin.

"Can't be!"

Was my mind playing tricks on me? I closed my eyes and looked again.

9.1 **George Hodel, 1974; Zodiac Composite, 1969**

Staring at me from the screen was a very strong likeness of my father circa 1974. Could this be possible? As I began to review the material I discovered that one of the most reliable eyewitnesses to the Zodiac killings, a San Francisco patrolman named Donald Fouke, had provided the following physical description of Zodiac:

> Male, White, American, 35 to 45 years, 5 foot 10 to 6 foot 2, 180 to 200 pounds, medium complexion, short brown or light-colored hair possibly graying in rear (may have been lighting that caused this effect). Navy blue jacket, brown pleated pants, baggy in rear (rust brown), possibly wearing low-cut shoes, wearing glasses.

On October 10, 1969 (the day before Fouke provided the above description), George Hodel celebrated his sixty-second birthday. But as all of us who knew him can attest, his physical condition and appearance belied his age. In fact, he could have easily passed for a man, say, in his mid-to-late forties. In 1969 he was strong and in excellent health. His physical description would have been as follows:

Male, White, American, 62 years, 6 feet tall 185 pounds, medium to dark complexion, short black hair with partial graying. Regularly wears black horn-rimmed glasses.

More frequently than not, George Hodel wore pleated slacks, which, while rarely seen on younger men in the late sixties, were the custom for older professionals. His glasses were identical to those worn by Zodiac in at least one of his murders.

I continued to stare at the monitor as my mind raced. Was it possible that the serial killer known and identified as the Black Dahlia Avenger left the United States for twenty years only to return and reinvent himself in San Francisco as Zodiac?

The intellectual part of me said, No! Dad was too old, and he didn't even live in the country during those years. Drop it and move on. But my gut, my cop's sixth sense, countered strongly: Serial killers don't stop until they're caught, go to prison, or die. Check it out.

Four years and several thousand investigative hours later, I can report that my intuition was correct. The evidence linking my father, Dr. George Hodel, to the Zodiac murders in the San Francisco area in the summer and fall of 1969 is exceptionally strong and compelling. And it adds fascinating layers to our understanding of a brilliant but vicious psychopath—a real-life Hannibal Lecter (including his credentialed degree in psychiatry) who received his utmost pleasure in terrorizing his victims and then taunting the police.

Cheri Jo Bates

Approximately sixty-five miles southeast of
Los Angeles lies the city of Riverside, California. Nestled in the barren San Bernardino
Valley, this center of California's citrus industry is the birthplace of Bobby Bonds,
prima ballerina Darci Kistler, and radio personality Don Imus. It also claims to own the
"World's Largest Paper Cup," which rises
sixty-eight feet in front of the Dixie Corporation warehouse on Iowa Street.

9.2

Back in 1966, Riverside was a quiet agri-
cultural center that rarely received national
attention.

On a warm Sunday night in 1966, the
day before Halloween, an eighteen-year-old former Ramona High
School cheerleader named Cheri Jo Bates climbed into her lime-green
Volkswagen Bug and drove to the Riverside City College Library.

After checking out some research books, the pretty blond coed
packed her bags and headed back to her car. She didn't know that while
she was studying, someone had opened the car's hood, ripped out the
distributor coil and condenser, then disconnected the middle wire of
the distributor. As she tried in vain to start the engine, a man appeared
and offered her a ride.

According to a confession letter sent to police and media by the
person claiming to be the killer, "She was . . . very willing to talk with
me. I told her that my car was down the street and that I would give her
a lift home."

That's when things turned ugly. "When we were away from the library, walking," the killer wrote, "I said it was (a)bout time. She asked
me 'About time for what'? I said it was about time for her to die."

Two separate witnesses reported hearing an "awful scream" at
around ten thirty, followed by "a muted scream, and then a loud sound
like an old car being started up." It wasn't until six thirty the following

morning that a campus groundskeeper found her body. She'd been choked and beaten about the face, stabbed multiple times in the chest and back, and slashed so violently across the throat that she'd nearly been decapitated.

It appeared from the churned-up ground that Cheri Jo Bates had fought hard. Hair follicles, likely belonging to the suspect, were found under her fingernails. Detectives also found a tuft of human hair clutched in her right hand. Riverside PD Chief of Detectives Captain Irwin Cross would later indicate that this, along with the rest of the physical evidence, was forwarded to the state laboratory in Sacramento and "preliminary analysis tends to show the murderer is a white male." If still available, this evidence could potentially be a strong source sample for the suspect's DNA. Shoe or heel prints found at the scene led detectives to believe that the suspect wore a size ten shoe.

Later that morning, Halloween, the following headline appeared in the *Riverside Press*:

RCC COED, 18, SLAIN ON CAMPUS

Riverside detectives recovered a man's Timex watch with a seven-inch wristband approximately ten feet from Cheri Jo's body. The time on its face read 12:23. Detectives speculated that the watch fell from the suspect's wrist during the struggle.

According to unconfirmed reports, authorities eventually traced the watch to a foreign military PX (post exchange), but the country of origin was never officially released.

It seemed that Cheri Jo Bates's attacker had escaped unseen. Her purse and identification were found at the scene. And the young woman had not been sexually assaulted.

Judging by the available evidence, detectives speculated that her murder was a crime of passion. They focused their investigation on possible suitors, ex-boyfriends, and men linked to Ms. Bates.

Then, almost one month after the attack, the case took a very bizarre turn. The Riverside Police Department and Riverside *Enterprise* received identical unsolicited confessions.

9.3 and (inset) 9.4

Experts determined that the letters had been typed using a portable Royal typewriter. The confession purportedly included a byline containing twelve blank characters representing the killer's name.

Riverside detectives concluded that the "confession" had been sent by Cheri's killer, because it contained details of the crime that had not been publicly revealed.

A reproduced copy of the letter, including unusual word usage and misspellings in bold, appears below:

THE CONFESSION
BY—-—-——-—-——-—-

SHE WAS YOUNG AND BEAUTIFUL. BUT NOW SHE IS BAT-
TERED AND DEAD. SHE IS NOT THE FIRST AND SHE WILL NOT
BE THE LAST. I LAY AWAKE NIGHTS THINKING ABOUT MY

NEXT VICTIM. MAYBE SHE WILL BE THE BEAUTIFUL BLOND THAT BABYSITS NEAR THE LITTLE STORE AND WALKS DOWN THE DARK ALLEY EACH EVENING ABOUT SEVEN. OR MAYBE SHE WILL BE THE SHAPELY BLUE EYED **BROWNETT** THAT SAID NO WHEN I ASKED HER FOR A DATE IN HIGH SCHOOL. BUT MAYBE IT WILL NOT BE EITHER. BUT I SHALL CUT OFF HER FEMALE PARTS AND DEPOSIT THEM FOR THE WHOLE CITY TO SEE. SO DON'T **MAKI** IT **TO** EASY FOR ME. KEEP YOUR SISTERS, DAUGHTERS, AND WIVES OFF THE STREETS AND ALLEYS. MISS BATES WAS STUPID. SHE WENT TO THE SLAUGHTER LIKE A LAMB. SHE DID NOT PUT UP A STRUG-GLE. BUT I DID. IT WAS A BALL. I FIRST PULLED THE **MIDDLI** WIRE FROM THE DISTRIBUTOR. THEN I WAITED FOR HER IN THE LIBRARY AND FOLLOWED HER OUT AFTER ABOUT TWO **MINUTS**. THE BATTERY MUST HAVE BEEN ABOUT DEAD BY THEN I THEN OFFERED TO HELP. SHE WAS THEN VERY WILL-ING TO TALK WITH ME. I TOLD HER THAT MY CAR WAS DOWN THE STREET AND THAT I WOULD GIVE HER A LIFT HOME. WHEN WE WERE AWAY FROM THE LIBRARY WALKING. I SAID IT WAS **BOUT** TIME. SHE ASKED ME, "ABOUT TIME FOR WHAT". I SAID IT WAS ABOUT TIME FOR HER TO DIE. I GRABBED HER AROUND THE NECK WITH MY HAND OVER HER MOUTH AND MY OTHER HAND WITH A SMALL KNIFE AT HER THROAT. SHE WENT VERY WILLINGLY. HER BREAST FELT VERY WARM AND FIRM UNDER MY HANDS. BUT ONLY ONE THING WAS ON MY MIND. MAKING HER PAY FOR THE BRUSH OFFS THAT SHE HAD GIVEN ME DURING THE YEARS PRIOR. SHE DIED HARD. SHE SQUIRMED AND SHOOK AS I **CHOAKED** HER. AND HER LIPS **TWICHED**. SHE LET OUT A SCREAM **OXCE** AND I KICKED HER HEAD TO SHUT HER UP. I PLUNGED THE KNIFE INTO HER AND IT BROKE. I THEN FINISHED THE JOB BY CUTTING HER THROAT. I AM NOT SICK. I AM INSANE. BUT THAT WILL NOT STOP THE GAME. THIS LETTER SHOULD BE PUBLISHED FOR ALL TO READ IT. IT JUST MIGHT SAVE THAT GIRL IN THE ALLEY. BUT THAT'S UP TO YOU. IT WILL BE ON YOUR

CONSCIENCE. NOT MINE. YES, I DID **MAXE** THAT CALL TO YOU ALSO. IT WAS JUST A WARNING. BEWARE . . . I AM STALK-ING YOUR GIRLS NOW.

    CC. CHIEF OF POLICE

    ENTERPRISE

9.5

A month later, a Riverside City College employee discovered a poem written on a desk that had been previously located inside the school library.

Sick of living/unwilling to die

cut.
clean.
if red/
clean.
blood spurting,
        dripping,
            spilling;
all over her new
dress.
oh well.
it was red
anyway.
life draining into an
uncertain death.
she won't
die.
this time.
Someone'll find her.
Just wait till
next time.
            rh

9.6

Police speculated that it could have been written by Cheri Jo Bates's killer, who said in his "confession" that he stalked her to the library, where he waited for her to finish studying. The poem was written in ballpoint pen and several of the words were overwritten so that they appear bold.

The poem read:

Sick of living/unwilling to die
cut.
clean.
if **red/**
clean.
blood spurting,
dripping,
spilling;
all **over** her new
dress.
oh well
it was red
anyway.
life draining into an
uncertain death.
she won't
die.
this **time**
someone ll find her.
just wait till
next time.
rh

Then, on the six-month anniversary of the crime, April 30, 1967, three separate and nearly identically worded notes were mailed to the *Riverside Press*, Riverside police, and Cheri Bates's father, whose address had been made public in the original coverage of the story. All three were mailed with double the amount of necessary postage—two four-cent stamps.

9.7

The large block printing written in pencil on lined paper, read:

BATES HAD TO DIE
THERE WILL BE MORE
Z

Riverside PD investigators racked their brains over the identity of "Z" as they continued to pursue the case with vigor. But no further communications from the killer arrived. And they were unable to develop significant new leads.

In the late sixties Riverside PD likely had only two or three full-time detectives assigned to Homicide. As time passed and the demand to solve new crimes increased, detectives assigned to the Bates investigation were forced to push it to a back burner. Back in those days, Riverside PD didn't have a "Cold Case Unit" that could take over.

The concept of a serial killer was not widely known or considered in those days. There had never been any indication that the Bates murder was anything other than the isolated brutal slaying of a beautiful young coed. Because of the time gap, Riverside detectives had no knowledge or reason to connect the Bates attack to the then unsolved Black Dahlia Avenger murders that had occurred in nearby Los Angeles some twenty years earlier. Had they known, they would have found a remarkable similarity in both MO and signatures:

- Taunting notes sent to the police, local newspapers, and relatives of the victims (Bauerdorf, Short, Kern)
- Confessions sent relating specifics of the crime (Bauerdorf, Short, Kern)
- The use of what seem to be deliberate misspellings (Short, Kern)
- Watches left at the crime scene (Short)
- Victim stabbed repeatedly and slashed across the neck (Kern)

Nor could they have been aware of a potentially important link to the murder and dismemberment of Lucila Lalu in Manila. The Bates killer in his multiple mailings made two separate promises. First, on the one-month anniversary of the Bates murder in Z's typed confession he wrote:

I SHALL CUT OFF HER FEMALE PARTS AND DEPOSIT THEM FOR THE WHOLE CITY TO SEE . . .

His second promise came on the six-month anniversary, April 30, 1967, in a taunting sadistic letter to the victims' parents and police. He raged:

THERE WILL BE MORE

Just three weeks after this promise, in faraway Manila, more came—in the form of that city's most brutal murder ever. Why the most brutal? Because, as horrible as Lucila's dissection and decapitation was, what made it top Manila's crime charts was its absolute savagery. The fact that the killer had deposited the victim's body parts for the whole city to see.

But none of this was known back then. Riverside homicide detectives continued to work their investigation, but after a few years with no new clues, the case went cold. Riverside detectives remained convinced that Cheri Jo Bates's murder was a standalone.

But that changed dramatically in 1970 when criminologists and crime reporters started to see the Cheri Jo Bates murder as part of a much larger story, a story that until then had been isolated farther north, in the Bay Area of California. As the November 16, 1970, headline in the *Los Angeles Times* stated emphatically:

ZODIAC LINKED TO RIVERSIDE SLAYING

9.7

Chapter Ten

All I have killed will become my slaves.

Zodiac

On a cold Friday night in December 1968, a seventeen-year-old high school wrestler and Eagle Scout named David Faraday borrowed his mother's 1961 two-tone Rambler station wagon to take sixteen-year-old Betty Jensen to a Christmas concert at Hogan High School in Vallejo, California—thirty miles northeast of San Francisco. Red-haired Betty wore her favorite lavender dress. It was their first date.

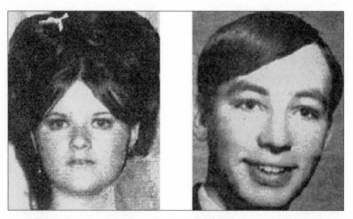

10.1 Betty Jensen, age sixteen; David Faraday, age seventeen

The teenagers never made it to the concert. Instead, they decided to stop at a local restaurant before driving out to an isolated "lovers lane" ten miles east of Vallejo, just off Lake Herman Road.

Shortly after eleven p.m. an unidentified suspect approached the young couple while they were seated inside the Rambler, pointed his handgun at David and Betty, and blew out the rear window. The terrified couple scrambled out the front passenger door.

David was immediately shot in the head and crumpled to the ground. Betty Lou attempted to run, but was stopped by five bullets in her back. She collapsed ten feet from the rear of the Rambler.

EMS personnel pronounced her dead at the scene thirty minutes later. David fought for his life for another twenty minutes before being pronounced DOA at the emergency room.

A "Double 187" (double homicide) call went out to the Solano County sheriffs. The sleepy, middle-class community of five thousand hadn't seen a murder in five years.

After studying the crime scene, the Solano County sheriff's detectives concluded that the suspect had fired a total of ten shots from a .22 caliber semiautomatic handgun. They found no indication of any type of sexual assault and concluded that the cold-blooded killer had finished his work in two minutes.

The question remained: Why?

An extensive investigation that included in-depth interviews with the victims' families and their friends yielded no leads, no physical description of the suspect, and no motive for the crime.

The murders seemed to be the work of a "crazed killer" working alone.

Six months later, he struck again.

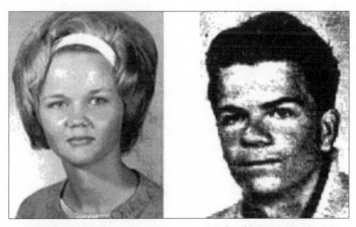

10.2 **Darlene Ferrin, age twenty-two; Michael Mageau, age nineteen**

The next crime took place just three miles east. At approximately five minutes to midnight on July 4, 1969, Darlene Ferrin, age twenty-two, and Michael Mageau, age nineteen, were seated in Darlene's light brown 1963 Corvair, in a secluded parking lot, adjacent to Blue Rock Springs Park.

As the two youngsters talked, a car pulled up behind them and parked. A male exited and approached the front passenger's side of the Corvair and shined a flashlight into Michael Mageau's face. Assuming it was a police officer, Michael reached for his identification.

Without warning, the stranger raised a handgun and fired. Bullets ripped into Michael's face and chest. In an effort to avoid further damage, the wounded teenager hurled his body into the backseat. Darlene, seated behind the steering wheel, was shot in both arms and in the back.

Without saying a word, the shooter turned and walked back to his car. Hearing Mageau cry out in pain, he did an about-face and coolly fired two more bullets into both Darlene Ferrin and Michael Mageau.

Mageau, bleeding profusely from multiple gunshot wounds, managed to open the passenger door and fall to the ground. As he looked up, he saw the suspect turn his car around and, as he later told police, the suspect "peeled tires and sped off toward the town of Vallejo at a high rate of speed."

Fifteen minutes later, passing motorists discovered the wounded couple and called the police. Darlene Ferrin died in an ambulance en-route to the hospital. Michael Mageau was rushed into surgery and despite his multiple wounds and heavy loss of blood, managed to survive.

He gave police a vague initial description of the shooter. "He was a white male. It was dark and I only saw his profile. I never saw his face from the front." When pressed for a further description Mageau said he "was unable to judge his age real well." His impression was of a man in his late twenties or early thirties, five foot nine, 195 pounds, "stocky, but not blubbery fat."

Investigators from the Vallejo Police Department determined that after leaving both victims for dead, the suspect drove directly to downtown Vallejo, where he used a pay telephone located at a Mobil gas station, just two blocks from the Vallejo Police Department, to call the police. The call was received at 12:40 a.m. on July 5, 1969, by a civilian police employee named Nancy Slover. According to Ms. Slover, the caller said:

> I want to report a double murder. If you will go one mile east on Columbus Parkway to the public park you will find the kids in a brown car. They were shot with a nine-millimeter Luger. I also killed those kids last year. Good-bye.

Ms. Slover, in her official Vallejo police report, also characterized the suspect's demeanor:

> I could distinguish no trace of accent in his voice. He seemed to be reading or had rehearsed what he was saying. He spoke with an even, consistent voice (rather soft but forceful). When I attempted to get information from him, his voice became louder, covering [up] what I was trying to say. He did not stop talking until his statement was complete. His voice was mature. The only real change in his voice was when he said, "good-bye." At that point his voice deepened and became taunting.

Vallejo police officers quickly confirmed that the weapon used was a 9mm handgun. They also learned that Darlene Ferrin had a husband and had worked as a waitress at Terry's Restaurant. Investigators questioned Dean Ferrin but eliminated him as a suspect when they established that he was working as a cook at Caesar's Restaurant at the time of the murder.

The similarities to the Jensen-Faraday double murder were striking. But after three weeks of searching for clues and interviewing the victims' families and friends, the trail to the killer turned cold.

Then on July 31, 1969, the Vallejo *Times-Herald*, the *San Francisco Chronicle*, and the *San Francisco Examiner* received hand-printed confessions and sections of a cryptogram. While the confession letters contained the same basic information, each section of the cryptogram was different. The killer informed the newspapers that the three parts had to be reassembled and, if deciphered, would reveal his identity.

Reproduced below are the letter and envelope with double postage, sent to the *San Francisco Chronicle*. While the suspect had yet to use the name "Zodiac," he did, for the first time, include his soon-to-be-infamous symbol of the cross and circle:

I have maintained the exact wording of the killer's letter to the *San Francisco Chronicle*, along with his punctuation and misspellings, with misspelled and unusual words bolded for easier identification:

10.3 Two-page letter and envelope received by the *San Francisco Chronicle*, July 31, 1969

Dear Editor

This is the murderer of the 2 **teenag-rs** last **Christmass** at Lake **He-man** & the girl on the 4th of July near the golf course in Vallejo to **Prove** I killed them I shall state some facts which only I & the police know.

Christmass

    1 Brand name of ammo Super X

    2 10 shots were fired

    3 the boy was on his back with his feet to the car

    4 the girl was on her right side feet to the west

4th July

    1 girl was wearing **patterned** slacks

    2 The boy was also shot in the knee.

    3 Brand name of ammo was Western

        Over

Here is part of a cipher the other 2 parts of this cipher are being mailed to the editors of the Vallejo times & S F Examiner. I want you to print this cipher on the front page of your paper. In this cipher is my **idenity**. If you do not print this cipher by the afternoon of **Fry**. 1st of Aug 69, I will go on a kill ram-Page **Fry**. night. I will **cruse** around all weekend killing lone People in the night then move on to kill again, **untill** I end up with a dozen people over the weekend.

On August 2, the *Chronicle* printed their section of the cryptogram. The following day, all three sections were released to the public, as shown in Figure 10.4.

Vallejo police chief Jack E. Stiltz rushed the coded message to a nearby navy base for analysis. In a ploy to elicit additional information from the suspect, Chief Stiltz announced that he wasn't sure that the correspondence came from the actual killer, and needed more proof.

The killer took the bait and im-

10.4 **Three-part cryptogram published by the *San Francisco Chronicle*, August 3, 1969**

mediately fired back a three-page handwritten response, introducing himself by saying, "This is the Zodiac speaking . . ." Received by the *San Francisco Examiner* on August 4, 1969, the letter is reproduced below as Figure 10.5, with all of its misspellings bolded for emphasis.

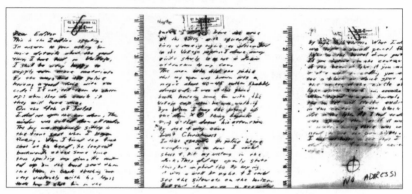

10.5 Three-page handwritten Zodiac letter received by the *San Francisco Examiner*, August 4, 1969

Zodiac's letter reads as follows:

Dear Editor

This is the Zodiac speaking. In answer to your asking for more details about the good times I have had in Vallejo,I shall be very happy to supply even more material. By the way, are the police **haveing** a good time with the code? If not, tell them to cheer up; when they do crack it they will have me. On the 4th of July: I did not open the car door. The window was rolled down **all ready**. The boy was **origionaly** sitting in the front seat when I began **fireing**. When I fired the first shot at his head, he leaped backwards at the same time thus spoiling my aim. He ended up on the back seat then the floor in Back thrashing out very violently with his legs; that's how I shot him in the knee. I did not leave the **cene** of the killing with **squealing** tires & **racing** engine as described in the Vallejo paper. I drove away quite slowly so as not to draw attention to my car. The man who told the police that my car was brown was a negro about

40-45 rather **shabbly** dressed. I was at this phone booth **haveing** some fun with the Vallejo cop when he was walking by. When I hung the phone up the **dam X O** thing began to ring & that drew his attention to me & my car. Last **Christmass** In that **epasode** the police were wondering as to how I could shoot & hit my **victoms** in the dark. They did not openly state this, but implied this by saying it was a well lit night & I could see the **silowets** on the horizon. Bullshit that area is **suronded** by high hills & trees. What I did was tape a small **pencel** flash light to the barrel of my gun. If you notice, in the center of the beam of light if you aim it at a wall or **celling** you will see a black or **darck** spot in the center of the circle of light about 3 to 6 in. across. When taped to a gun barrel, the **bu llet** will strike exactly in the center of the black dot in the light. All I had to do was spray them as if it was a water hose; there was no need to use the gun sights. I was not happy to see that I did not get front page cover age.

No Address

Military and civilian experts were unable to decipher Zodiac's cryptogram. But a high-school teacher named Donald Harden and his wife, Bettye, did. Working together over a long weekend, they broke most of the coded message and mailed their results to the *San Francisco Chronicle*, which printed Zodiac's deciphered message. I have bolded the undeciphered or misspelled words. It read:

I LIKE KILLING PEOPLE BECAUSE IT IS SO MUCH FUN IT IS MORE FUN THAN KILLING WILD GAME IN THE FOREST BECAUSE MAN IS THE MOST **HONGERTUE** ANIMAL OF ALL TO KILL SOMETHING **ERYETHEYC** A THRILLING EXPERIENCE IT IS EVEN BETTER THAN GETTING YOUR ROCKS OFF WITH A GIRL THE BEST PART OF IT **I ATHAE** WHEN I DIE I WILL BE REBORN IN **PARADICE** AND ALL THE I HAVE KILLED

WILL BECOME MY SLAVES I WILL NOT GIVE YOU MY NAME
BECAUSE YOU WILL **TRS** TO **SLOI** DOWN OR **ATOP** MY COL-
LECTING OF SLAVES FOR MY AFTERLIFE **EBEO RIET EMETH
HPITI**

A few days later a professor at the Stanford Research Center in Menlo
Park contacted Vallejo detectives and advised them that the references
in the Zodiac's message of "collecting slaves for the afterlife" was a concept that originated in Southeast Asia, particularly in Mindanao in the
Southern Philippines. The professor advised that the "suspect could
possibly be of Southeast Asian extraction, or be someone familiar with
the area."

In the 1950s and '60s my stepmother, Hortensia Hodel Starke, owned
a large sugar plantation in the Southern Philippines known as Haciendo
Bino. In 1959–60, while stationed at Subic Bay, I visited and toured the
plantation with my father. I believe the land remains in Hortensia's
name and ownership to this day.

The next six weeks passed uneventfully as Vallejo County deputies
and city police sifted through hundreds of tips and potential leads.
Then, on September 27, 1969, Zodiac struck again.

Chapter Eleven

I think I shall wipe out a school bus some morning. Just shoot out the front tire & then pick off the kiddies as they come bouncing out.

Zodiac, October 13, 1969

On a peaceful Saturday afternoon in late September 1969, two young college students lay on a blanket admiring the pristine beauty of Lake Berryessa, fifty miles northeast of San Francisco, near Napa Valley.

11.1 Cecelia Shepard, age twenty-two; Bryan Hartnell, age twenty

Cecelia Shepard, age twenty-two, and Bryan Hartnell, age twenty, had driven to the secluded spot in Bryan's Karmann Ghia. They'd parked just off the road, walked several hundred yards down a dirt path that led to the peninsula, and spread their blanket under a tree at the water's edge. While talking about the future and waiting for the sun to set, Cecelia noticed a man watching them from behind a tree. A few seconds later, she saw him move closer and gasped, "Oh my God. He's got a gun."

The terrified students turned to face a man wearing what appeared to be a black cloth executioner's hood and tunic, with eyeholes cut out of the hood and clip-on sunglasses attached to further conceal his identity. A strange white cross and circle about three inches in diameter had been sewn or drawn on the tunic, and a bayonet-style knife hung from the stranger's left side inside a homemade sheath, which was wrapped with white tape.

11.2

Pointing a large blue-steel automatic at Bryan's head, the masked man said, "I want your car keys and money. My car is hot."

The man then removed precut lengths of clothesline from his back pocket and ordered Cecelia to tie her boyfriend. She complied. Next, the masked man bound Cecelia's hands and feet. Bryan, hoping to keep the man calm, attempted to engage him in conversation. According to Bryan, the stranger said:

> I just escaped from prison in Montana. I had to kill a guard breaking out. Don't try and grab my gun, you don't want to try and be a hero. I'm flat broke and I'm heading for Mexico.

The masked man forced Bryan onto his stomach and hogtied his hands and feet. A second later, without warning, Bryan felt a knife blade plunge into his back. The attacker thrust his knife into him again and again; five more times. One stab punctured a lung.

Then the attacker turned on a horrified Cecelia, stabbing her ferociously, first perforating the front of her body, then the back.

A bleeding Bryan lay still and feigned death. He watched the masked man slowly walk away and disappear.

Five to ten minutes passed before Bryan heard a boat engine on the lake and shouted, "Get help!" He received no response. Bleeding profusely from multiple wounds, the young man managed to untie himself and crawl up the path to look for aid.

Nearly an hour elapsed before the wounded couple was found. Emergency workers rushed Bryan and Cecelia to Napa Queen of the Valley Hospital in critical condition, where both underwent emergency surgery. Cecelia died forty-eight hours later. Bryan miraculously survived.

Just as he had done in the Ferrin/Mageau Blue Rock Springs assault, the attacker drove downtown and telephoned police headquarters. Officer Dave Slaight received the call at 7:40 p.m. Printed below is his verbatim recollection of their conversation:

> Slaight: Napa Police Department, Officer Slaight.
> Caller: I want to report a murder—no, a double murder. They are two miles north of Park Headquarters [actually about only a half mile]. They were in a white Volkswagen Karmann Ghia.
> [There is a long pause.]
> Slaight: Where are you?
> Caller: I'm the one that did it.

Napa County police traced the call to a booth outside the Napa Car Wash, four and a half blocks from the station.

A day after the attack, Bryan Hartnell, though sedated and weak, told detectives that he'd only been able to catch a glimpse of the attacker's face, in profile, through the eyehole of the mask. Though unsure of his age, height, and weight, Bryan provided the following description based on the masked man's profile and sound of his voice:

> Male, white, 5 feet 8 inches to 6 feet, possibly 20 to 30, possibly 225 (unable to determine weight due to loose clothing), dark brown hair, dark blue or black lightweight windbreaker jacket, dark blue or black pleated slacks ("old-fashioned type"), moderate voice, neither high or low-pitched. Unsure if he was wearing gloves or not.

An examination of the Lake Berryessa crime scene produced some significant discoveries. As lead detective Sergeant Kenneth Narlow of the Napa County Sheriff's Office approached Bryan Hartnell's white 1956 Karmann Ghia, he noticed writing on the right front door panel. Pointing his flashlight at it, he read:

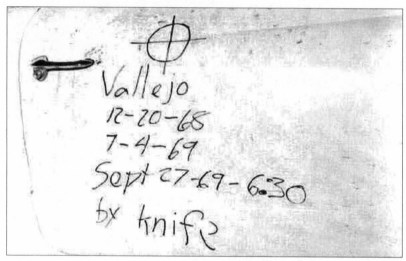

11.3 **Right front door panel of victim's 1956 Karmann Ghia**

The macabre message had been printed in large bold letters, using a black felt-tip pen. At the top, the attacker had drawn a replica of the cross and circle the victims had seen sewn on his tunic. It was the same symbol that had been included in the letter to the *San Francisco Examiner* following the Vallejo crime.

Under the symbol, the suspect had written the dates of the attacks in Vallejo and Lake Herman Road, as well as the date and time of his most recent murder "by knife."

The following day, detectives studying the crime scene discovered clearly defined shoeprints (measuring "approximately 13 inches in length, 4½ inches at the widest point of the sole"), which they believed had been left by the suspect. They speculated that the imprint could have been created by a military-style wing-walker boot, which was available for purchase by either military or civilians in sizes 10½ R (military) or 10½ D (civilian). After canvassing a dozen shoe stores, detectives determined that "the imprint could have also been made by a shoe or boot of foreign import."

Based on their investigation, Napa sheriffs were convinced that this crime was connected to the vicious killer who called himself "Zodiac." Further evidence supporting this belief arrived nine days later, when on October 7, 1969, Sherwood Morrill, questioned document examiner and court-certified expert in the field of handwriting comparison, rendered his expert opinion:

> The person who hand printed the message on the victim's vehicle at Lake Berryessa was the same individual who had sent the hand-printed letters to the *Vallejo Times Herald,* the *San Francisco Chronicle,* and the *San Francisco Examiner* claiming to have murdered three persons in Solano County.

As investigators searched for further evidence and panic spread throughout the Bay Area, Zodiac struck again.

On Saturday evening, October 11, 1969, a twenty-nine-year-old San Francisco State graduate student named Paul Stine waited in the Yellow Cab he drove part-time.[12] He'd parked in front of the St. Francis Hotel near Union Square in downtown San Francisco.

After receiving a call for a fare on nearby Ninth Avenue, Stine turned from Powell Street onto Geary, where he had to slow for a crowd pouring out of the

11.4 **Paul Lee Stine**

12 The 1944 Avenger murder of socialite Georgette Bauerdorf occurred late night on October 11, 1944, which would have made it the same date. In a typed letter to the press, written nearly a year after his crime, the Avenger references the anniversary of his Bauerdorf killing as being "October 11." Both of these killings are committed the day after George Hodel's birthday, which is October 10.

Curran Theatre's hit production of *Hair*. A man hailed his cab and got in. Paul Stine logged the destination address as "Washington Street and Maple" in Presidio Heights.

As the cab entered the upscale neighborhood, the passenger in the backseat instructed Stine to proceed up Washington another block to Cherry Street. Stine braked the car to a stop between two trees on the corner, directly in front of 3898 Washington.

"That'll be six twenty-five," Stine said. His passenger answered by placing a 9mm handgun to Stine's right temple and pulling the trigger. Paul Stine died instantly.

Three young teenagers, inside a residence across the street, happened to look outside their second-story window. They saw the taxi driver slumped over on the front seat and watched as a man leaned over him and appeared to be rifling through his clothing. The man then began wiping down the interior of the cab with a white cloth or handkerchief. Believing the cab driver was being robbed, one teen placed an emergency call to the police as the other two continued their surveillance. Next the man began to wipe down the exterior doors on both the passenger's and driver's side of the cab. Cool and deliberate, the shooter then slowly walked away, northbound on Cherry Street toward the Presidio.

According to the initial San Francisco police report, the teens gave the following description:

> Male, white, early forties, 5 foot 8, heavy build, reddish-blond "crew cut" hair, wearing eyeglasses, dark brown trousers, dark (navy blue or black) parka jacket, dark shoes.

It is worth noting several discrepancies in the historical record of the suspect's description. The first report of the teenagers' description to appear in the *San Francisco Chronicle* on October 12, 1969, contains a key discrepancy when compared to the police report cited above—the suspect's weight is estimated to be approximately 170 pounds. And Officer Fouke's previously cited estimation of the man's height was different on the night in question, when he described him as being in the six to six-two range. In a later media interview Officer Fouke would state that "the suspect appeared older than represented in the original composite drawing."

In any event, confusion ruled the night: Police dispatchers immediately alerted "all units in the area" with the suspect's description. But due to a miscommunication, the shooter was described as a black male.

San Francisco patrol officers Donald Fouke and his partner, Eric Zelms, responded quickly. Approaching the scene of the crime in their cruiser, the two officers observed a lone man walking east on Jackson Street. Officer Fouke got a good look at the man, but claimed he made no attempt to stop him, since they'd been told to look for a black male and the man they saw was white.

In recent years Officer Fouke's denial of stopping and talking to the Zodiac suspect has come under serious scrutiny. In a 2007 film interview he adamantly denied ever stopping or talking to the suspect. Tragically, Fouke's partner, Officer Zelms, was shot and killed by a burglar just ten weeks after the Stine shooting. It is reported that Officer Zelms's widow provided statements that in the weeks following the Stine shooting her husband admitted to her that he and his partner, Officer Fouke, had in fact stopped and spoken with Zodiac. Apparently, Zelms's fear of department and public criticism, along with his concern that as a rookie officer he might lose his job, prevented him from reporting it to superiors. Naturally, there was the added pressure of what others, his peers, might think. What patrol officer would want the career stigma of being remembered as "the guy who Q&R'd (questioned and released) Zodiac."

A short time later, dispatchers issued a correction advising all units that the suspect was actually a white male. Fouke and Zelms turned around and returned to Jackson, but the suspect was no longer there.

Suspecting that the shooter may have fled into the Julius Kahn Playground to hide in the dense undergrowth of the Presidio, police quickly sealed off the area and all seven of San Francisco's K-9 police dogs were pressed into service. San Francisco officers and military police searched long and hard, but to no avail. The suspect had been lucky. Had it not been for a mistake in the initial description, the SFPD would have had their man.

Since cabdriver robberies were common at the time, detectives at first speculated that the Stine murder was another taxicab heist gone bad. Most ended when the drivers handed over their money. Occasionally a nervous suspect or a hyped-up drug addict would pull the trigger.

This case, however, contained a big anomaly. Along with removing the victim's wallet in an apparent robbery, the suspect also took the time to cut or tear out a large section of the victim's bloody shirttail, which he took with him.

Why?

The answer came posthaste, mailed to the *San Francisco Chronicle* using double postage, written with a blue felt-tip pen.

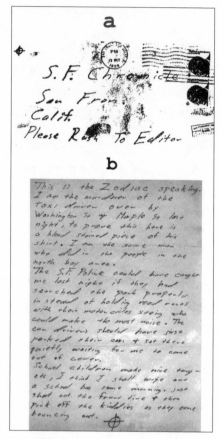

11.5 October 13, 1969, Zodiac letter and envelope

On the front of the envelope, the sender underscored his sarcasm with a polite "Please Rush To Editor."

Received only two days after the shooting, it began with what would soon become Zodiac's trademark salutation:

This is the Zodiac speaking. I am the murderer of the taxi driver over by Washington St & Maple St last night, to prove this here is a blood stained piece of his shirt. I am the same man who did in the people in the north bay area. The S.F. Police could have caught me last night if they had searched the park properly instead of holding road races with their **motorcicles** seeing who could make the most noise. The car drivers should have just parked their cars & sat there quietly waiting for me to come out of cover. School children make nice targets , I think I shall wipe out a school bus some morning. just shoot out the front tire & then pick off the kiddies as they come bouncing out.

Ballistics experts examined the spent slug and casing found in the Yellow Cab and determined that the weapon used to kill Paul Stine was a 9mm automatic. But in their opinion, it was a different 9mm from the one used three months earlier at the Blue Rock Springs shooting of Darlene Ferrin and Michael Mageau.

Based on Zodiac's letter to the *Chronicle* and his macabre inclusion of a small cutout section of the victim's bloody shirt, SFPD homicide detectives Bill Armstrong and Dave Toschi concluded that they were dealing with a psychotic egomaniac who thrived on publicity.

11.6 SFPD criminalist John Williams examines Stine shirt

11.7 The *Los Angeles Times*, October 16, 1969

Evidence assembled from the multiple crime scenes now included fingerprints, the suspect's probable shoe size, a pair of men's size 7 leather gloves left in the Stine cab, extensive handwriting samples, spent slugs and casings from three separate weapons for ballistic comparison, and several police composite drawings of the suspect's physical descriptions.

In the hope that people who knew or had seen the suspect would come forward, the SFPD released a composite sketch, based on both the teenagers' and patrolman Donald Fouke's descriptions. It was published in the *San Francisco Chronicle* on October 15, 1969, and amended slightly by sketch artists three days later.

In an internal SFPD memo dated November 12, 1969, submitted a month after the shooting, Officer Fouke described the man he had seen on Jackson Street as taller and thinner:

White, male, American, 35-45 years, 5-10, 180-200, medium-heavy build, Barrel-chested, medium complexion, light colored hair possibly graying in rear, may have been lighting that caused this effect, Navy blue jacket, brown pleated pants, baggy in rear (Rust Brown). Possibly wearing low-cut shoes.

11.8 SFPD Supplemental Bulletin "amending" Zodiac description

As hundreds of leads poured in, SFPD detectives had reason to feel confident that they would soon arrest the killer who called himself Zodiac. No one at the time imagined that four decades later the case would remain unsolved.

Chapter Twelve

> We should bear in mind that, in general, it is the object
> of our newspapers rather to create a sensation—to make
> a point—than to further the cause of truth. The latter
> end is only pursued when it seems coincident with the
> former.
>
> Edgar Allan Poe, "The Mystery of Marie Rogêt"

Back in October 1969 as happy songs like "Sweet Caroline" by Neil
Diamond and "Build Me Up Buttercup" by the Foundations dominated
the AM airwaves, an evil foreboding hung over the Bay Area like a thick,
sickening fog. The crazed killer who called himself Zodiac was on the
loose and no one had any idea where he'd strike next.

From Napa to San Francisco people heeded his threats. Police units
in Napa and Solano County rode on school buses or followed closely
behind in unmarked cars. Teachers showed terrified schoolchildren
what to do if their bus driver should yell out, "Hit the floor!" Cabdrivers
in San Francisco stopped working the night shift, forcing nervous visitors to brave the streets by foot. Young lovers throughout the area kept
their romantic assignations indoors.

A lone homicidal maniac had burned his weird circle-and-cross
symbol into the public psyche. Then, following the same pattern he used
in Riverside, the killer started playing elaborate mind games with authorities through the mouthpiece of the local newspaper. This time he
had chosen the *San Francisco Chronicle*.

He was egged on in part by *Chronicle* investigative reporter Paul
Avery, who threw the first provocative punch on October 18, 1969, with a
front-page article entitled "Zodiac—Portrait of a Killer." Avery claimed:

> The killer of five who calls himself "Zodiac" is a clumsy criminal,
> a liar, and possibly a latent homosexual . . . that's the opinion of

homicide detectives assigned to bring in the boastful mass murderer.

If Avery wanted a riposte from Zodiac, he got it. Two and a half
weeks later, Zodiac fired back with the following letter and cipher:

12.1

12.2

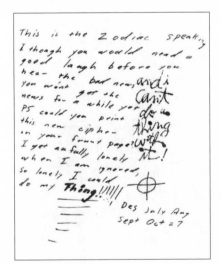

12.3

12.4

Figure 12.3 reads:

This is the Zodiac speaking I **though** you would need a good laugh before you **hea-** the bad news you won't get the news for a while yet PS could you print this new **ciphe-** in your **frunt** page? I get **au fully** lonely when I am ignored, so lonely I could do my **thing** !!!!!!
  (and I can't do a thing with it!)

⊕

Des july Aug
sept Oct = 7

The letter contained the same taunting tone and deliberate misspellings as the missives mailed by the killer of Elizabeth Short, Gladys Kern, Suzanne Degnan, and Cheri Jo Bates. Accompanying the letter was a cipher that was feverishly worked on by military and civilian experts but was never broken.

A day later, November 9, 1969, Zodiac mailed another letter to the *Chronicle*. This time he upped the ante. After more bragging about his cleverness, he delivered an elaborate bomb threat.

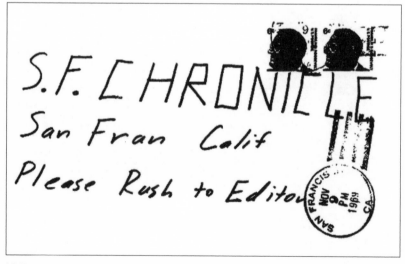

12.5

1/6

This is the Zodiac speaking up to the end of Oct I have killed 7 people. I have grown rather angry with the police for their telling lies about me. So I shall change the way the collecting of slaves. I shall no longer announce to anyone. when I comitt my murders, they shall look like routine robberies, killings of anger, + a few fake accidents, etc.

The police shall never catch me, because I have been too clever for them.
1 I look like the description passed out only when I do my thing, the rest of the time I look entirle different. I shall not tell you what my descise consists of when I kill
2 As of yet I have left no fingerprints behind me contrary to what the police say

2/6

in my killings I wear transparent finger tip guards. All it is is 2 coats of airplane cement coated on my finger tips - quate unnoticible + very efective.
3 my killing tools have been bought through the mail order outfits before the ban went into efect. except one & it was bought out of the state.
So as you see the police dont have much to work on. If you wonder why I was wipeing the cab down I was leaving fake clews fr the police to run all over town with, as one might say, I gave theecops som busy work to do so keep them happy. I enjoy needling the blue pigs. Hey blue pig I was in the park - you were useing fire trucks to mask the sound of your cruzeing prowl cars. The dogs never came with in 2 blocks of me + they were to the west + there was only 2

12.6

3/6

groops of parking about 10 min apart then the motor cicles went by about 150 ft away going from south to north west. ps. 2 cops pulled a goof abot 3 min after I left the cab. I was walking down the hill to the park when this cop car pulled up + one of them called me over + asked if I saw any one acting supicisous or stranye in the last 5 to 10 min + I said yes there was this man who was runnig by waveing a gun + the cops peeled rubber + went around the corner as I directed them + I dissapeared into the park a block + a half away never to be seen again.
Hey pig doesnt it rile you up to have your noze rubed in your booboos?
If you cops think Im going to take on a bus the way I stated I was, you deserve to have holes in your heads.

4/6

Take one bag of ammonium nitrate fertilizer + 1gal of stove oil + damp a few bags of gravel on top + then set the shit off + will positivily ventalate any thing that should be in the way of the blast.
The death machine is allready made. I would have sent you pictures but you would be nasty enough to trace them back to developer + then to me, so I shall descibe my masterpiece to you. The nice part of it is all the parts can be boyght on the open market with no quest ions asked.
1 bat. pow clock - will run for aprox 1 year
1 photoelectic switch
2 copper leaf springs
2 6V car bat
1 flash light bulb + reflector
1 mirror
2 18" cardboard tubes black with shoe polish inside + oute

12.7

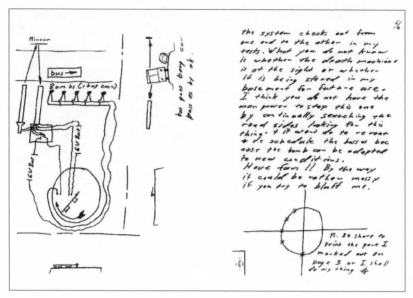

12.8

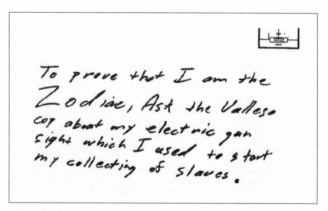

12.9

The letter reads:

(Page 1/6)

This is the Zodiac speaking Up to the end of Oct I have killed 7 people . I have grown rather angry with the police for their telling lies about me. So I shall change the way the collecting of slaves. I shall no longer announce to anyone. when I **comitt** my murders, they shall look like routine robberies , killings of rage-, & a few fake accidents, etc. the police shall never catch me, because I have been too **cleve-** for them. I look like the description passed out only when I do my thing, the rest of the time I look **entirle** different. I shall not tell you what my **descise** consists of when I kill

As of yet I have left no fingerprints behind me contrary to what the police say

(Page 2/6)

in my killings I wear transparent **finger tip** guards. All it is is 2 coats of **air plane** cement coated on my **finger tips**—quite **unnoticible** & very **efective.**

my killing tools have been **boughten** through the mail order outfits before the ban went into **efect**. except one & it was bought out of the state. So as you see the police don't have much to work on. If you **wonde-** why I was **wipe ing** the cab down I was leaving Fake **clews fo-** the police to run all ove- town with, as one might say, I gave cops **som bussy** work to do to keep them happy. I enjoy needling the blue pigs. Hey blue pig I was in the park—you were **useing** Fire trucks to mask the sound of your **cruzeing** prowl cars. The dogs never came with in 2 blocks of me & they were to the west & there was only 2

(Page 3/6)

groups of barking about 10 min apart then the **mot or cicles** went by about 150 ft away going from south to **north west**. ps. 2 cops pulled a goof **abot** 3 _____ min **afte-** I left the cab. I was **walk ing** down the hill to the park when this cop car pulled up & one of **the m** called me over & asked if I saw any one acting **supicisous** or strange in the last 5 to 10 min & I said yes there was this man who was **runnig** by **waveing** a gun & the cops peeled rubber & went **a-ound** the **co-ne-** as I directed them & I **dissap- eared** into the park a block & a half away never to be seen again.[13] _____
Hey pig doesnt it rile you up to have your **noze rubed** in your

13 Zodiac wrote in the left margin between above marked spaces, "Must print in paper-"

booboos? If you cops think **Im** going to take on a bus the way I stated I was, you deserve to have holes in your heads.

(Page 4/6)

Take one bag of ammonium nitrate **fertlizer** & 1 gal of stove oil & dump a Few bags of gravel on top & then set the shit off & will **positivly ventalate** any thing that should be in the way of the Blast. The death **machiene** is **all ready** made . I would have sent you pictures but you would be nasty enough to trace them back to **de-velope-** & then to me, so I shall **desc-ibe** my **master piece** to you. The nice part of it is all the parts can be bought on the open market with no questions asked. 1 bat. pow clock—will run for approx 1 year 1 photo electric switch 2 **coppe-** leaf springs

2 6V ca- bat

1 flash light bulb & reflector

1 mirror

2 18" cardboard tubes black with

shoe polish inside & **oute**

(Page 5/6)

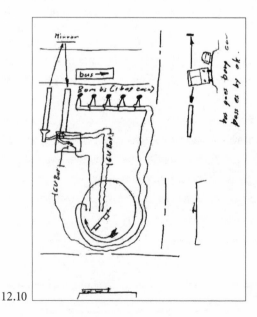

12.10

(Page 6/6)

the system checks out from one end to the other in my tests. What you do not know is whether the death **machiene** is at the **sight** or **whethe-** it is being stored in my basement **fo- futu–e** use. I think you do not have the **man power** to stop this one by continually searching the **road sides** looking **fo-** this thing. & it **wont** do to **re root & re schedule** the **busses bec ause** the bomb can be adapted to new conditions. Have fun !! By the way it could be rather messy if you try to bluff me.

PS. Be **shure** to print the part I marked out on page 3 or I shall do my thing

To prove that I am the **Zodiac, Ask** the Vallejo cop about my electric gun sight which I used to start my collecting of slaves.

Bay Area detectives took Zodiac's "death machine" seriously. Besides trying to locate it, they stepped up their surveillance of schoolbus routes and checked on the recent sales of ammonium nitrate fertilizers.

Investigators knew they weren't dealing with a run-of-the-mill killer. Zodiac was unique, and by November 1969 was even out-headlining his Southern California competition, Charlie Manson and family, who'd left a paranoid, drug-induced trail of blood through L.A. just three-months earlier. What did Zodiac want? He seemed driven by a deep psychosis that manifested itself as savagely misdirected rage. Although he'd succeeded in instilling terror and attracting attention, he expressed no political or personal agenda, except collecting slaves as part of some bizarre plan for the afterlife.

Criminologists and columnists speculated that the killer was a Renaissance man educated in military tactics, chemistry, mathematics, cryptography, and music. He was highly intelligent, but tried to disguise his sophistication with clumsy misspellings.

Following the exact same pattern that the Black Dahlia Avenger employed in his letters to Los Angeles newspapers after the death of Elizabeth Short in 1947, Zodiac now made noises about turning himself in.

The first of his coy offers was sent to celebrity defense attorney Melvin Belli on December 20, 1969—exactly one year after the murders of David Faraday and Betty Lou Jensen in Vallejo. It included another bloody swatch of cabdriver Paul Stine's shirt.

Mr. Melvin M. Belli
1228 Mtgy
San Fran Calit

Dear Melvin

This is the Zodiac speaking I wish you a happy Christmass. The one thing I ask of you is this, please help me. I cannot reach out for help because of this thing in me wont let me. I am finding it extreamly dificult to hold it in check I am afraid I will loose control again and take my nineth & posibly tenth victom. Please help me I am drownding. At the moment the children are safe from the bomb because it is so massive to dig in & the triger mech requires much work to get it adjusted just right. But if I hold back too long from no nine I will loose complet all controol of my self & set the bomb up. Please help me I can not remain in control for much longer.

12.11

Dear Melvin

    This is the Zodiac speaking I wish you a happy **Christmass** . The one thing I ask of you is this, please help me. I cannot reach out for help because of this thing in me **wont** let me. I am finding it

extreamly dif- icult to hold it in check I am afraid I will **loose** control again and take my **nineth** & **posibly** tenth **victom**. Please help me I am **drownding**. At the moment the children are safe from the bomb because it is so massive to dig in & the **triger mech** requires much work to get it adjusted just right. But if I hold back too long from **no nine** I will **loose** ~~complet~~ all **controol** of **my self** & set the bomb up. Please help me I can not remain in control for much longer.

$$\oplus$$

The publication of the letters generated thousands of tips from people who believed they had some clue to the madman's identity. Some were sheer speculation. Others were hunches or fears about an oddball neighbor. An average of ten per week came from women who were convinced that Zodiac was a former husband or ex-boyfriend.

Investigators meticulously checked each tip. More than two thousand suspects were pursued and questioned, some as far away as Cleveland, Atlanta, and Germany. They included a wealthy San Francisco businessman and a former Harvard lecturer. In the decades following Zodiac crimes, theorists attempted to link Zodiac to the Unabomber, members of the Manson family, Texarkana's "Phantom Killer," a mysterious and taunting letter writer calling himself "Scorpio," and most recently to Wichita's "BTK Strangler."

The California State Bureau of Criminal Identification and Information (CII) held weekly Zodiac update meetings in Sacramento, where representatives of the nine Bay Area counties discussed leads and cross-checked information. Meanwhile, CII personnel searched through thousands of profiles of Californians trying to isolate a manageable sample based on factors that included appearance, age, anger at the police, and certain skills.

They came up with nothing concrete, only theories: Zodiac's dead. He's in jail. He's institutionalized. He's overseas. He's lying in wait to "do his thing."

Chapter Thirteen

If the Blue Meannies are evere going to catch me, they
had best get off their fat asses and do something.

Zodiac

The letters continued into 1970 and arrived periodically up until 1978. In the end, they totaled twenty-five, written in the same grandiose tone with barbs of increasing sarcasm thrown at the police. In several, Zodiac had the audacity to urge Bay Area residents to wear buttons with his circle-and-cross symbol.

Was this his idea of a joke? Did he ever seriously consider blowing up a school bus filled with children? It was hard to tell.

What we do know is that the letters followed the same pattern of threats, boasts, pleas for attention, and misspellings. Some included additional cryptograms that were never decoded.

The entire set of twenty-five letters can be viewed on my Web site (www.stevehodel.com). But certain features of some of the letters are worth pointing out.

13.1

For example, Letter #12, postmarked San Francisco, April 28, 1970, is notable because of its use of double postage—the same practice followed by the Black Dahlia Avenger in Los Angeles and by the killer of Cheri Jo Bates in Riverside.

In Letter #15 (mailed in San Francisco on July 26, 1970), Zodiac revealed a musical facet of his persona, reciting lyrics from Gilbert and Sullivan's comic opera *The Mikado*. The song he references, entitled "As Some Day It May Happen," is sung by the character of Ko-Ko the Lord High Executioner. In it, he claims to have a "little list," which serves as his hit list of "society's offenders." These are the types of people Ko-Ko (or Zodiac) finds objectionable enough to be worthy of death. As noted in chapter 1, young musical prodigy George Hodel loved Gilbert and Sullivan and knew their music and lyrics by heart. Also as a radio host and programmer for the *Southern California Gas Company's Music Hour* he would have played Gilbert and Sullivan's popular *Mikado* on a regular basis.

In this particular letter, Zodiac—after cataloguing the tortures he's going to inflict on the thirteen slaves who are waiting for him in paradise—offers his take on "As Some Day It May Happen," which starts at the top of page three.

13.2

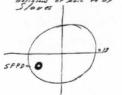

13.3

13.4

The letter reads:

This is the Zodiac speaking Being that you will not wear some nice ⊕ buttons, how about wearing some nasty ⊕ buttons. Or any type of ⊕ buttons that you can think up. **If** you do not wear any type of ⊕ buttons **I** shall (on top of every thing else) torture all 13 of my slaves that I have **wateing** for me in **Paradice**. Some I shall tie over **ant hills** and watch them scream & **twich** and squirm. Others shall have pine splinters driven under their nails & then burned. Others shall be placed in cages & fed salt beef **untill** they are gorged then I shall listen to their **pleass** for water and I shall laugh at them. Others will hang by their thumbs & burn in the sun then **I** will rub them down with deep heat to warm

(page 2)

them up. Others I shall skin them alive & let them run around screaming . And all billiard players I shall have them play in a **dark ened**

dungen cell with crooked **cues & Twisted Shoes**. Yes I shall have great fun **in flicting** the most delicious of pain to my **Slaves**.

$\oplus$ = 13

SFPD = 0

(page 3)

As some day it may **hapen** that a **victom** must be found. I've got a little list. I've got a little list, of society offenders who might well be underground who would never be missed who would never be missed. There is the **pest- ulentual nucences** who **whrite** for au- tographs , all people who have flabby hands and **irritat- ing** laughs. All children who are up in dates and implore you with **im platt**. All people who are **shakeing** hands shake hands like that. And all third persons who with unspooling take **thoes** who insist. They'd none of them be missed. They'd none of them be missed. There's the banjo **seranader** and the others of his race and the piano **orginast I** got him on the list. All people who eat **pepermint** and **phomphit**

(page 4)

in your face . they would never be missed They would never be missed And the **Idiout** who **phraises** with **in- thusastic** tone of centuries but this and every country but his own. Find the lady from the **provences** who dress like a guy who doesn't cry and the **sin- gurly abnomily** the girl who never kissed . I don't think she would be missed **Im shure** she wouldn't be missed. And that nice **impriest** that is rather rife the **judicial hummerest** I've got him on the list All funny fellows, **commic** men and clowns of private life. They'd none of them be missed. They'd none of them be missed. And **uncom- promis e ing** kind such as **wachamacallit, thingmebob**, and **like wise**, well- **nevermind** , and **tut tut tut tut**,

(page 5)

who, but the task of filling up the blanks I rather leave up to you. But it really doesn't matter whom you place upon the list , for none of them be missed, none of them be missed.

ps. the Mt. Diablo code concerns Radians & inches along the radians

It's a slight variation on the Gilbert and Sullivan original:

As some day it may happen that a victim must be found, I've got a little list, I've got a little list of society offenders who might well be underground, and who never would be missed, who never would be missed! There's the pestilential nuisances who write for autographs, all people who have flabby hands and irritating laughs, all children who are up in dates, and floor you with 'em flat, all persons who in shaking hands, shake hands with you like that, and all third persons who on spoiling tête-à-têtes insists, they'd none of 'em be missed, they'd none of 'em be missed. . . .

In *The Mikado*, we learn that Ko-Ko was once condemned to death for flirting, but reprieved at the last moment and raised to the exalted rank of Lord High Executioner. According to Gilbert and Sullivan's own lyrics:

And so we straight let out on a bail, a convict from the county jail, whose head was next, on some pretext, condemned to be mown off, and made him Headsman, for we said, who's next to be decapitated, cannot cut off another's head until he's cut his own off.

Because of some perceived wrong in his own life, it seems that Zodiac came to identify himself with the character of Ko-Ko, who acts in the play as a combined judge, jury, and executioner.

Bay Area detectives, alert to any possible clue to the killer's identity, started examining programs and interviewing people involved in local productions of *The Mikado*. Their efforts led them into yet another dead end.

Four years later, in January 1974, the *Chronicle* received another mailing from Zodiac, referencing a different *Mikado* song, also sung by Ko-Ko Lord High Executioner.

13.5

I saw + think "The Exorcist" was the best saterical comidy that I have ever seen.

  Signed, yours truley :

He plunged him self into the billowy wave and an echo arose from the sucides grave
    tit willo   tit willo
        tit willo

Ps. if I do not see this note in your paper, I will do something nasty, which you know I'm capable of doing

Mc - 37
SFPD - 0

13.6

The letter reads:

I saw & think "The Exorcist" was the best **saterical comidy** that I have ever seen.

Signed , yours **truley** :

He plunged him self into the billowy wave and an echo arose from the **sucides** grave **titwillo tit willo tit willo**

Ps. if I do not see this note in your **pape-** , I will do something nasty, which you know I'm capable of doing

Me - 37

S F P D - 0

After calling the horror movie *The Exorcist* the best satirical comedy he's ever seen, Zodiac quoted directly from the song "Willow, Tit-Willow," which is a threat by Ko-Ko to his lover that he might die of a broken heart and "plunge himself into the billowy wave" if she rejects his overture of love. In a line of dialogue that follows, Ko-Ko states that he "finds beauty in bloodthirstiness."

Apparently, Zodiac wanted authorities to believe that he was contemplating entering "suicide's grave." Was he leaving a clue, either consciously or subconsciously, to his other crimes?

In 2000, during the early stages of my Dahlia investigation, I came across the following article printed in the *Los Angeles Times.* According to the article, someone claiming to be the Black Dahlia Avenger staged a possible suicide on the two-month anniversary of Elizabeth Short's murder. The man left his clothes and a penciled handwritten suicide note at the water's edge on Venice Beach to create the impression that he'd plunged to his death.

'Suicide' Revives 'Dahlia' Inquiry

13.7

From the March 15, 1947, *Los Angeles Times* article:

A man's clothing and a note scrawled in pencil on a bit of foolscap found by the ocean's edge at the foot of Breeze Ave., Venice, yesterday revived the lagging investigation of the mutilation murder of Elizabeth Short, 22, the "Black Dahlia."

If the note is authentic, it indicated that the person who brutally slew Miss Short and left her body in a Norton Ave. lot last Jan. 15 had committed suicide, driven to walk into the sea by the shadow of his crime.

The pile of clothing was first seen by a beach caretaker, who reported the discovery to John Dillon, lifeguard captain. Dillon immediately notified Capt. L. E. Christenson of West Los Angeles Police Station.

"Too much of a coward."

The note, tucked inside one of the shoes, read:

> To whom **in** may concern: I have waited for the police to capture me for the Black Dahlia killing, but have not. I am too much of a coward to turn myself in, so this is the best way out for me. I couldn't help myself for that, or this. Sorry, Mary.

It was not signed.

Nothing else—not even a laundry or cleaning mark—was found in the clothes that might give any hint of the identity of their owner. "Mary" also remained a mystery.

During the early stages of my Dahlia investigation, I had originally disregarded the note as a probable hoax, assuming it had been written by a prankster or emotionally disturbed individual temporarily caught up in the sensationalism of the Dahlia story. But now I think it's worthy of a closer consideration.

Why? Because it appears to be an interesting part of the Avenger/Zodiac's MO. In several other instances he suggested he would either turn himself in or commit suicide, sometimes on the anniversary of a particular murder.

In the 1944 Los Angeles Georgette Bauerdorf note, the Avenger had claimed he would "appear in person at the Hollywood Canteen, on or about October 11, the one-year anniversary of her murder." I believe this confirms the Avenger's interest in anniversary dates, and it may be no coincidence that this date is a day after George Hodel's birthday of October 10. October 11 was also the day Paul Stine was killed by Zodiac.

In 1946, the Degnan suspect wrote, "If you don't ketch me soon, I will cummit suicide. . . . You may find me at the Club Tavern at . . . Please hurry now."[14]

Twenty years later in Riverside, California, "Z" sent a "confession letter" for the Cheri Jo Bates murder on the one-month anniversary of her death. Five months later, on the murder's six-month anniversary, he dispatched a second note that said "Bates had to die."

Thus, it seems that Zodiac's *Mikado* reference hinting at suicide out of "blighted affection," along with his mailing of notes on the anniversary dates of his kills, follows a pattern that echoes through Chicago, L.A., and Riverside.

Before we leave Zodiac's letter dated January 29, 1974 (#21), I want to turn your attention to the notation at the bottom: "Me - 37; SFPD - 0." This would appear to be a tally of thirty-seven murders committed to this point. If so, it might not be an exaggeration. By my count, if we link all of the murders to my father, George Hodel's total killings could well approximate Zodiac's boastful claim of thirty-seven.

Zodiac's letter of January 1974 isn't the first or last time he mentioned popular movies, either. In letter number eighteen (postmarked February 13, 1971) he references the Blue Meanies from *Yellow Submarine*. Letter number twenty-four (postmarked July 8, 1978) offered his personal critique of the Terrence Malick movie *Badlands*, a fictionalized

---

14 Zodiac, in a 1969 letter, misspelled this same word, albeit in a different way, when he wrote, "I shall no longer announce to anyone when I comitt my murders."

version of the murder spree conducted by teenagers Charles Stark-weather and Caril Ann Fugate in Nebraska and Wyoming during 1958.

Missive sixteen (a postcard sent on October 5, 1970) is of interest because of its use of cut-and-paste letters, a practice employed by the Black Dahlia Avenger in his letters to the press following the Elizabeth Short murder in L.A.

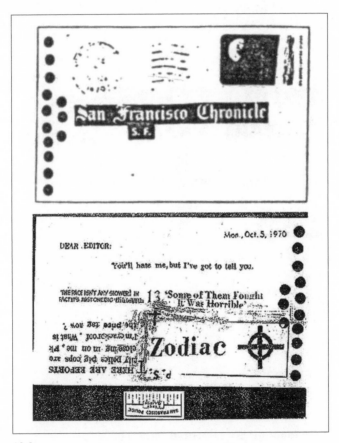

13.8

On October 12, 1970, the *Los Angeles Times* headlined an article NEW ZODIAC BOAST: CLAIMS 13 VICTIMS IN TWO NOTES. An excerpt from that article described the postcard as having "... a Christian cross carefully drawn in blood and then cut out along its outline and pasted to the card. Police said the blood appears to be human." Figure 13.9 shows an enlargement of the section containing the "Christian cross." This is reminiscent of the September 21, 1945, *Los Angeles Times* article that referenced a typed note sent in by the killer of Georgette Bauerdorf. The sheriff's crime lab upon analyzing the note determined that the suspect had smeared iodine on the note to simulate blood. If in fact Zodiac's 1970 note is human blood, it could be another potential source of DNA and or blood type.

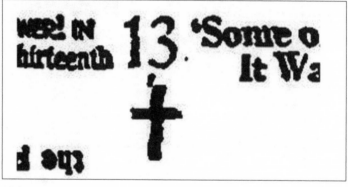

13.9

The postcard reads:

Mon. Oct. 5, 1970
DEAR EDITOR:
      You'll hate me, but I've got to tell you. THE PACE ISN'T ANY SLOWER! IN FACT IT'S JUST ONE BIG THIRTEENTH 13 **'Some of Them fought It Was Horrible'** (cross) (inverted)
      P.S. THERE ARE REPORTS city police pig cops are **closeing** in on me, Fk I'm **crackproof**. What is the price tag now ?

ZODIAC

It appears that Zodiac might have been trying to leave a hint about his L.A. murders that investigators seemed to have missed. On March 16, 1971, a copy boy sorting through the mail at the *Los Angeles Times* came across a white envelope with the urgent message: "Please rush to editor." It had been mailed from Pleasanton in Alameda County, some four hundred miles north. The letter inside was classic Zodiac.

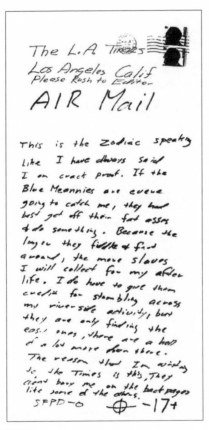

13.10

This letter to the *Los Angeles Times* reads:

This is the Zodiac speaking Like I have **allways** said I am crack proof. If the Blue **Meannies** are **evere** going to catch me , they had best get off their fat asses & do something. Because the longer they fiddle & **fa-t** around , the more slaves I will collect for my **after life**. I do have to give them credit for stumbling across my riverside activity, but they are only finding the easy ones, there are a hell of a lot more down there. The reason that **Im** writing to the Times is this, they don't bury me on the back pages like some of the others.

SFPD - 0 ⊕ - 17+

Not only does he refer to police discovering his "riverside" activity—namely the murder of Cheri Jo Bates—he also states, "they are only finding the easy ones, there are a hell of a lot more down there."

Investigators never made the connection between Zodiac and the Black Dahlia Avenger, despite the fact that detectives, criminologists, psychiatrists, Zodiac fanatics, cryptologists, and amateur sleuths have spent thousands of hours poring over the twenty-five letters, searching for clues to Zodiac's identity.

Nor have they ever found anything in the letters that they believe links them to a specific individual. After carefully analyzing all twenty-five missives, most experts agree that they reveal the following attributes of the killer who called himself Zodiac:

- He displays an enormously warped sense of superiority over other human beings and a mad desire to "show it off."
- He has a strong Jekyll-Hyde complex that causes him to kill his "slaves" with insane ferocity one moment and blend into society by acting normal the next.
- He hates cops and all constituted authority and enjoys taunting them for their "stupidity." He sometimes referred to them in the slang of the time as "blue pigs."
- His clumsy use of vernacular of the late '60s and early '70s, combined with his use of slang expressions that had been out of use for a quarter of a century, may indicate an older man in his fifties or sixties.
- He's well educated and well read, and demonstrates familiarity

with *The Egyptian Book of the Dead*, the Greek alphabet, and early Native American and Asian hieroglyphics.

- He's interested in culture, can quote lyrics by Gilbert and Sullivan, and has an interest in current movies.
- He claims to have killed many more than the five victims the police have attributed to him, and chides authorities to look further.

Chapter Fourteen

I'm gonna keep you guessin.
Zodiac, 1990

There's no doubt that the handwriting and content of the notes provide significant clues to the identity of the man who called himself Zodiac. With that in mind, I again contacted questioned document examiner Hannah McFarland in the spring of 2008 and asked her to compare them to several dozen samples of my father's handwriting.

Reproduced below is her report:

Hannah McFarland
HANDWRITING & DOCUMENT EXAMINER
May 29, 2008
Steve Hodel
Studio City, California 91604
RE: Examination of Zodiac documents
Dear Mr. Hodel:
I am providing this report pursuant to your request.

Assignment
I examined 34 photocopy documents associated with the Zodiac murder cases in San Francisco, California. These questioned documents include letters, notes and envelopes. Most of these questioned documents are executed in lowercase printing. Three are executed in uppercase printing. I am informed these documents were produced between 1966 and 1990.

I understand that another document examiner has examined these original documents and concluded that they were all produced by the same person. By comparing these photocopy documents with each other I found evidence indicating that most of them could have been produced by the same person.

Exemplars

I compared these questioned documents to documents that you have represented to me as having been authored by George Hill Hodel. These are the same documents that I list in my report to you dated May 7, 2003 (K-1 through K-9). Following are additional hand-printing samples that you have represented to me as having been authored by George Hill Hodel:

1. "Steve and Dad, April 1961 Baguio" from photograph of Steve and George Hodel
2. Section of art document referencing items to be sold in auction, Jan. 11, 1999
3. Section of document referencing military experience, no date indicated
4. Lowercase hand printing inserted in letter addressed to you, dated 6/4/80
5. Section of death certificate from Los Angeles, dated Dec. 24, 1949
6. One page from Passport, no date indicated
7. Envelope addressed to Dorothy Barbe

Finding

I found many significant similarities between the exemplars of George Hill Hodel and the Zodiac documents. Therefore, based upon the available evidence it is my professional opinion that George Hill Hodel probably authored 19 of the Zodiac documents.

My opinions are subject to review should the original questioned Zodiac documents become available for examination.

Many of the Zodiac documents appear to be disguised. There

was a deliberate attempt to hand print in such a way as to avoid being identified.

Attached as Exhibit A is an illustration with a section of a questioned Zodiac note and samples of George Hill Hodel.

Exhibit A

QUESTIONED ZODIAK SAMPLE FROM

As some day it may hapen
that an victom must be found.
I've got a little list. I've
got a little list, of society
offenders who might well be
underground who would never

EXEMPLARS OF GEORGE HILL HODEL
Medical Diary from 1943

INC. PERIODS, "etc".
INF. DISEASES

Envelope from 1986   **Note from 1961**

O'FARRELL   BAGUIO

to join these
n mate their flight   with them and continue

14.1

Following are similarities between the Zodiac documents and the exemplars of George Hill Hodel:

1. Wide spacing between the end of a word and the punctuation that follows the word as shown by arrow 1 in Exhibit A;

2. The letter "O" begins and ends on the left portion of the circle shown by arrow 2 in Exhibit A;

3. The letter "S" is enlarged shown by arrow 3 in Exhibit A;

4. The initial stroke on the lowercase letter "e" is extra long as shown by arrow 4 in Exhibit A;

5. The letter "U" does not have a downstroke on the right side of it;

6. The capital letter "M" has a u shape between the two vertical strokes;

7. The number "4" has a short horizontal stroke;

8. The number "2" does not have a loop at the bottom;

9. The letter "O" is often reduced in size;

10. The letters "D", "P", and "B" are sometimes open at the bottom;

11. Spacing of individual letters, between letters and between words;

12. Letter proportions;

13. A Greek-style E;

14. Some of the lower extensions are extra long and move toward the left

Theoretical Bases

Many people learn the same system of handwriting in school. In spite of this, no one completely adheres to the system they were taught. Everyone develops a unique set of handwriting characteristics. A particular writer can be identified or eliminated from having written a questioned handwriting by identifying the combination of handwriting traits that are unique to one person only.

I declare under penalty of perjury under the laws of the State of Washington that the foregoing is true and correct to the best of my knowledge.

EXECUTED this 29th day of May 2008, in Port Townsend, Washington.

HANNAH McFARLAND

To repeat, in Hannah McFarland's professional opinion "George Hill Hodel probably authored 19 of the Zodiac documents."

The following is a summary of her analysis and expert opinion on authorship of all questioned writings relating to my multiple investigations over the past eight years (2000–2008):

1. 1945 Frances Brown Note in lipstick on wall: "Indications it was written by George Hodel."
2. 1946 Suzanne Degnan Ransom Note: "Probably written by George Hodel."
3. 1943–1946 (Unknown date) Elizabeth Short photo album snapshots: "Probably written by George Hodel."
4. 1947 Elizabeth Short Avenger Notes: "Highly probably written by George Hodel.
5. 1947 Jeanne French lipstick message on body: "Highly probably written by George Hodel."
6. 1948 Gladys Kern Note: "Probably written by George Hodel."
7. 1966 Bates Notes: "Indications written by George Hodel."
8. 1969–1990 Zodiac Notes: "Probably written by George Hodel."

Zodiac Returns—The 1990 Missive

On March 2, 2007, the motion picture *Zodiac* was released in the United States. Directed by David Fincher, the film examines the impact of the investigation on four men, Paul Avery, Robert Graysmith, and Detectives David Toschi and Bill Armstrong—all of whom became obsessed with trying to solve the serial killings.

During the preproduction phase of the movie, the *San Francisco Chronicle* offered to let the filmmakers look into their thirty-five-year-old Zodiac files. As a result, a new, previously overlooked Zodiac letter came to public attention. It was a Christmas card mailed to "Editor, San Francisco Chronicle," postmarked from Eureka, California, and dated 1990.

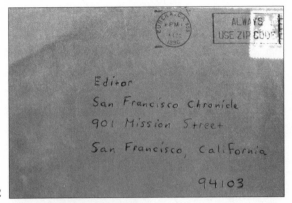

14.2

14.3

This newly discovered evidence immediately generated a new wave of excitement
among Zodiac researchers. Tom Voigt of
zodiackiller.com, who in my opinion is one
of the most knowledgeable and balanced
Zodiacologists, went on record as saying
that he believes "the 1990 Christmas card
is a legitimate Zodiac mailing." I tend to
agree for the following reasons:

14.4

1. The card's envelope (14.2) appears to be in Zodiac's hand printing, and the writing characteristics are identical in all respects to
   those of my father, Dr. George Hodel.

The card (14.3) is identical in design to another holiday card (14.5) mailed to the *Chronicle* by Zodiac in 1970, which also used the theme "From Your Secret Pal." (The holiday in that case was Halloween.) In that 1970 mailing some investigators have speculated that Zodiac's printed format may have been a subtle clue to his last name—possibly a monogram with the words forming the letter "H" as seen below.

14.5

2. As in many of Zodiac's previous correspondences, this 1990 card contains a riddle wrapped in a mystery that conceals Zodiac's familiar taunt, "catch me if you can." The card (14.3) depicts the "Secret Pal" as a Christmas snowman disguised as the well-known film, radio, and television comedian Groucho Marx. In 1960 Marx starred in the NBC television special Bell Telephone Hour performance of *The Mikado*. His role? Ko-Ko, Lord High Executioner. Groucho sang both the Titwillo and "As Some Day It May Happen," songs cannibalized by Zodiac in his written taunts to the press and police. The 1990 Christmas card appears to be another of his mind games that takes us from Zodiac to Groucho, to Ko-Ko, back to Zodiac, running us in circles.

3. Included with the card is a Xerox copy of two post office box keys (14.4). The numbers on the keys appear to be 79408 and 59851, or 58851. They may be a ruse, or they could have the potential to provide future leads for law enforcement follow-up. Knowing

that there is a reason and purpose to every Zodiac communication, I cannot help but think the photocopied keys may be a link to a victim. Could the keys belong to cabdriver Paul Stine or one of the other original victims? Has this "new evidence" been checked out by today's law enforcement? Or could the keys belong to a yet unidentified victim in Eureka? Why mail the card from Eureka, a small town that is a three-hour-drive north of San Francisco?

4. The 1990 card has an additional clue that has been brought to my attention by Tom Voigt and the "collective detectives" at zodiackiller.com—namely, a subtle and distinctive "saddle M," which was frequently used by Zodiac. This unique writing characteristic (one of fourteen) was also independently identified by QDE Hannah McFarland in her handwriting comparison report of George Hodel to Zodiac. From her report: "The capital letter 'M' has a 'U' shape between the two vertical strokes."

Figure 14.6 shows five selected samples from Zodiac's previous handwriting using this swayback "saddle M."

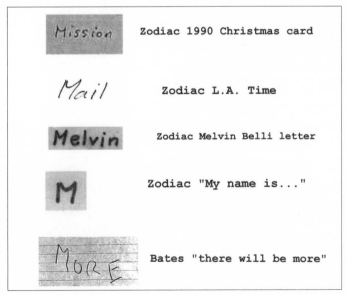

Zodiac 1990 Christmas card

Zodiac L.A. Time

Zodiac Melvin Belli letter

Zodiac "My name is..."

Bates "there will be more"

14.6

Figure 14.7 below shows samples of the "saddle M" from known samples of my father's hand printing.

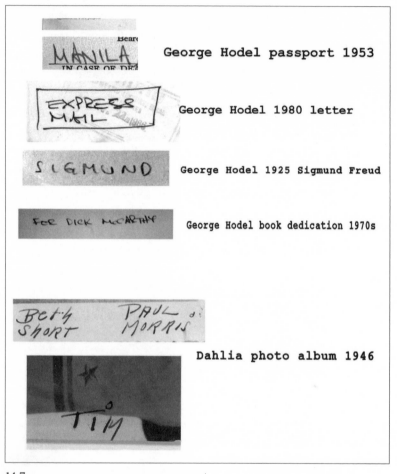

14.7

The exhibit on the following page shows a side-by-side comparison between three separate lowercase handwritten murder notes:

1. 1948 Gladys Kern "Avenger confession"
2. 1966 Cheri Jo Bates "Confession note"
3. 1990 Zodiac "Keep You Guessin" card

In my opinion the similarities in the individual letters are dramatic.

14.8

In 1990, after nearly forty years of expatriate life with residences in Manila, Tokyo, and Hong Kong, George Hodel at age eighty-three made a decision to "come home" to San Francisco—the city of his youth. Several months after his return, I believe he couldn't resist mailing the Christmas card (14.3) from nearby Eureka. His message was clear: I'm back.

And who better to break the news than his old pen pal and former employer, the *San Francisco Chronicle*? The old panther, long of tooth, too frail now to even include a threatening note, must have been saddened to discover that his name and reputation were all but forgotten. His final taunt was now reduced to a subtle whisper, never publicized in his lifetime: "I'm gonna keep you guessin."

Chapter Fifteen

The devil is in the details.

Gustave Flaubert

So far we've learned that, in the opinion of a court certified handwriting expert, the writings of Dr. George Hodel link him to L.A.'s Black Dahlia Avenger, the Chicago Lipstick Killer of the 1940s, and his 1960s California counterparts "Z" and Zodiac. Before we move on, let's take a minute to consider some of the numerous and distinct similarities between the various communications:

- cut-and-pasted letters
- block printing, appearing very similar in style
- multiple mailings (Avenger, 14; Zodiac, 25)
- taunting words and childlike pictures
- deliberate misspellings, feigned illiteracy
- double postage
- sadistic and misogynistic content
- addressed to police and press
- avenger theme (wronged or scorned by a woman)
- demands for publicity
- piece of victim's clothing and or personal effects mailed to press to prove he was the killer
- postmortem messages written in lipstick on the wall of a victim's residence, on a post outside "the murder room," on a victim's body and in marker pen on a victim's vehicle

There are, in addition, several fascinating anomalies found in the penmanship, word usage, and even type of paper used by Zodiac that are obvious even to the untrained eye. Since the common threads that run through the notes are so important, I'm going to take the time to illustrate these characteristics one by one.

1. Letters "C" and "G"

Figure 15.1 shows examples of George Hodel's highly unusual double-looped letter G in a 1999 document signed weeks before his death, and double-looped C's and G's and in two samples from 1949 (Figure 15.2). The same double-looped C's and G's appear in the "Corporal Guy" notation on an Elizabeth Short photo and the Frances Brown lipstick writings (Figure 15.3).

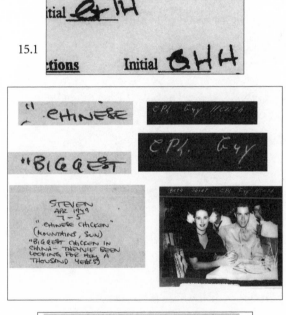

Figure 15.4 is the brown wrapping paper that contained a human ear that was addressed and mailed to Mrs. Degnan in 1946. At first glance the handwriting style, with its flared letters, appears quite different from George Hodel's. However, closer scrutiny reveals a curious similarity to the double-looped letter "C" in the word "Chicago." Compare that to the known cursive samples of the letter "G" in George Hodel and G. Hill Hodel, which also contain double loops.

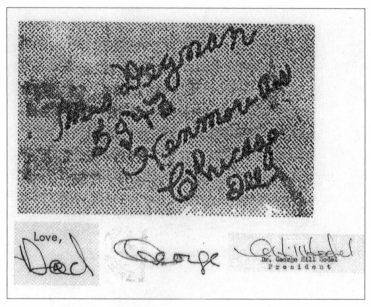

15.4

2. Dots and circles over lowercase letter "i"

Figure 15.5 illustrates the Zodiac's tendency to use a circle rather than a dot or period. Evidence of this is seen in the "Exorcist" and "L.A. Times" missives. Compare these to my father's notations in Elizabeth Short's photo album (Figure 15.6).

was the best saterical comidy that I have ever seen.

He plunged him self into
the billowy weve
and an echo arose from
the sucides grave
tit willo   tit willo
tit willo

The L.A. Times
Los Angeles Calif
Please Rush to Editor
AIR Mail

15.5 Zodiac handwriting from the *San
Francisco Chronicle* and *Los Angeles Times*

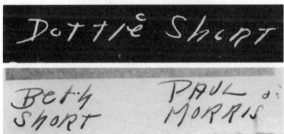

15.6

3. Lowercase "i"

The following mailings from Zodiac and the Black Dahlia Avenger span more than twenty years. In each note the killer printed in uppercase with the sole (and unusual) exception of the letter "i."

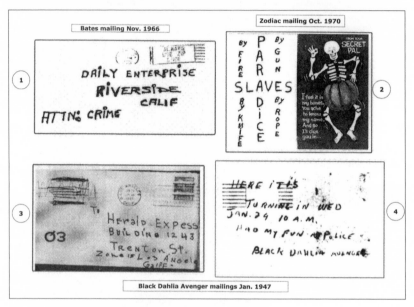

15.7

1. Zodiac's Bates confession envelope—1966
   DAiLY ENTERPRiSE RiVERSiDE CALIF ATTN : CRiME
2. Zodiac's Halloween Card—1970
   BY FiRE—BY KNiFE—PARADiCE
3. George Hodel "Avenger" envelope—1947
   BUiLDiNG
4. George Hodel "Avenger" surrender note—1947
   HERE iT iS TURNiNG iN WED JAN. 29 10 A.M.
   HAD MY FUN AT POLiCE
   BLACK DAHLiA AVENGER

4. Dot inside letter "O"

Figure 15.8 on page 179 shows examples of Zodiac's characteristic dot inside the letter "O" as seen in the Bates poem and various San Francisco mailings. Researchers have speculated that Zodiac intentionally inserted the universally acknowledged symbol for the sun. But I believe there's a more mundane explanation.

Figure 15.9 was written by my father on the back of a photograph, which he mailed to my mother, Dorothy "Dorero" Hodel, at Christmas, 1981.[15] At first glance the letter "O" in the word "Love" appears to be a circle with a dot. Closer examination reveals that George Hodel formed the letter "O" beginning at the nine o'clock position and ending at the eleven o'clock, where it curves inward and terminates inside itself. Figure 15.10 was written by George Hodel and mailed from Manila to San Francisco in 1986. At normal size it appears to be a dot inside a circle, but when enlarged (as seen at the bottom of Figure 15.10), we can see that the dot is actually the termination of his letter O. Many of the Zodiac letter O's appear to have been written this way.

15.8

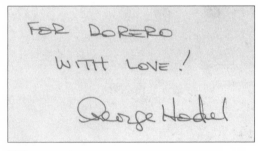

15.9

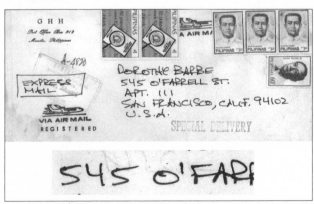

15.10

15 Dorero was my father's nickname for my mother—his own contraction of the Greek word dor (gift) and Eros (god of passion).

5. Typewriter "e"

Handwriting samples taken from Brown, Degnan, Black Dahlia Avenger, Elizabeth Short's photo album, Kern, Bates, and Zodiac all show the consistent use of the "typewriter e," which matches the known handwriting of George Hodel.

15.11 Samples of the typewriter letter "e"

6. Mathematical < "less than" symbol

At the bottom of George Hodel's 1990 "June Hodel Conference Notes" (Figure 15.12) he uses this rather unusual symbol: "Look frwd to day with anticip- to endure pain <" Beside it is a reproduction of Zodiac's handwritten cryptogram mailed to the press in 1969 in which he employs the same symbol six times. Though rarely seen, this symbol is commonly used by two types of professionals: mathematicians and medical doctors.

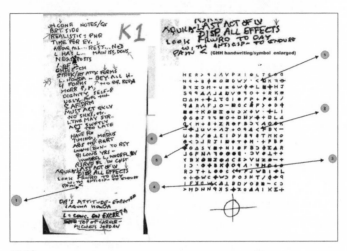

15.12

7. "A friend"

Though their taunts to the press were separated by more than twenty-five years, both the Black Dahlia Avenger and Zodiac mailed letters to their respective city editors offering information and signing it "a friend." Both suspects also used a lowercase "a." In my opinion, the killer's use

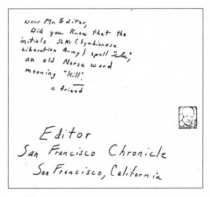

15.13

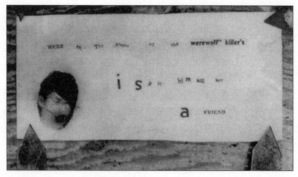

15.14

of this unique signature is neither casual nor accidental. He could be referencing the works of Edgar Allan Poe, who repeatedly used the term "a friend" throughout his short stories. See especially "The Murders in the Rue Morgue," "The Gold Bug," and "The Purloined Letter."

8. "Squirm, Twich [sic] & Scream"

It wasn't enough for Zodiac/BDA/Lipstick to perpetrate his sadistic crimes upon his victims. He also delighted in extending his perversity by providing detailed verbal descriptions of his crimes to the public. In the cases of Suzanne Degnan and Cheri Jo Bates he even mailed letters directly to the victim's family.

The killer's message in the Cheri Jo Bates case shows a pattern of word usage and misspelling that was used again four years later by Zodiac.

BRUSH OFFS THAT SHE HAD GIVEN ME DURING THE YEARS PRIOR. SHE DIED HARD. SHE
SQUIRMED AND SHOOK AS I CHOAKED HER, AND HER LIPS TWICHED. SHE LET OUT A SCRE
ONCE AND I KICKED HER HEAD TO SHUT HER UP. I PLUNGED THE KNIFE INTO HER AND I
BROKE. I THEN FINISHED THE JOB BY CUTTING HER THROAT. I AM NOT SICK. I AM
INSANE. BUT THAT WILL NOT STOP THE GAME. THIS LETTER SHOULD BE PUBLISHED FOR

*of my slaves that I have
wateing for me in Paradice.
Some I shall tie over ant hills
and watch them scream + twich
and squirm. Others shall have*

15.15

Figure 15.15 shows a section of the typed Bates letter compared to Zodiac's subsequent (*Mikado*) "little list" letter written by hand.

Bates:

"She **squirmed** and shook as I **choaked** her, and her lips **twiched**. She let out a **scream**. . . .

Mikado:

"Some I shall tie over ant hills and watch them **scream & twich** and **squirm**."

Not only does the killer use the same exact words in a single sentence in these separate writings, but he also misspells the same word "twich," omitting the letter "t" in both.

9. Bates confession paper and signature

The original crime summary of the Cheri Jo Bates investigation states that the suspect typed his "confession letter" on teletype paper cut from a roll of a "UP model 15 Teletype machine." He also typed "THE CONFESSION" at the top using all capital letters and, according to some investigators, included a signature line comprised of spaces for 12 letters, as shown below.

THE CONFESSION BY _ _ _ _ _ _ _ _ _ _ _ _

Not having access to the original documents, I'm unable to confirm the accuracy of these statements.

Figure 15.16 shows three of my father's legal signatures. They read: (1) G. Hill Hodel M.D.; (2) Dr. G. Hill Hodel; and (3) George H. Hodel. All three contain 12 letters. It is not a stretch to imagine Zodiac, due to his megalomaniacal ego, would not be able to resist using the actual number of letters in his name.

or hope of receiving assistance in securing such

Ca Hill Hodel MD
(Signature of affiant)

ffirmed) before me this JUL 11 1942

The bearer should also fill in blanks below as
indicated.

c/o DR. G. HILL HODEL

CANCELLED

Bearer's address in the United States

IN WITNESS WHEREOF, this Agreement has been executed
in three (3) counterparts, any one of which may be considered
the original.

George H. Hodel

George H. Hodel

GHH sig sample 12/21/92

15.16

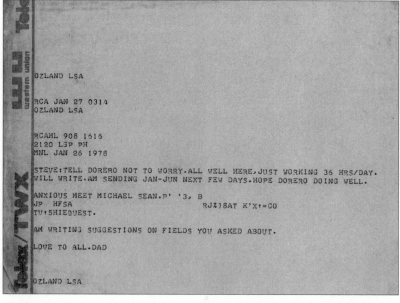

```
OZLAND LSA

RCA JAN 27 0314
OZLAND LSA

RCAML 908 1616
2120 L3P PH
MNL JAN 26 1978

STEVE:TELL DORERO NOT TO WORRY.ALL WELL HERE,JUST WORKING 36 HRS/DAY.
WILL WRITE.AM SENDING JAN-JUN NEXT FEW DAYS.HOPE DORERO DOING WELL.

ANXIOUS MEET MICHAEL SEAN.P' '3, B
JP   HFSA                    RJ%I8AT K'X+=CO
TV+SHIEQUEST.

AM WRITING SUGGESTIONS ON FIELDS YOU ASKED ABOUT.

LOVE TO ALL.DAD

OZLAND LSA
```

15.17

Figure 15.17 is a reproduction of a Telex teletype sent to me by my father in January 1978. I know for a fact that he had Telex machines (unknown models) installed in all of his fifteen branch market research offices throughout Asia, and received and sent dozens of teletypes a week.

Telex teletype paper would have been foreign and inaccessible to most people who were considered suspects (including past boyfriends and students) in the Bates murder. Yet it was a commonly used item, handled many times a day by business executive George Hill Hodel.

10. Use of "Z" signature Bates/Zodiac
The following is a comparison of the "Z" signature in the "Bates Had To Die . . ." message to the "Z" signature used by Zodiac as his return address for the "Paul Averly [sic], San Francisco Chronicle" letter.

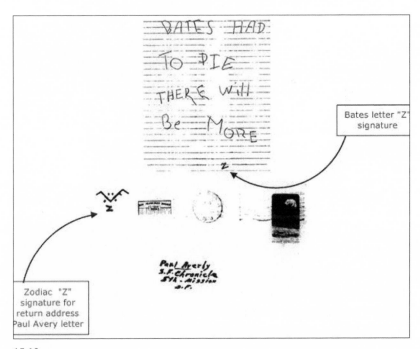

15.18

11. The Bates Poem

Compare the top line of George Hodel's 1998 "June Hodel Conference Notes" (which was really a poem of sorts, a collection of his thoughts justifying his intended suicide by pills) to the first line of Cheri Jo Bates's killer's poem, which he wrote just minutes before following her outside the library and cutting her throat. Both are divided by a slash "/".

George Hodel—"JH CONF. NOTES/Qs

Zodiac—"Sick of living/unwilling to die."

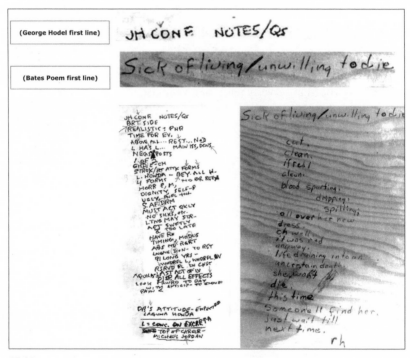

15.19

12. Underscores and exclamations

Figure 15.20 shows the Black Dahlia Avenger's use of exclamation marks and underscoring (top row) and compares it to Zodiac's (bottom row).

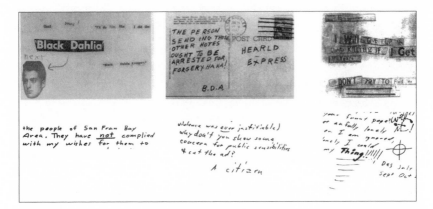

15.20

Taken on their own, any individual piece of the foregoing evidence may be explained away as a coincidence. But at what point does a preponderance of coincidence equal proof? That is typically up to a jury to decide. I, for one, based on twenty-four years as a homicide detective and experience on more three hundred murders, believe coincidences as numerous as these are not accidental and should be examined further.

Chapter Sixteen

Please help me I can not remain in control for much
longer.

Zodiac

Back in 1969, SFPD and other Bay Area investigators, despite an abundance of physical evidence from five crime scenes, still had no leads.

Their lack of progress in putting the pieces together only added to their frustration. The heat was on from the press, the public, and the mayor's office. The entire Bay Area demanded an immediate arrest.

The Zodiac notes, while presenting good handwriting evidence, nevertheless yielded few specific clues pointing to Zodiac's identity. SFPD believed their best hope lay in the eyewitness composite sketches. Law enforcement remained confident that the drawings bore a strong likeness to Zodiac.

Zodiac's physical description as shown on page 189 was obtained by a police sketch artist from the three teenagers who watched from the second-floor window of their residence during the San Francisco shooting of taxicab driver Paul Stine. A second follow-up "amended" sketch was obtained from SFPD patrolman Donald Fouke and his partner, Eric Zelms, who, while enroute to the shooting, had seen Zodiac walking away.

For the sake of comparison, I've included two photographs of my father from 1962 and 1974. In the '74 photo he's seen wearing his own glasses, which appear identical to those worn by Zodiac in the composite drawing. In Figure 16.2, on the far right, I've added glasses for easier comparison.

In my research, I came across a second composite of Zodiac on the now-defunct Web site "This Is the Zodiac Speaking" run by Jake M. Wark. Jake Wark, like Tom Voigt and others, has done extensive research and assembled a thorough and objective summary of the crimes.

16.1 SFPD Zodiac composite compared to
George Hodel

16.2

The following composite (Figure 16.3) appeared on Wark's Web site with
the comment: "It is unknown why Sonoma County would issue a Zodiac sketch, as no Zodiac crimes are acknowledged in that area." Follow-
up research indicated that this composite could have been made of a

suspect in an attempted kidnapping of a woman in her vehicle, a crime that some investigators believe was committed by Zodiac.

16.3 **Sonoma composite; George Hodel, 1962**

Jake Wark's site features yet another police composite (Figure 16.4) that's remarkable because of its detail and resemblance to my father. As referenced in an earlier chapter, this third composite was also used on the cover for a book entitled *Great Crimes of San Francisco*, an anthology of San Francisco area true-crime essays edited by Dean W. Dickensheet.

16.4 **George Hodel, 1974; Zodiac as represented on paperback cover of 1974** *Great Crimes of San Francisco* (Ballantine Books, New York)

Because of the sketch's striking similarity to my father (including his black horn-rimmed glasses) I was determined to find its source. Was I looking at an artist's imaginary rendition or a reproduction of an actual police drawing from official files? If the Zodiac composite was simply the publisher's decision to take "creative license," then why place it on an official SFPD Police Bulletin connected to an otherwise completely factual true-crime story? On the other hand, if the composite was an official police drawing, why had it not surfaced earlier?

I found the answer with the help of a confidential source who contacted the author of the essay on Zodiac in *Great Crimes of San Francisco*, Duffy Jennings. Jennings, a former *San Francisco Chronicle* crime reporter, confirmed that "the composite originated with law enforcement," but couldn't recall the specific agency. Since the sketch includes the correct date (October 18) and number [90-69] of a known San Francisco Police Department bulletin, it would appear that this composite originated from the files of the SFPD.[16]

Zodiac Shoe Size

At both the Riverside (Cheri Jo Bates) and the Napa County (Shepard/Hartnell) crime scenes, investigators were able to find, measure, and preserve footprints that they believed were left by Zodiac. Analysis based on photographs and plaster castings showed the suspect wore a man's size 10. Napa detectives after a follow-up investigation concluded that "The shoe print was possibly made by a military style wing-walker boot or a shoe or boot of foreign import." Their findings indicated either a size 10½ R (military) or a 10½ D (civilian).

Figure 16.5 shows an actual shoe, owned and worn by my father, Dr. George Hodel. It was manufactured in Switzerland by Bally's, size 10E.

---

16 Despite Jennings's acknowledgment and the fact that it is an almost picture-perfect likeness to George Hodel, I still have some doubts about this third composite. When I attempted to locate editor Dean W. Dickensheet, I discovered that he died in the 1990s. Further attempts to confirm Duffy Jennings's recollection that this was an official police composite are being made through Dickensheet's original publisher.

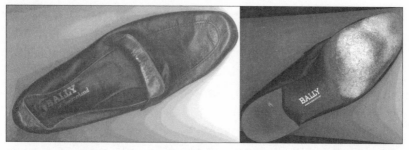

16.5 **Left dress shoe of Dr. George Hodel**

Figure 16.7 shows an enlargement of George Hodel's right shoe. Visible inside is a typed label inserted by my father, identifying the model as Bally Long. Written on the label in green ink, in my father's handwriting, are the words "injured toe in Tokyo." How many people do you know who would have thought to write this? I point this out as an interesting aside and another peek into Dr. George Hodel's strange and unique mind.

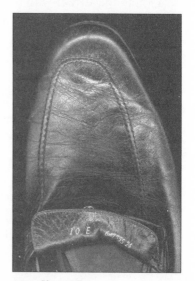

16.6 **Size 10E**

16.7 **Label reads: "Bally Long (injured toe in Tokyo)"**

Bryan Hartnell—the young college student who was severely wounded at Lake Berryessa and managed to survive—provided a detailed description of his attacker's strange attire. Based on Hartnell's recollections, law enforcement developed a sketch (Figure 16.8) that shows Zodiac in a military-type getup.

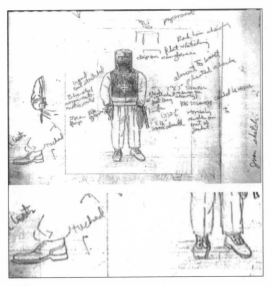

16.8

Hartnell told police that the suspect carried a semiautomatic handgun and wore a bayonet knife in a twelve-inch wooden sheath. Figure 16.8 shows the man who called himself Zodiac with his pants tucked into ankle-high boots, infantryman-style. Legible in the enlarged figure is the artist's description, "tucked."

My father was obsessed with all things military. He maintained a military bearing throughout his long life and had a powerful emotional need to always be in control. His 1946 nine-month tour in China as an honorary lieutenant general assigned to UNRRA briefly fed that need.

In Hankow, UNRRA had provided "Lieutenant General" Hodel with a small staff and a military jeep complete with a three-star UNRRA flag. Figure 16.9 is a photo and two close-ups of Lt. Gen. George Hodel (sitting, second from right) taken in China in 1946. In it, he wears ankle-high boots with the pants tucked into them infantry-style. Could these be the same style (or even the very same) size-10 military-style boots worn by Zodiac?

16.9

The *Chronicle* Connection

Bay Area investigators have often speculated that Zodiac seemed to have a special relationship with the *San Francisco Chronicle*. According to the book *Great Crimes of San Francisco*, "Zodiac began his publicity campaign with several Bay Area papers, but he soon began to concentrate on one: the *San Francisco Chronicle*."

Many experts suspect that Zodiac had a direct, personal connection to the newspaper. Perhaps he was related to someone who worked at the *Chronicle* or had once been an employee himself.

Zodiac's Halloween card of October 20, 1970 (Letter #17), was addressed directly to "Paul Averly, [sic] San Francisco Chronicle." In his final letter (#25, dated April 24, 1978), Zodiac took the time to acknowledge Herb Caen, one of San Francisco's most beloved columnists, as though they were old friends.[17] He wrote:

> This is the Zodiac speaking, I am back with you. Tell herb caen, I
> am here. I have always been here. That city pig toshi is good but I
> am ~~bu~~ smarter and better he will get tired then leave me alone. I am
> waiting for a good movie about me. who will play me. I am now in
> control of all things.
>
> yours truly :

On the surface, Zodiac's message can be taken as just another taunt to San Franciscans, reminding them that he's a local boy and still on the prowl. But the person who carefully composed these letters and risked being discovered isn't someone who says things casually. Everything that issues from his complex, enigmatic, psychotic mind alludes to a deeper meaning as he plays his dangerous double game—relying on his superior intellect to outsmart the police while at the same time feeding his massive ego that demands he leave subtle clues to his identity.

In the earlier biographical summary of my father's life, I mentioned his experiences as a young journalist, first in Los Angeles as a crime reporter for the *Los Angeles Record*, then later, while he was living in and

17 In 1978, several months after the receipt of this letter, a controversy arose when it was learned that Inspector Toschi had anonymously written himself some "fan mail" letters and sent them to a friend at the *San Francisco Chronicle*. This caused some to wonder if the "I am back." letter was genuine. Toschi adamantly denied writing the Zodiac letter and was backed by command staff on the SFPD. On July 16, 1978, an article appeared in the *New York Times* headlined POLICE OFFICIALS ON COAST DENY INSP. FORGED ZODIAC LETTERS. I quote in part from that article: "Police officials have emphatically denied reports that Insp. Dave Toschi, who has investigated the Zodiac killer case for nine years, ever was suspected of forging the latest letters attributed to the murder. . . . Mr. Toschi was reassigned from homicide to the pawn shop detail Monday after admitting that he used fake names to write self-flattering fan mail to a former *San Francisco Chronicle* columnist."

attending medical school in San Francisco. It was during this time that he was employed as a columnist for the *San Francisco Chronicle.*

Beginning on Valentine's Day, February 14, 1932, George and his (first) wife, Emilia Hodel, wrote a weekly Sunday column in the *San Francisco Chronicle* entitled "Abroad in San Francisco." The following insert, printed next to their first co-bylined article, "Little Italy, Like Naples, Leans Over Azure Bay; Breath of Mediterranean," shows how George and Emilia Hodel were introduced to San Franciscans back in 1932:

16.10 *San Francisco Chronicle* columnists George and Emilia Hodel with son Duncan, circa 1932.

> Editor's note—This series of articles, by George and Emilia Hodel, deals with the foreign colonies of San Francisco. The various foreign quarters—Chinatown, the Latin Quarter, Little Greece, and the rest are veritable cities within a city. There are more than twenty of them, with a combined population of over 190,000. Each Sunday you will explore, with the Hodels, one or another of these colonies. The foreign populations of San Francisco have merged their interests inseparably with those of all San Francisco. In many respects life in the "colonies" is indistinguishable from that of the entire American scene. Nevertheless, each group has brought over with it its old-world heritage— customs, festivals, philosophies, foods. The old ways have in many cases been carefully preserved, and each now lends its special color to the life of San Francisco.

Each subsequent Sunday, George and Emilia described the sights, sounds, customs, and tastes of another ethnic enclave within the city. These included Italy, Yugoslavia, Portugal, Spain, Greece, Denmark, Norway, Sweden, Russia, Japan, Germany, China, and France. Accompanying the articles were photographs showing traditional dress and interviews by George Hodel featuring a prominent citizen.

After reading the "Abroad in San Francisco" series of articles, one comes away with two distinct impressions of George Hodel. One, he was a man who loved things that were different and exotic. Two, he was an astute observer who saw everything and remembered every detail.

16.11

George Hodel left the *Chronicle* in 1932, after writing fourteen articles over a five-month period. Herb Caen, nine years younger than George, didn't begin writing for the newspaper until 1938.

Herb Caen went on to become the *Chronicle*'s greatest journalist and wrote about the city he loved for almost sixty years. While my father encouraged San Franciscans to explore the cultural diversity of their own city, Caen spoke to them much more directly. His message: let's laugh at ourselves and the vagaries of our time and in the process learn to accept one another in our splendid diversity.

While Herb Caen was likely completely unaware of George Hodel, I suspect George followed Caen's career with interest. Given the enormity of his ego, he probably considered himself to be Caen's predecessor. As he read Caen's column, he probably thought to himself, "I've been there and done that, said that before you."

In his cryptic message to Caen, the author adopts a familiar tone. It no longer sounds like the Zodiac pontificating, but former *San Francisco Chronicle* columnist George Hodel talking to a colleague, as he says:

> I am back with you. Tell herb caen, I am here. I have always been here.

16.12
Location 1: Paul Stine murder crime scene, Washington and Cherry Streets (1969)
Location 2: George and Emilia Hodel residence, 2275 Jackson Street (1934)
Location 3: George Hodel residence, 715 Bush Street (1931 pre-med)[18]
Location 4: George Hodel residence, 1567 Willard Street (1929 and 1933–1936)
Location 5: UCSF Medical School, George Hodel attended (1933–1936)
Location 6: Point Bonita, George Hodel's gravesite (1999)

18　In February 1932, George Hodel also showed a listed residence address of 1627 Oxford Street, Berkeley, California, just a few blocks from his UC Berkeley pre-med campus.

George Hodel: A resident of the Presidio

The Presidio area of San Francisco was George Hodel's neighborhood for most of his school years (1929–1936). The map on the previous page identifies his three separate San Francisco residences as well as the Stine murder scene.

I know from several car trips I took with my father through his old neighborhoods that he and Emilia also lived together in a small home on the winding road to Coit Tower. On one of my visits in 1997, I recall we drove by this house and he spoke of it with particular affection.

It's worth noting that the distance from George Hodel's Jackson Street residence to the Stine murder is 1.3 miles; and it's 2.7 miles from the Stine murder site to his UCSF Medical School.

Police speculated that the Stine suspect seemed very familiar with the area, which helped explain how he was able to elude their massive search. They were right.

Chapter Seventeen

I have with me two gods, Persuasion and Compulsion.

Themistocles

We know that the Zodiac murders occurred on October 30, 1966; October 20, 1968; July 4, 1969; September 27, 1969; and October 11, 1969. The mailings, on the other hand, began in 1966 and lasted until 1990.

Zodiac Mailings

Year	Number	Date sent
1966	2	11/29
1967	3	4/30
1969	8	7/31, 8/4, 10/13, 11/8, 11/9, 12/30
1970	6	4/20, 4/28, 6/26, 7/24, 7/26, 10/27
1971	1	3/13
1974	4	1/29, 2/14, 5/18, 7/8
1978	2	4/24, 5/2
1990	1	December

One of the first questions I asked myself when I started this investigation was, "Is it possible that my father was physically present in the United States to commit these crimes?" My initial response was, "No, probably not."

However, after examining the time intervals of the crimes and notes, coupled with the knowledge of my father's high-frequency travel to and from the United States, I changed my mind. For decades, law enforcement and researchers have speculated that Zodiac could have been a member of the military or merchant marines, a man who spent long periods abroad punctuated by brief but frequent trips to the Bay Area. Instead of limiting his movements to the belly of a tanker or transport ship, isn't it just as likely that Zodiac may have conducted his international travel in the first-class section of a Boeing jet?

From the mid-1950s until 1988, George Hodel based his home and business in the Philippine capital of Manila. As the president of an international market research firm, International Research Associates (INRA) Asia, with clients that included Boeing, the World Tourism Organization, and major airlines and hotel chains, he traveled regularly and frequently to the United States, primarily San Francisco, Los Angeles, and New York.

I remember my father showing me his passport on several occasions and smiling with pride. It was literally three inches thick because of the many entrance stamps, visas, and millions of miles he had accumulated in his travel to and from Europe, Asia, and the United States. As president of INRA-ASIA, all of my father's worldwide first-class air travel and five-star hotel lodgings were gratis.

His profession provided him with the perfect cover to carry out his crimes and then quietly return in comfort to his home base in Southeast Asia as a business executive.

My attempts to establish and document the exact travel dates for my father's regular and frequent trips to the United States have been hampered by lack of available records from the 1960s and '70s. The financial, credit card, and medical records I've discovered only go back to 1990. U.S. entry/exit records from the period do not exist. My father's personal passport, if it still exists, would be among the personal effects I do not as yet have access to.

My father always kept his life cloaked in secrecy.

I, like all his children, was never informed in advance of his trips to the United States. Instead, every so often I'd receive a phone call out of the blue: "Hello, Steven, this is your father speaking. I am in Los Angeles for just a day or so. Please contact your brothers and meet me at my hotel for dinner."

After talking with my half-sister Tamar, I've pieced together a chronology of those trips to the States when my father actually contacted us. They place him in California in the following years: 1965, 1966, 1967,

1968, 1969, 1971, 1972, 1974, 1978, 1979, 1982, 1983, 1987, and 1988. He returned for good from 1990 to 1999. But I know there were many more occasions over the decades when my father passed through town on business without ever notifying members of his family.

1965: Visit with Kiyo (my ex-wife) and me in Los Angeles at the Biltmore Hotel.

1966 or 1967: Visit with Tamar and Deborah, her eleven-year-old daughter, in San Francisco.

1968: Meeting at Century City Hotel in Los Angeles. The following day, I took Father on a private tour of LAPD's Parker Center Police Building, showing him the Scientific Investigation Division (SID) Unit, followed by a lunch at the Police Academy restaurant in Elysian Park.

April 1969: George has a Beverly Hills luncheon with his daughter Tamar and then a later dinner with his granddaughter Deborah.

July–August 1971: George visits with Tamar in Honolulu, Hawaii, while enroute either to or from the United States.

1971 or 1972: George and his then girlfriend June are in Los Angeles.

1974: Father is admitted to his alma mater hospital, UCSF, where his personal physician performed an operation on his gall bladder called a cholecystectomy.

1978 or 1979: My father visits my family at our home in Eagle Rock, in northeast Los Angeles.

June 28, 1982: George and June are secretly married in Reno, Nevada.

1983: I receive an unexpected call from my father requesting I take a few days off and drive up from L.A. to meet him and June in San Francisco.

1987 or 1988: San Francisco. I visit with George and June at their downtown hotel, by my recollection the St. Francis.

1990: George and June Hodel relocate to the United States, choosing downtown San Francisco as their permanent residence.

Comparing the years I know my father was in the United States against the years in which there was known Zodiac activity, there is only one year that doesn't line up: 1970. As busy as my father was with international travel, it is my belief that he made many dozens or even hundreds of trips through California in the 1960s, '70s, and '80s without calling any of his children. Though this of course falls far short of any kind of proof, I believe it demonstrates enough opportunity to be consistent with the theory that George Hodel could have been behind the killings and mailings attributed to Zodiac.

Dr. George Hill Hodel—Horologist

My father had a thing for watches. Throughout his life, he bought and collected expensive timepieces, including the expensive Breitling Navitimer, seen in Figure 17.1 that he gave me two years before his death. It was equipped with a navigational computer that allowed military pilots (and those few civilians with the mental know-how) to manually calculate the speed of the aircraft they were flying.

17.1 Dr. George Hodel's Breitling Navitimer watch believed worn by him at the time of the Zodiac killings

What significance did watches hold for George Hodel? I'm not sure. What I do know is that melting, malleable watches figured prominently in the symbology of surrealist art, and that disabled watches were left at two Avenger/Zodiac crime scenes.

In *Black Dahlia Avenger* I explained how Elizabeth Short's body was carefully posed as a tribute to my father's friend the surrealist artist

Man Ray. As mentioned before, two of Man Ray's works in particular, *The Minotaur* and *The Lovers* are paid homage to in the arrangement of the arms and the slashed smile. Could there be another surrealist homage connecting the Dahlia crime scene to the Cheri Jo Bates crime scene years later? I believe so.

During my Dahlia investigation I discovered that a man's military watch had been recovered from the crime scene on Norton Avenue. What I didn't know but discovered later was that the watch had initially been placed inside the cavity of Elizabeth Short's body, as a detailed examination of enlarged crime scene photographs made clear to me.

This appears to be the same watch found by police recruits who canvassed the crime scene a week after the body's removal.

Quoting from *The Washington News*, January 21, 1947: "The police department's homicide squad figuratively starting from scratch, was augmented by 100 additional policemen and began a widespread search for new clues to the girl's murderer. Half of them combed the area where the bisected body was found . . . the search turned up a military-type watch, still unidentified."

Had the watch gone unnoticed and fallen into the grass when the body was moved to the coroner's wagon? It seems so. We know that the LAPD found and recovered a man's wristwatch at the Dahlia crime scene and booked it into evidence. In 2004 when asked about the watch, LAPD was forced to acknowledge that the watch, along with the rest of the physical evidence, "had disappeared from the locked property room."

Why did my father place it there? It seems that disabled watches and other representations of time figure prominently in numerous surrealist works, including Man Ray's *Object of Destruction*. Perhaps the most famous of these is Salvador Dalí's *The Persistence of Memory*.

According to art critic Dawn Ades, "the soft watches [in Dalí's

17.2 *The Persistence of Memory,* Salvador Dalí, 1931

painting] are an unconscious symbol of the relativity of space and time, a surrealist meditation on the collapse of our notion of a fixed cosmic order." Certainly George Hodel, like his mentors Man Ray and Salvador Dalí, used his "art" to challenge our belief in a rational, orderly, rule-bound world.

17.3–17.4 **Bates crime scene watchband**

I believe George Hodel repeated this signature act some twenty years after the death of Elizabeth Short, when a second watch was ripped apart and left at the scene of the Bates murder in Riverside, California. According to Special Agent Melvin Nicolai of the California Department of Justice, "Evidence found at the scene of the crime consisted of

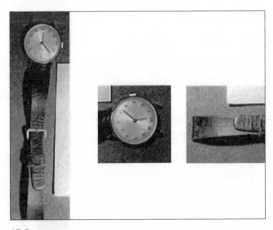

17.5

a Timex wristwatch with the fastener on one side of the strap torn off. . . ."

Initially investigators speculated that the watch fell off the suspect's wrist during the struggle. Figures 17.3 and 17.4 show Riverside detectives in October 1966 pointing to a portion of the watchband strap found at the Bates crime scene.

One strap of the watchband appears to have been ripped from the body of the watch. In the evidence photo Figure 17.5, likely taken for identification purposes at the police station, the torn strap is seen in close-up.

We know from our discussion of the Riverside investigation in chapter 6 that detectives were able to trace the watch to a military base PX overseas. Could it have been a PX in the Philippines, Dr. George Hodel's home base from the mid-1950s to the 1980s?

In 1966, there were two main U.S. military bases in the Philippines on the island of Luzon. One was the Navy base at Subic Bay, where I was stationed from 1959 to 1960, and the second was Clark Air Force Base. Most Americans, including civilian businessmen like my father who resided in Manila, regularly made their purchases from one of these two duty-free military bases. Clark AFB was only forty miles northwest of Manila and was the largest U.S. overseas military base ever constructed.

In his Cheri Jo Bates investigative summary, Department of Justice special agent Melvin Nicolai made two other connections that should be noted:

> Mr. Sherwood Morrill concluded that the three envelopes and letters, along with the printed poem on the desk, had been prepared by the same person responsible for the Zodiac letters. . . .
>
> During the investigation, information was received to the effect that the concept that persons killed will be the killer's slaves in the life hereafter originated in South East Asia and particularly in Mindanao in the southern Philippines. . . . Suspects from groups having similar beliefs were investigated, including all male members of the Charles Manson Family.

Combined efforts by law enforcement agencies have failed to uncover the identity of the "Zodiac" killer. . . .

Investigation continuing.

Melvin M. Nicolai
Special Agent

Chapter Eighteen

The map coupled with this code will tell you where the
bomb is set.

                                        Zodiac

An element that runs through all the murders I attribute to George
Hodel, from the Black Dahlia Avenger to Suzanne Degnan to Zodiac,
are the elaborate cat-and-mouse games he played with authorities. Probably the most perplexing of these was a mysterious Phillips 66 gas station map and compass diagram sent by Zodiac in 1970. Since its arrival
at the *San Francisco Chronicle*, SFPD detectives and expert cryptogra-
phers have spent endless hours racking their brains, trying to figure out
what it means.

18.1

The letter reads:

This is the **Z**odiac speaking I have become very upset with the
people of San Fran Bay Area. They have **not** complied with my
wishes for them to wear some nice⟊buttons. I **promiced** to

punish them if they did not comply , by **anilating** a full School **Buss**. But now school is out for the summer, so I punished them in **an** another way. **I** shot a man sitting in a parked car with a .38.

- 12 SFPD - 0

The Map coupled with this code will tell you where the bomb is set. You have **untill** next Fall to dig it up.

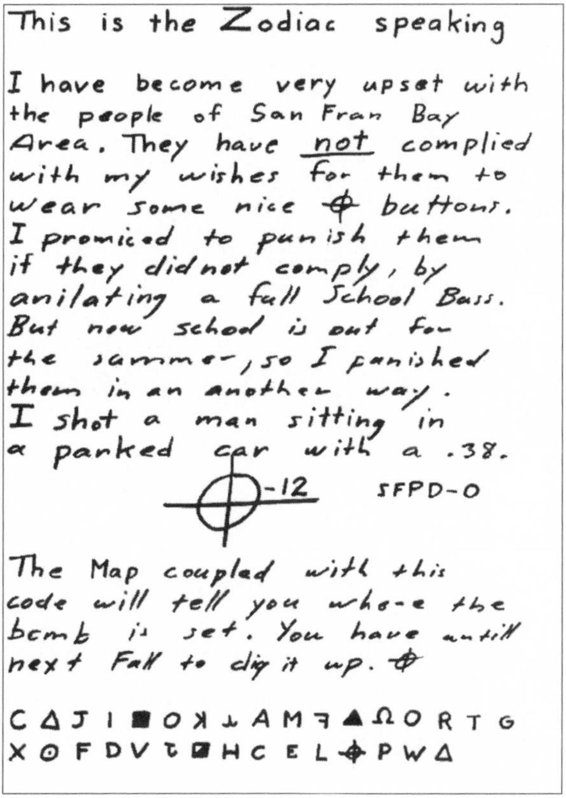
This is the Zodiac speaking

I have become very upset with the people of San Fran Bay Area. They have not complied with my wishes for them to wear some nice ⊕ buttons. I promiced to punish them if they did not comply, by anilating a full School Buss. But now school is out for the summer, so I punished them in an another way. I shot a man sitting in a parked car with a .38.

⊕-12 SFPD-0

The Map coupled with this code will tell you where the bomb is set. You have untill next Fall to dig it up. ⊕

C Δ J I ■ O ꓘ ⊥ A M ꓶ ▲ Ω O R T G
X ⊙ F D V Ꞇ ◪ H C E L ⊕ P W Δ

18.2

The code in this letter was never broken, and no bomb was ever found. But a month later, in his July 26, 1970, *Mikado* "little list" letter, Zodiac referenced the map again:

PS. The Mt. Diablo code concerns Radians & # inches along the radians.

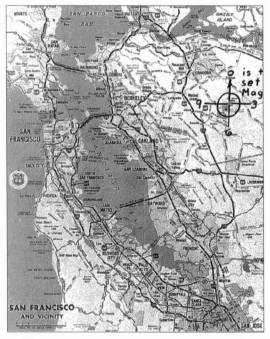

18.3

The map with its obscure notations was first brought to public attention in a November 1981 article published in *California* magazine, entitled "Portrait of the Artist as a Mass Murderer." Author Gareth Penn, who wrote under the pen name George Oakes, is the son of an Army cryptographer who was a former employee of the California Attorney General's Office. Gareth is a member of Mensa—the most famous high-IQ society in the world.

18.4

In his *California* magazine article, Penn theorized that Zodiac had used his crimes to create a form of land art. Land Art, also known as Earthworks, is a movement said to have been launched in October 1968 with the group exhibition "Earthworks" at the Dwan Gallery in New York. Zodiac's first Bay Area murder occurred just one month later, in December 1968. If Zodiac was influenced by the Earthworks movement, it might mean he had carefully selected his murder sites and positioned his victims to create his own masterpiece. If George Hodel was Zodiac, working his crimes into a piece of art only he could fully understand would continue the tradition he began when he posed Elizabeth Short as his surreal masterpiece.

As Penn (Oakes) states in the article:

Seen from the perspective of outer space, the Zodiac murders make a certain kind of sense. They show, in fact, a degree of precision and a consistency of design that, combined with the savagery and viciousness of the crimes, is downright blood chilling.

In a book he published in 1987, *Times 17*, Gareth Penn defined the term "radian."

A radian is a unit of angular measurement frequently used by engineers, mathematicians, and some people in the physical sciences. . . . In more familiar terms, it is 57.2957795131. . . . or 57 degrees, 17 minutes, 44 seconds.

He then goes on to describe his process of discovery:

I was curious to discover what the Zodiac had meant by this rather bizarre suggestion. I bought a sheet of clear acetate and a marking pen. Using a protractor and a straightedge, I drew an angle of between 57 and 58 degrees on the acetate and then laid the acetate over a map of the Bay Area. I placed the apex of the angle on Mount Diablo, then rotated the angle around until one leg passed through the scene of the murder at Blue Rock Springs. . . . The other leg of the angle went straight through Presidio Heights in San Francisco where the Zodiac had murdered the cabby. It was the most shocking experience of my entire life.

Penn said he knew in an instant why cab driver Paul Stine was killed where he was—and why he, a cabdriver, had been chosen as Zodiac's final known victim. Who would be easier to direct to a specific location before committing a murder than a cabdriver? Penn also understood why no one before him had grasped Zodiac's plan. It had to be viewed from the perspective of outer space by someone with knowledge of what a radian is.

Penn deemed Zodiac "a genius . . . coldly calculating and incredibly evil."

Then he concluded:

I knew then that everything he had done or written, as mad as it might appear, had to have a discoverable sense.

Figure 18.5, below, shows Zodiac's original notations on the Phillips 66 map with dotted lines extended at an angle of one radian to visually represent Gareth Penn's discovery. As you can see, the northern radian passes through the crime scene at Blue Rock Springs in Vallejo, and the southern line intersects Presidio Heights, where Paul Stine was murdered in his cab.

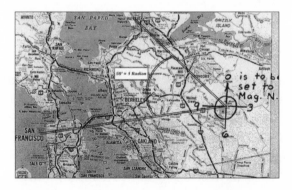

18.5

Using Zodiac's 1970 letter and map, investigators searched the Bay Area for the "bomb" Zodiac claimed to have buried along the radian lines. Nothing was found. But was the "bomb" actually an oblique reference to something else of interest buried along the radians shown in Figure 18.5? I wondered if "bomb" was meant metaphorically and whether some other feature of the map intersected with the radian lines in any interesting way. This thought, when combined with a piece of information brought to light by my book *Black Dahlia Avenger*, would provide one of the most chilling details of my entire investigation.

When I wrote *Black Dahlia Avenger*, my early research showed that Elizabeth Short had been buried near her sister's home in Oakland, California.

On October 10, 2006, I received the following e-mail and photos from a reader:

Mr. Hodel,

I recall seeing a picture in your book of your father in his later years with a view of the SF city skyline in the background. The picture looked familiar to me because I had a friend who lived in a condo in SF with a similar vantage point, that of looking out over the city and able to see the Transamerica pyramid and across the bay to Oakland.

My father happens to be buried at Mountain View Cemetery in Oakland with a fantastic view of the SF skyline across the bay. Then I learned Elizabeth Short rests in the same cemetery. Where the strange coincidence comes into play is the view from the slight hill where Elizabeth Short is buried. Attached are some photos from the hill where she rests. It appears your father may have had a commanding view, albeit from a distance of Elizabeth's final resting place.

Your book is quite compelling and for what it is worth has me convinced. It is surely a sad tale.

Regards,

S. M.

Reno, NV

It's true that my father owned a high-powered telescope mounted on a tripod that stood in the window of his thirty-eighth-floor penthouse apartment in San Francisco in the final years of his life. It's also true that he kept the telescope pointed in the general direction of the Mountain View Cemetery in Oakland across San Francisco Bay. How many times during his nine-year residency did he focus his telescope on Elizabeth Short's gravesite? It's impossible to tell.

18.6 Elizabeth Short's gravesite at Mountain View Cemetery, Oakland, California (Courtesy of S.M., Reno, NV). Photo of June and George in their 38th floor penthouse suite, taken by author in 1998.

When and if he did, was he filled with a perverse, gloating pride to be looking down on his masterpiece? We can only wonder.

But looking at Zodiac's map in the context of his radian comments and Penn's "Land Art" theory, something far more remarkable became clear. Elizabeth Short's final resting place in Oakland's Mountain View Cemetery is precisely intersected by Zodiac's lower radian (seen in Figure 18.7)—the same one that extends through the Paul Stine crime scene.

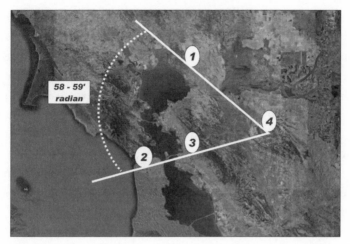

18.7
1. Blue Rock Springs (Ferrin/Mageau crime)
2. Paul Stine crime scene
3. Elizabeth Short (Black Dahlia) burial site (Mountain View Cemetery)
4. Mt. Diablo

Could it be a coincidence that Elizabeth Short happened to be buried along the radian line purposely established by Zodiac when he directed Paul Stine to his specific place of execution? The mathematical probability of it being coincidence is infinitesimal. The Zodiac murders and the murder of Elizabeth Short must have been connected.

Clearly Zodiac knew what he was doing. He wasn't simply offering authorities a geometric map of his crimes. He was providing them with a very telling and taunting clue that, if solved, would reveal a link to his identity as the 1947 Black Dahlia Avenger. The "bomb" mentioned in the letter was no literal bomb, but rather a *bombshell* of information that, if decoded, would have connected California's two most famous and enduring sequences of serial killings as the work of the same man.

Knowing that Paul Stine was directed to a specific location in the Presidio before being killed, and considering George Hodel's penchant for choosing his precise landmarks using street names, I wondered whether there were further surprises left by Zodiac all those years ago for me to discover. As illustrated in chapter 7, the placement of Elizabeth Short's body tied her bisection and murder in Los Angeles in 1947 to the murder/dismemberment of Suzanne Degnan in Chicago one year earlier. Twenty years later, Lucila Lalu's cut-up body was dumped on or very near Zodiac Street in Manila, an eerie link to the murder of Cheri Jo Bates in Riverside and the Zodiac crimes that would follow.

I was working on the theory that my father used street names to create a ghoulish forensic map to his crimes. The pattern was repeated too often to ignore:

1. Victim Suzanne Degnan: After surgical bisection, body parts (arms bent at elbows and posed upward) placed in sewer at Hollywood Avenue.
2. Victim Elizabeth Short: After surgical bisection, body parts (arms bent at elbows and posed upward) placed in vacant lot adjacent to Degnan Avenue.
3. Victim Lucila Lalu: After surgical bisection, body parts placed at or near Zodiac Street.

Did this peculiar signature end in Manila? Or did the San Francisco–area killer who called himself Zodiac place his victims in a way that referenced his other crimes?

On the night of October 11, 1969, Zodiac flagged down Paul Stine's cab in front of the St. Francis Hotel at Mason and Geary in downtown San Francisco and directed Stine to drive him to a specific location. We know that location to be Washington Street and Maple Street from the letter Zodiac sent (10/13/69) in which he takes credit for the murder. Arriving at that address, he apparently instructed Stine to proceed approximately four hundred feet west, which is where he committed the murder.

Police were able to confirm this specific location a few days later when Zodiac mailed in a bloody swatch cut from the victim's shirt. In

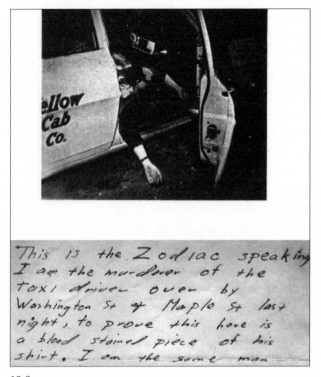

18.8

the accompanying message he called out the address of the crime as "Washington St. & Maple St."

Stine's probable route after picking up Zodiac at Mason and Geary to Washington and Maple in Presidio Heights comprises a total driving distance of about three miles.

What's the significance of that address? And why was Zodiac so precise? Is there anything that specifically connects George Hodel to Washington and Maple other than the fact that he lived a mile away on Jackson Street in 1934?

The answer is yes, and comes to us from one of the many bits of unexplained activity in the final weeks of Elizabeth Short's life.

On January 12, 1947, three days before the bisected body of Elizabeth Short was found in the vacant lot, a man fitting my father's description and calling himself Mr. Barnes checked into a hotel in downtown Los Angeles a mile south of my father's medical office. Accompanying Mr. Barnes was an attractive young woman. Barnes told manager William Johnson that they "were married and had just moved from Hollywood."

Mrs. Barnes was never seen again by either the manager or his wife, both of whom were present when the couple checked in.

Late in the morning of January 15, Mr. Barnes returned to the hotel alone. Mr. Johnson, upon seeing his guest, remarked that he "hadn't seen him or his wife in three days" and joked, "We thought you must be dead."

Upon hearing these words, Mr. Johnson reported that Mr. Barnes became visibly flustered and quickly left the hotel. On that same morning (January 15, 1947) simultaneous to the eleven a.m. Johnson and Barnes conversation at the hotel, LAPD homicide detectives were arriving at a new crime scene. The vacant lot at Thirty-ninth and Norton/Degnan was just two miles southwest of the hotel—a short five-minute drive. It would be more than a week before detectives would make the link and establish that the victim, Elizabeth Short, and Mr. Barnes had checked into the Washington Boulevard Hotel on January 12, some three days before her body was found. A week into the Black Dahlia investigation, police investigators showed the Johnsons photographs of Elizabeth Short. Both husband and wife identified her as the woman who had checked into their hotel as Mrs. Barnes. They also positively identified Mr. Barnes from one of the photographs found in Elizabeth's luggage.

Since the LAPD contends that this photograph and others have "disappeared from the files," it's impossible to know or establish if it was my father. But we do know from law-enforcement files released after the publication of *Black Dahlia Avenger* that my father dated Elizabeth Short and witnesses saw them together shortly before her murder.

The downtown hotel that "Mr. and Mrs. Barnes" checked into in January 1947 still remains intact. Sixty years later it's an apartment building known as the Hirsh Apartments at 300 East Washington Boulevard, near the intersection with Santee Street, approximately four hundred feet west of Washington and Maple.

Figure 18.9 shows aerial maps of both the San Francisco (Paul Stine) and Los Angeles (Elizabeth Short) Washington and Maple locations. Coincidence, many will say. Unlikely. Instead it seems that the Los

18.9 *(top)* Location of victim Short's Los Angeles Hotel stay, 400° west of the intersection of Washington and Maple; *(bottom)* location of victim Stine's San Francisco murder, 400° west of the intersection of Washington and Maple

Angeles hotel near the intersection of Washington and Maple was the last place my father stayed with Elizabeth Short before he took her life.

Twenty years later, as Zodiac, he needed to position his last murder in San Francisco's Presidio Heights District according to the grid of radians he'd previously worked out. He'd plotted them carefully to intersect the cemetery where Elizabeth Short is buried. With one last flourish, he would complete his forensic map with signposts linking his crimes in Chicago, Los Angeles, Manila, and San Francisco.

As a former San Francisco cab driver, my father was familiar with Presidio Heights. He knew it contained a Washington-Maple intersection just like the one in L.A.

Enjoying his own cleverness, I believe he instructed Paul Stine to take him to Washington and Maple, and then had him pull forward half a block, approximating the location of the Los Angeles hotel. His pawn now in place, Zodiac coolly removed his 9mm handgun from his jacket pocket, placed it against Paul Stine's head, and pulled the trigger. Another feature of his macabre map was complete.

Chapter Nineteen

Where love rules, there is no will to power; and where power predominates, there love is lacking. The one is the shadow of the other.

Carl Jung, *On the Psychology of the Unconscious*

The term "serial killer" didn't enter the popular vernacular until the mid-seventies when the crimes of Ted Bundy and David Berkowitz (Son of Sam) made the evening news. A serial killer is generally defined as a person, usually a man, who murders more than three people with a cooling-off period between each murder and who is motivated by a variety of psychological factors, primarily power and sexual compulsion.

FBI profilers separate this type of criminal into two categories: organized/nonsocial offenders and disorganized/asocial offenders. The latter are often of low intelligence and commit their crimes impulsively. They tend to be extremely introverted people with few friends and a history of mental problems. When captured they often have little insight into their crimes and sometimes, even, block out memories of having committed the murders.

Generally, organized/nonsocial offenders are of high intelligence and plan their crimes methodically. Armed with knowledge of forensics and maintaining a high degree of control over their crime scenes, they're able to skillfully cover their tracks. They often regard their crimes as some sort of grand project and follow them proudly in the media. When they're caught, it's often discovered that they've been leading a somewhat normal social life with friends, lovers, and even a wife and children.

Without question, the Black Dahlia Avenger, Zodiac, and the Lipstick Killer in Chicago all fall into the category of organized offenders, as the murders were carefully planned to disguise the identity of the killer. But even within that classification there are specific MOs that make each serial murderer unique and that are used by law enforcement to develop a specific profile of each killer.

Beginning to believe that these three killers were the same man, I developed a list of MOs for each and then combined them into one master list to see how much overlap I would find. The list of shared characteristics is remarkable:

1. Geographically preselects specific crime-scene location by plotting coordinates on a map, then randomly murders victim(s) who by happenstance enter his "killing zone," or

2. Geographically preselects specific crime-scene location by plotting coordinates on a map, then has unwitting victim (taxi driver) drive him to that location, where victim is then shot and killed, or

3. Forcibly kidnaps female victim, strangles her to death, and dismembers body with surgical skill and precision. Then poses body parts in public view at a specific location (street name) that provides taunting clue related to the crime or suspect.

4. In three separate murders medical coroner's office declares suspect to be a "skilled surgeon." Suspect performs a "hemicorpectomy" surgical operation on the victims. Using a scalpel, he bisects the bodies between the second and third lumbar vertebrae.

5. Uses ruse and abduction.

6. Brutal assault and overkill, particularly savage with female victims.

7. Taunting notes, hand-printed and/or cut-and-pasted and typed, sent to press and police. Extremely sadistic in nature, with threats of additional harm to specific named victims, and/or children and the community in general. Includes cryptograms, puns, and "word games" in his public messages.

8. Places taunting telephone calls to press and police after the crime is committed. Written taunts continue for decades.

9. Suspect's taunting communications indicative of a suspect of high intelligence and reveal he possesses extensive knowledge of

PART FIVE

DR. GEORGE HILL HODEL'S SIGNATURE: MURDER AS A FINE ART

Chapter Twenty

I'd say yes, but facts say maybe.
Charlie Chan, *Charlie Chan*
at Treasure Island

I felt confident at this point that the circumstantial case linking Dr. George Hodel to Zodiac was strong. The facts and signatures were overwhelming. But I had to probe deeper and try to establish motive. Because I wanted to understand better how my father's sick mind worked and what compelled him to kill.

I knew that the only way to accomplish that was to get inside his head. It's something I'd trained myself to do over decades of working the Hollywood beat as a homicide detective. As I tracked down suspects, I'd learned to think like a wife beater, a street pimp, a jealous boyfriend, a hype in withdrawal from heroin in need of a fix.

But this wasn't just another suspect. It was my father—the man who gave me life—who claimed to love me and called me his favorite son.

On the surface, Dr. George Hodel lived a storybook life. Successful Hollywood doctor, friend to the rich and famous, beautiful and talented wife, architecturally significant house, lovely children. But something monstrously bitter lurked beneath the surface. It's what compelled him to commit incest with his fourteen-year-old daughter and savagely butcher Elizabeth Short.

Who was this monster that he kept largely hidden? This murderous Mr. Hyde behind his Dr. Jekyll public face? Why did it peek out when it did? How did it operate within his persona? How could the erudite doctor justify the monster living inside him?

We know that as both the Black Dahlia Avenger and Zodiac, my father offered to turn himself in to authorities, but never did. That suggests that on some level he was aware of the terrible crimes he had committed. Yet he was able to live with himself. To kill by night and function as a sophisticated international businessman by day. How?

These were the questions that kept me up at night. The answers, I knew, lay in the intricately layered and terrifying mind of Dr. George Hodel. That's where I needed to go.

I felt like I had no choice. I owed it to myself, my family, the victims, and the hundreds of other people my father had hurt.

To accomplish this, I relied on an investigative technique that identified the points of similarity between what was known about a suspect's life, body of knowledge, and interests and compared it to the evidence the killer left behind. The result was something that I called a "thoughtprint"—a unique mental paradigm pieced together from an individual's known thoughts, beliefs, and actions.

In a textbook by Dr. Richard H. Walton, *Cold Case Homicides: Practical Investigative Techniques,* I described thoughtprints this way:

> While our actions may appear simple, routine and automatic, they really are not. Behind and within each of our thoughts is an aim, an intent, a motive. The motive within each thought is unique. In all our actions, each of us leaves behind traces of our self. Like our fingerprints, these traces are identifiable.[19]

Using the large body of evidence left by Zodiac, the Black Dahlia Avenger, the Lipstick Killer in Chicago, and the Jigsaw Murderer in Manila, I started to delve. My initial focus was the mysterious Zodiac symbol and name.

Why a circle and cross? Why Zodiac's stated mission of collecting slaves for the afterlife? What did these mean to George Hodel?

Joe Barrett, an artist who knew my father well and rented a room in his house on Franklin Avenue in Hollywood during the late 1940s, once told me that my father had a photographic memory but was not creative. Original ideas did not spring from his consciousness, Joe said. Instead,

19 CRC Press, Taylor & Francis, 2006, 109.

my father was expert at absorbing information and ideas and restating them to appear as his own.

As I've said before, my father exuded an air of self-importance and was highly educated, well read, and culturally sophisticated. His formal

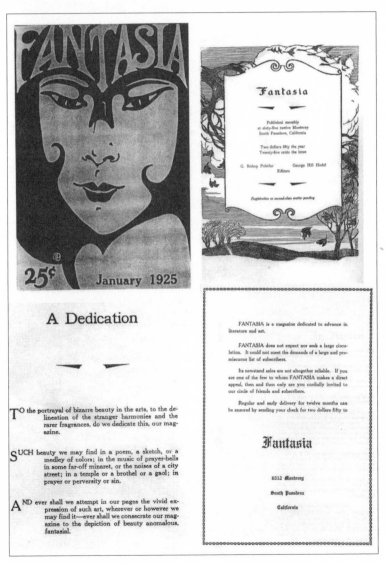

20.1

education lasted twenty-two years and was complemented by an abiding interest in music, literature, and film. Especially film. Dad loved movies and was a devotee—a cinephile. His tastes in film and literature leaned toward the intellectual, dark, and bizarre.

This penchant for the unusual was clearly expressed in the editorial statement of the debut issue of his literary magazine, *Fantasia*:

A Dedication
By George Hill Hodel, editor

To the portrayal of bizarre beauty in the arts, to the delineation of the stranger harmonies and the rarer fragrances, do we dedicate this, our magazine.

Such beauty we may find in a poem, a sketch, or a medley of colors; in the music of prayer-bells in some far-off minaret, or the noises of a city street; in a temple or a brothel or a gaol; in prayer or perversity or sin.

And ever shall we attempt in our pages the vivid expression of such art, wherever or however we may find it—ever shall we consecrate our magazine to the depiction of beauty anomalous, fantasial.

Seeing himself as a young surrealist, George cultivated friends who shared his interest in exploring fantasies having to do with forbidden sex and violence. One of these was film director John Huston, who started his career as a screenwriter and wrote the dialogue for Universal's 1932 adaptation of Poe's "Murders in the Rue Morgue." Huston's wife, Dorothy—who later married George and became my mother—while married to John also worked on movie scripts for Universal, MGM, and RKO.

In 1939, while dating my mother, George Hodel returned to UCSF's Parnassus campus to take a postgraduate course in the treatment of venereal disease. As a means of supplementing his income, he worked as attending physician at the San Francisco World's Fair on Treasure Island. Also known as the San Francisco Golden Gate Fair, it was an international exhibition that honored the building of the world's two largest suspension bridges, the Golden Gate Bridge and the Oakland Bay Bridge. Located on man-made Treasure Island, the fair featured architectural structures representing many of the world's countries. Most prominent was the Tower of the Sun, with a separate statue placed at each of its four cardinal points (north, south, east, and west), representing: science, agriculture, industry, and art.

I found out that soon after my father joined the fair's staff, attending to the medical needs of visiting tourists from around the world, 20th Century Fox began filming an installment of its popular Charlie Chan detective film series. This one was to be called *Charlie Chan at Treasure Island*. They used the fairground with its dramatic architecture and Pacific Ocean backdrops as a colorful on-site location. I have no doubt that as a film buff and astute observer, my father took a serious interest in a film being shot on location where he worked.

What did he learn? The movie *Charlie Chan at Treasure Island* opens aboard a China Clipper flight from Hawaii to San Francisco. As the famous private detective Charlie Chan (Sidney Toler) and his son, Jimmy Chan (Victor Sen), prepare to land, a flight attendant discovers that Chan's good friend and novelist Paul Essex has been found dead in his seat. Chan learns that during the flight, Essex received a radiogram message that read:

SIGN OF SCORPIO INDICATES
DISASTER IF ZODIAC OBLIGATIONS IGNORED.
UNSIGNED

Essex then dispatched the following in-flight radiogram to his wife:

CAN'T ESCAPE ZODIAC. GOOD-BYE MY LOVE.
PAUL

Chan concludes that Essex took his own life. The question is: why? And who is the mysterious Dr. Zodiac, and what is his connection to

Charlie Chan's good friend? As Charlie Chan ponders these questions, the world-famous detective flags down a Yellow Cab taxi to take him to the St. Francis Hotel.

The connections are too comprehensive to be coincidence. George Hodel as a young student in both Los Angeles and San Francisco was a taxicab driver for Yellow Cab. Zodiac preselected one of his victims to be a Yellow Cab taxi driver, Paul Stine, hailing him just outside the same St. Francis Hotel. Zodiac then ordered Stine to drive to a specific location, where he shot and killed him.

Back to the movie plot. When Chan gets in the cab, he's surprised to find two men already occupying the backseat. They order him to get in. Chan thinks he's being kidnapped, but soon discovers that the "thugs" are San Francisco Police detectives pulling a joke on him, on behalf of their chief.

The detectives tell Chan that Dr. Zodiac is a renowned San Francisco psychic and seer, who claims to have the ability to channel three-thousand-year-old Egyptian high priestesses from the Great Beyond. The master sleuth doesn't buy it.

Next the film introduces Peter Lewis (Douglas Fowley), a reporter for a local San Francisco newspaper, and the "Amazing Rhadini," a professional magician who is headlining a show at the Treasure Island Fair. He's played by a young, debonair Cesar Romero. Rhadini and reporter Lewis are united in their desire to expose Dr. Zodiac as a fraud.

To that end, Rhadini publicly challenges Dr. Zodiac to a showdown. Reporter Lewis writes the challenge and his paper headlines the story:

RHADINI CHALLENGES DR. ZODIAC TO TEST!
PSYCHIC TO WIN $5,000 IF MAGICIAN CANNOT EXPOSE DOCTOR'S CLAIM

Based on what he's heard about Dr. Zodiac's personality, Charlie Chan concludes:

Dr. Zodiac is a man of great ego. He enjoys using power to dominate lives of others.

In diagnosing Dr. Zodiac's psychological disorder, detective Chan describes him as suffering from "Pseudologia Fantastica." From a book in the film entitled *History of Psychiatry,* Chan reads the following definition:

> Pathological liars and swindlers suffer from exaggerated fantasy, unleashed vanity, and great ambition, which robs them of caution known to saner men.

One of the challenges facing Chan is revealing the conjurer's true identity. Dr. Zodiac keeps his face hidden behind a mask, turban, and beard.

One night Detective Chan decides to break into Dr. Zodiac's residence/office. He's joined at the last minute by reporter Lewis and magician Rhadini, who offer to help him search for clues.

Chan discovers a vault, which leads to a secret room that contains hundreds of files on Zodiac's clients. Inside the files are dark secrets about his clients' pasts. Chan learns that Zodiac has been blackmailing them. Four of his clients, including Chan's friend Paul Essex, have already committed suicide out of fear of being exposed.

In Zodiac's personal file on Essex, Chan finds Essex's secret:

PAUL ESSEX GETS 3 YEARS FOR SWINDLE

Determined to put an end to Zodiac's extortions, Chan removes the client files from the metal cabinets and stacks them on the floor with the following Chan-ism: "In humble opinion, suicide induced by blackmail is murder."

Then, striking a match, he sets the client files ablaze, and says, "We are destroying web of spider; now let us find spider."

And find him he does, by issuing a challenge in the San Francisco newspapers, to which Dr. Zodiac responds with a handwritten, anonymous note. In the closing scene, back at the World's Fair on Treasure Island, the truth is revealed. Detective Chan unmasks Dr. Zodiac as the man we least suspected: the Amazing Rhadini!

It seems to me that my father would have been fascinated by the filming of this movie, especially its themes of duplicity and hidden identity. The dark deeds of Rhadini/Dr. Zodiac, witnessed at close range during filming, must have appealed to him on a deep psychic level. Could this film have planted the seeds that grew into Zodiac's methods years later? Could it have inspired other behavior in my father's life?

During the course of my Black Dahlia investigation and as summarized in *Black Dahlia Avenger*, I learned from Joe Barrett that my father was involved in the extortion of his clients and patients. In addition to being the venereal disease control officer for all of Los Angeles County, Father owned and operated the First Street Clinic in downtown Los Angeles, where in the years before penicillin (pre-1945), call girls, cops, politicians, and people from the film world came to be treated for their indiscretions. DA surveillance captured George Hodel admitting to performing abortions—"lots of them." Clearly, he had the key to the skeleton closet of the rich and famous and would certainly use it if necessary.

Barrett revealed that during a conversation with my mother in 1949, prior to Father's arrest for incest, she said, "Yes, the clinic made for some interesting income." According to Joe Barrett, she was suggesting that George was using highly sensitive medical information about his patients as a form of blackmail or extortion, just like Dr. Zodiac.

My father often spoke knowingly of mysteries wrapped in enigmas. Is *Charlie Chan at Treasure Island* one of them? Did he draw his inspiration for the murderous Zodiac from the 1939 film?

I strongly suspected so. And as I probed further and found that he was influenced by other 1930s movies and popular stories, I became even more convinced.

Chapter Twenty-one

Only after the kill does man know the true ecstasy of
love.

Count Zaroff

I believe a fairly strong case has been made that George Hodel could well
have obtained his inspiration for the name Zodiac (as well as some of his
signature acts) from the 1939 film *Charlie Chan at Treasure Island*. Especially considering the fact that he was physically "on location" at Treasure Island the entire time it was being filmed in San Francisco Bay.

Let's stay with this premise and examine a second period film, the
1932 classic *The Most Dangerous Game*. That film was adapted from a
short story by the same name written by Richard Connell.

In 1924, the year it was first published, it won the prestigious O.Henry
Memorial Award for short fiction and was quickly recognized as a literary adventure classic and compared with the work of Jack London and
Rudyard Kipling. It was reprinted in the June 7, 1925, Sunday edition of
the *Los Angeles Times*, where it would have been seen and probably read
by hundreds of thousands of people, including George Hodel, who on
that same date was a young investigative crime reporter working across
town at the *Los Angeles Record,* one of the *Times*'s chief competitors.

The story revolves around two characters. The protagonist, Sanger
Rainsford, is a world-class big-game hunter from New York who, in the
opening pages, while returning from a power-yacht cruise in the Carib-
bean, accidentally falls overboard. He yells for help but isn't heard, and
saves himself by swimming toward the sound of gunshots echoing in
the distance. Though exhausted, he manages to swim ashore, and he
finds himself on a remote jungle island.

There, Rainsford finds .22 casings on the ground and shoe prints left
from a man's hunting boot. Through a clearing, he sees a palatial cha-
teau with pointed towers, perched on a high bluff overlooking the sea.

21.1 *Los Angeles Times,* June 7, 1925

Inside, Rainsford meets the lord of the manor and antagonist of the story, Count Zaroff. Zaroff, like Rainsford, is a highly skilled professional hunter. He's described this way in the text:

> Rainsford's first impression was that the man was singularly handsome; his second was that there was an original, almost bizarre quality about the general's face.

The cultured Zaroff provides Rainsford with clothing and shelter. After an elegant dinner, the men discuss their favorite pastime, hunting. Zaroff says that he's hunted everything, "grizzlies in your Rockies, crocodiles in the Ganges, rhinoceroses in East Africa . . . even jaguar in the Amazon." The sport now bores him, he says, because wild animals are no match for a hunter with his wits about him and a high-powered rifle. In desperation he's invented a new game.

Again, from the original story:

"I wanted the ideal animal to hunt," explained the general.

"So I said, 'What are the attributes of an ideal quarry?' And the answer was, of course, 'It must have courage, cunning, and, above all, it must be able to reason.'"

"But no animal can reason," objected Rainsford.

"My dear fellow," said the general, "there is one that can."

Later in the conversation, Zaroff offers his philosophy:

Life is for the strong, to be lived by the strong, and, if needs be, taken by the strong. The weak of the world were put here to give the strong pleasure.

Zaroff promises that if Rainsford can elude him in the jungle for three days, he'll grant him his freedom and safe passage from his island. The game begins.

In the closing scene, Rainsford, after eluding Zaroff and his rifle for nearly three days, is finally cornered on a ridge. With Zaroff and his dogs closing in, Rainsford jumps from the cliff into the sea, presumably to his death.

Zaroff looks down at the vast green-blue expanse, shrugs his shoulders, then takes a shot of brandy from a silver flask, lights a cigarette, and hums of few bars of *Madama Butterfly*.

With the game over, the madman returns to his castle, where he enjoys a sumptuous solitary dinner in the paneled dining hall, complete with "a bottle of Pol Roger and half a bottle of Chambertin," and finally "soothes himself by reading from the works of Marcus Aurelius."

Eight years later, in 1932, *The Most Dangerous Game* was made into a motion picture and released in the United States. In the Hollywood adaptation, the character of Eve Trowbridge (played by actress Fay Wray) was introduced to provide Rainsford with a love interest.

I have no doubt that by the end of 1932, George Hodel, an erudite, twenty-five-year-old medical student and part-time San Francisco newspaper columnist, had both read and seen *The Most Dangerous Game*. Its surreal, fatalistic theme was right up his alley.

The film version makes it clear from the get-go that Count Zaroff is a full-blown psychopath, who first psychologically tortures his guests and then ritualistically stalks them through the forest like animals.

After cornering his prey, the mad hunter slays them using his weapon of choice: a rifle, handgun, or bow and arrow. Then, he dresses down his kills and mounts their heads on the walls of his trophy room.

Strong sexual fetishes are presented the moment Rainsford approaches the castle. The movie still shown below left focuses the viewer's attention on the unusual doorknocker, which depicts a Minotaur-like demon with an arrow piercing his heart. In his arms he holds an unconscious woman. The still to the right shows Rainsford grasping hold of the female captive's supine body in order to announce himself.

21.2

A second, more ominous fetish is introduced when Rainsford climbs the stairway, escorted by Count Zaroff's mute manservant, and gazes at an unusual wall hanging. Woven into the tapestry is a Minotaur-like monster, half-man, half-beast, carrying an unconscious maiden through

21.3

the forest—suggesting a kidnap and the probable rape and murder of an innocent woman.

Zaroff forecasts Eve's fate in no uncertain terms by reciting a Russian proverb, "Hunt first the enemy then the woman." With lustful eyes focused directly on Eve, he says, "It is after the chase only that man revels."

Being a man who plays by the rules, Zaroff makes it clear that he will only have his way with Eve after he's tracked down and slain her mate.

The style of the 1932 film is surreal. The location, the sets, the characters are all otherworldly and bizarre. Danger and eroticism are omnipresent.

21.4 Salvador Dalí, 1936; Count Zaroff, 1932

In appearance, Count Zaroff strongly resembles the famous surrealist artist Salvador Dalí.

Salvador Dalí was born in Catalonia, Spain, in 1904 and was two years older than George Hodel. The photograph seen above (*Time* magazine, December 1936) was taken by Man Ray in Paris in 1929. Man Ray was a good friend to both Dalí and my parents, Dorothy and George Hodel. Simultaneous to the release of *The Most Dangerous Game,* Dalí's painting *The Persistence of Memory* (featuring his famous melting clocks) was shown at New York's Julien Levy Gallery. The following year, that same gallery opened Dalí's first one-man show. Art collectors and fans worldwide, which certainly included both Man Ray and George Hodel, formed a group to subsidize the Catalan artist. They named their organization *Zodiaque*—The Zodiac Group.

None of this would have been lost on young George Hodel— modernist, avant-garde intellectual, poet, and publisher of "bizarre beauty" and "stranger harmonies." My father was a devotee of the surrealist movement in art and literature and shared its goal "to spit in the eye of the world." Like them, he was attracted to the physical and psychological power of the Minotaur myth. He read and collected their official magazine, *Le Minotaure* (1933–39), named in homage to the half-man, half-beast.

In my opinion, *The Most Dangerous Game* is essentially a modern retelling of the ancient Greek myth. Count Zaroff represents the Minotaur; and his jungle island is the labyrinth. Rainsford stands in for Theseus. Stalked and hunted by the Minotaur, he must survive by his wits. In the film version of the story, Eve is the equivalent of Ariadne, daughter of King Minos, who falls in love with Theseus and is determined to help him escape.

21.5 **Theseus slaying the Minotaur**

In the final reel of the film, Theseus, as Rainsford, survives the leap into the ocean, slays the Minotaur (Zaroff), and gets the princess.

In real life, however, the story had a different ending. Dr. George Hodel cast himself in the role of Zaroff-Minotaur-Avenger. Throughout the 1940s, he stalked, played with, and eventually slew young maidens. As a macabre homage to his fellow surrealists he even went as far as to re-create Man Ray's 1933 photograph of the Minotaur (himself) using victim Elizabeth (Black Dahlia) Short's body as his subject in 1947.

But the Minotaur was neither captured nor slain. Instead, he discarded his Avenger persona and fled to a foreign land. After years of exile, the aging beast emerged from his island hideout and chose San Francisco and its Bay Area as his new killing labyrinth. There he resumed the hunt, tracking and murdering his prey and broadcasting the Minotaur's new identity to the public with the words: "This is the Zodiac speaking."

Zodiac's strange and unique "introduction" has taken on a special and very personal significance. During my childhood years (age five to eight) at the Franklin house while my brothers and I and our half-sister Tamar were playing in our "castle," Father would on occasion get on the intercom and in a loud, melodious voice announce, "This is God speaking . . ." This would be followed by specific orders such as, "Children, you all must be dressed and ready to go at five forty-five p.m. God will be taking you to hear Burl Ives sing at the Hollywood Bowl. Those not ready will be left behind." During his always-unexpected phone calls to me, even up until his death in 1999, my father would invariably begin his call with "Hello, Steven, this is your father speaking . . ." and follow with something like "I'm in town for just a day or two. I would like you to call your brothers and we can all meet at my hotel. . . ." After five years of Zodiac research my father's unique introduction has become a very personal and powerful thoughtprint.

In his mailings, Zodiac left what I believe were three separate references to his "most dangerous game." The first was pre-Zodiac and found in "the confession" mailed to Riverside police and the press on November 29, 1966. After recounting his murder of Cheri Jo Bates, he wrote:

I AM NOT SICK. I AM INSANE. BUT THAT WILL NOT STOP THE GAME.

On the five-month anniversary of the crime, April 30, 1967, the killer dispatched a sadistic hand-printed note to the victim's father signed with a simple "Z," which suggests that the Zodiac persona wasn't fully realized. Perhaps the killer was paying homage to another hunter and a stalker. A man who, like himself, knew the game and played it with precision: Zaroff, the Minotaur's alter ego.

The second reference to both the short story and the film arrived three years later, hidden in the Zodiac's three-part cryptogram mailed to San Francisco newspapers. Deciphered by the high-school teacher Donald Harden and his wife, the excerpted portion reads:

I LIKE KILLING PEOPLE BECAUSE IT IS SO MUCH FUN IT IS MORE FUN THAN KILLING WILD GAME IN THE FOREST BE-CAUSE MAN IS THE MOST **HONGERTUE** ANIMAL OF ALL TO KILL . . .

The third and final reference is found in Letter 19, mailed in 1971 and printed in the May 8, 1994, *San Francisco Chronicle* article "On the

Trail of the Zodiac, Part I," along with a cipher that remains unbroken. Zodiac wrote:

> I'LL DO IT TO BECAUSE I DONE IT 21 TIMES I CANT STOP BE-CAUSE EACH THAT I KILL MAKES IT WORSE AND I MUST KILL MORE MAN IS THE MOST PRIZED GAME ILL NEVER GIVE MY NAME BECAUSE YOU DONT UNDERSTAND NEXT TIME I WILL SEND A PATCH OF HUMAN SKIN IF **THEIR** IS SOME LEFT OVER.

Finally, there's the matter of Zodiac's costume and choice of weapons, especially in his September 27, 1969, Lake Berryessa assault on Bryan Hartnell and Cecelia Shepard. Most of the items worn and used by Zodiac are borrowed from either author Richard Connell's original story or the 1932 film adaptation. They include:

RKO 1932: *The Most Dangerous Game*

21.6 Leslie Banks "in uniform" as Count Zaroff with knife in sheath

All-black clothing, a long-bladed knife worn at his side in a sheath, hunting boots [only possible, as shoe print could also be foreign import], the use of .22 caliber weapon *and* a 9mm German Luger [used in the film version].

The only things missing were the executioner's hood and the cross and circle sewn or drawn on the chest. But George Hodel didn't have the luxury of owning a private island like Zaroff. He had to reinvent his labyrinth in the midst of modern society with its police watchdogs.

As the psychopath played out his mad fantasy, he hid behind masks and elaborate codes so as not to get caught. Unlike Zaroff, Dr. George Hodel was both hunter and hunted. In his October 5, 1970, postcard to the *Chronicle*, he boasted: "I'm crackproof."

It was all part of the game.

Chapter Twenty-two

A cryptogram is a piece of writing to which a meaning exists but is not immediately perceptible; its intelligibility is concealed, hence mysterious or occult.

William F. Friedman, *The Index of Coincidence and Its Application in Cryptography*

The Gold Bug

In addition to his love for fine art, my father was also a man of literature and letters, a true scholar with a voracious appetite for reading. He loved both poetry and prose.

One of his favorite authors was Edgar Allan Poe, the dark genius of American literature who died under mysterious circumstances in October 1849 at age forty. Poet, editor, literary critic, and inventor of detective fiction, Poe, like Zodiac, was obsessed with codes, cryptograms, puns, and hidden meanings. During his lifetime he was called "the most profound and skillful cryptographer who ever lived."

Poe claimed he could solve any cryptogram or cipher devised by the human mind, and published a challenge in several popular magazines, including *Alexander's Weekly Messenger* and *Graham's* magazine.

His interest in the subject is most notably represented in the 1843 short story "The Gold Bug," which I believe is the fictional blueprint for an elaborate game my father played with San Francisco Bay Area investigators 127 years later.

Poe's story written in 1843 is set on Sullivan's Island, near Charleston, South Carolina—a sliver of sea sand three miles long and a quarter mile wide.

There are only three characters. The narrator is an anonymous physician and friend of the protagonist, Mr. William Legrand. Legrand, a thinly disguised stand-in for Poe, is described as a once-wealthy man from an ancient Huguenot family, who "through a series of misfortunes was reduced to want."

Legrand lives in a small hut with an old black man named Jupiter. According to the story:

> His [Legrand's] chief amusements were gunning and fishing, or sauntering along the beach and through the myrtles, in quest of shells or entomological specimens; his collection of the latter might have been envied by a Swammerdamm.

Poe describes Legrand as well-educated and brilliant, but infected with misanthropy and subject to perverse moods of alternating enthusiasm and melancholy.

The plot centers around Legrand's discovery of a gold bug, a rare *scarabaeus*, in the island's sand. The *scarabaeus* in Legrand's estimation is not just a bug but a clue to real treasure. As he tells the narrator-physician, "Since fortune has thought fit to bestow it on me, I have only to use it properly, and I shall arrive at the [real] gold of which it is an index."

Both Jupiter and the physician believe that Legrand might have been bitten by the bug and is going insane. But he proves them wrong and, with the help of Jupiter and a piece of parchment that he uses to wrap the bug, finds a vast fortune of diamonds, rubies, emeralds, and gold buried on the island by the pirate Captain Kidd.

The narrator, now "dying with impatience for a solution to the riddle," asks Legrand to explain how he knew where to find the treasure. It all started by accident, Legrand says, when he held the piece of parchment in which he used to wrap the bug up to a candle. At first, the drawing of a skull appeared, then a goat.

He speculated that the goat might be some sort of pun or hieroglyphic signature for Captain Kidd, since a baby goat is a "kid" and according to local legend, Captain Kidd and his pirates had roamed the area and possibly even buried their valuable plunder. For more than a hundred years, people near and around Charleston had searched the coast for clues.

Then Legrand heats the ancient parchment further and holds it up to his friend. Magically, a series of symbols and notes appear in reddish ink midway between the skull and the goat:

"53‡‡†305))6*;4826)4‡.)4‡);806*;48†8
¶6o))85;1‡(;:‡*8†83(88)5*†;46(;88*96
?;8)‡(;485);5*†2:*‡(;4956*2(5*—4)8
¶8*;4069285);)6†8)4‡‡;1(‡9;48081;8:8‡
1;48†85;4)485†528806*81(‡9;48;(88;4
(‡?34;48)4‡;161;:188;‡?;"

22.1

Poe, through the character of William Legrand, goes on to explain in minute detail just how he deciphered the code using a secret alphabet he discovered by combining deductive reasoning with numeric probabilities. This is precisely how high school teacher Donald Harden and his wife, Bettye, broke the Zodiac cryptogram, which had mystified both military and civilian experts.

In Poe's story, the enigmatic message reads:

A good glass in the bishop's hostel in the devil's seat twenty-one degrees and thirteen minutes—northeast and by north—main branch seventh limb east side—shoot from the left eye of the death's-head—a bee-line from the tree through the shot fifty feet out.

Next, Legrand explains how he spent several days "making diligent inquiry, in the neighborhood of Sullivan's Island," which resulted in his discovering some historical references that, when pieced together, ultimately solved the riddle. In speaking to one of the oldest women on the island, he learned that the reference to "bishop's hostel" was actually a long-forgotten location, some four miles distant, near the northern tip of the island, once known as Bessop's Castle, which was neither a castle nor a tavern, but a high rock.

I made no doubt that here was the 'devil's-seat' alluded to in the MS., and now I seemed to grasp the full secret of the riddle.... Of course, the 'twenty-one degrees and thirteen minutes' could allude to nothing but elevation above the visible horizon, since the horizontal direction was clearly indicated by the words, 'northeast and by north.' This latter direction I at once established by means of a pocket-compass; then, pointing the glass as nearly at an angle of twenty-one degrees of elevation as I could do it by guess, I moved it cautiously up or down, until my attention was arrested by a circular rift or opening in the foliage.... Adjusting the focus of the telescope, I again looked, and now made it out to be a human skull.

Finally, Legrand recounts how he instructed Jupiter to climb the ancient tree to its seventh limb and pass the gold bug through the hol-

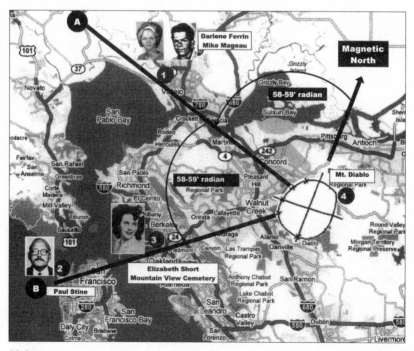

22.2

low eye of the skull so that it fell on the exact spot where Captain Kidd buried the treasure.

Now, let's fast-forward 125 years to San Francisco, California. Zodiac has recently shot and killed cabdriver Paul Stine and is threatening to bomb a school bus and shoot the children as they get off the bus. In separate letters he attaches clues like the aforementioned Phillips 66 map, and goes as far as to draw, mark, and highlight points along the arc of his now infamous cross-and-circle symbol. And what does he do? He instructs authorities to go to the apex of Mt. Diablo (Devil Mountain)—Poe in his story uses "the devil's seat"—and, with the help of a compass, find true north.

Zodiac says that by calculating radians and inches along the radians, we can discover the thing that he's buried. But in this case it's not pirates' gold and doubloons. Nor is it an actual bomb. As we've already discovered, it's a bombshell: his surreal masterpiece, Elizabeth Short.

Chapter Twenty-three

Nil sapientiae odiosius acumine nimio (Nothing is more hateful to wisdom than excessive cleverness.)

Edgar Allan Poe, "The Purloined Letter"

In 1983, I received an unusual call from my father. He and his fourth wife, June, were in San Francisco on business and wanted to know if I could join them for a few days and possibly drive them back to Los Angeles.

At the time I was a senior detective at Hollywood homicide and had just reached my twenty-year mark with the LAPD. Anxious to see my father and wanting to road test a new car, I accepted his invitation.

Soon after I arrived in San Francisco, my father announced, "I have a surprise." He went on to tell me about a hot-air-balloon trip he'd arranged for the following morning.

"A balloon trip?" I asked. To my knowledge, my father had never taken a hot-air-balloon trip before and had never expressed the slightest interest.

"Yes, a balloon trip. We have to leave the hotel at six a.m."

My father had always been a hard person to read. And he rarely, if ever, explained himself. For some reason he was excited about the upcoming trip.

The next morning greeted us with perfect weather. As we went aloft, the view from the balloon was spectacular.

For more than an hour my father, June, and I glided silently across the Napa/Sonoma valley. From our high vantage point we could see the entire Bay Area, with Vallejo and Mt. Diablo to the southeast and the Presidio and downtown San Francisco to the southwest.

I gazed down at the bay, the bridges, and the valley's patchwork-quilted wineries, then up at my father's very satisfied expression. Seeing how much he was enjoying himself pleased me, too.

More than two decades later, armed with the fuller knowledge of who my father was and how his mind worked, I now see the balloon trip for what it was. Not an unusual way for a father to share time with his son but rather a cat-and-mouse game and his private joke. The satisfaction I saw on his face that day was actually the gloating smile of a serial killer. My father was giving his son, the big-city homicide detective, a tour of his Zodiac killing fields!

According to the popular expression, a picture is worth a thousand words. The photo below of that day speaks them eloquently. I'm the one in the middle wearing the down vest and sunglasses. I appear proud to be with my father. My father's Japanese wife, June, stands smiling for the camera to my left, unaware of her husband's sinister agenda. My father looms to my right in an elegant tweed jacket with a handkerchief in the pocket, a fancy turtleneck sweater, and an expensive watch.

How would you describe his expression? The cat that ate the canary? Or, even better, the man who knows he's gotten away with murder?

Or maybe Zodiac saying to himself, "There, Steven, right in front of you, but you don't have the eyes to see it! I'm crackproof!"

23.1 **Author wearing sunglasses (center) between George and June Hodel,** circa 1983 (pilot and copilot unidentified)

Landgrowth

The 1983 balloon tour wasn't the first time my father had tried to involve me in his ruse. A decade earlier, in 1972, I was approaching my ten-year anniversary with the LAPD. In a few months, I would be halfway to my goal of retiring with 40 percent of my police pension, at the relatively young age of forty-one.

I would have been young enough to have begun a new career.

Knowing this, my father contacted me from Manila, where he had reinvented himself as an international marketing expert. He told me he was developing some "new and exciting opportunities" and needed someone he could trust to serve as president of a fledging company with responsibilities throughout Asia and the potential to make millions.

It sounded good. Divorced, with no children and few responsibilities, I took the bait and after obtaining special permission from the LAPD to take an extended vacation, I spent the next two months with my father traveling through Asia as he explained his vision for his new company.

Instead of joining his market-research company INRA-ASIA, he wanted me to take the helm of his new company, Landgrowth, and manage the sale of several hectares of vacation property in Tagaytay—a resort situated some thirty miles south of Manila, adjacent to an active volcano known as Lake Taal.

The offer was tempting. Exotic lands, beautiful women, a handsome living, and I could start at the top.

But my mind was flooded with second thoughts. First, I enjoyed working homicide and the challenge of solving crimes. And the prospect of early retirement was hard to pass up.

But my main concern was dear old Dad. Though I loved and respected him, I couldn't ignore his tremendous need to control and dominate. And I couldn't help noticing how he frequently kept visitors waiting two hours or more and constantly moved employees around like pieces on a chessboard. I passed.

Though disappointed, my father proceeded with his plan without me. Landgrowth was his baby, and he supervised everything, from formulating the entrepreneurial concept to writing the business plan and designing the letterheads and logo. Then he introduced the investment opportunities Landgrowth would offer to the public in a full-page ad (Figure 23.2).

23.2

The ad included a rather attractive company logo—a cross within a circle. Take a closer look.

My father had this variation of the Zodiac symbol printed on his stationery, envelopes, and business cards. It is as if Zodiac were saying, "There it is, right in front of you, but you don't have eyes to see it."

23.3

Consider the audacity: He was offering his son, the LAPD homicide cop, a job as president of Landgrowth Corporation, which had as its logo a variation of the symbol he used as the serial killer Zodiac who, at that very time, was mailing taunting notes to the SFPD.

INTRI-San Francisco

To give himself an added thrill, he publicly displayed his Zodiac logo a second time, seventeen years later.

In 1989, at age eighty-two, Dr. George Hodel decided that he needed a change. Most people would have kicked back and retired after a demanding life filled with exotic travel and eighteen-hour workdays.

Ever the entrepreneur, my father chose to relocate and work full-time in San Francisco. So, in 1990, George and June, then living in Hong Kong, packed their bags and moved to a thirty-eighth-floor condominium on Bush Street, in the heart of the downtown financial district.

After securing his business license and designing his logo, my father mailed me the particulars. He'd named his new company INTRI— International Travel Research Institute. Home office: 333 Bush Street West, Suite 3808, San Francisco, California.

No stretch of the imagination is needed here. This time the

23.4

megalomaniacal Dr. George Hodel had placed the Zodiac logo resting on top of the world.

I came across these logos in July 2005 as I was looking for samples of my father's handwriting. When I'd first seen them thirty-three years earlier, they had no meaning. Only after I was deeply immersed in the Degnan/Zodiac investigations and my father's pathological need to conceal clues as purloined signatures was I able to comprehend another of his inside jokes.

The Medicine Wheel

We'll probably never know what the cross with a circle emblem meant to my father. But I do think I know where he found it. Anthropologists refer to the symbol as the "sun cross" or "solar cross" and it appears in Asian, American, European, and Indian religious art from the dawn of history.

As mentioned in chapter 1, my father's first assignment as a doctor in 1936–37 was as a district public health officer, assigned to the Indian reservations in New Mexico and Arizona. He served as physician to the Hopi and Navajo tribes and established a friendship with Tom Dodge, chief of the Navajo Nation.

Later in his life, Dad regaled me with stories about his drinking bouts with the Native Americans and how he used to race his twelve-cylinder touring car up and down the deserted Arizona highways. During his stay in the Southwest, Dad accumulated an enormous collection of authentic Hopi Kachina dolls, which he proudly displayed at the Franklin house in Hollywood.

My mother told my brothers and me how she and my father were granted the special privilege of witnessing the secret tribal sun and rain dance rituals, as well as the creation of beautiful Navajo sand paintings. Featured at the center of most Navajo sand paintings is a medicine wheel (seen in Figure 23.6), which symbolizes the four movements or phases of a person's life—birth, childhood, adulthood, and death.

Back in 1937 when my father worked on the Navajo and Hopi reservations, he would have seen medicine wheels like the one shown in

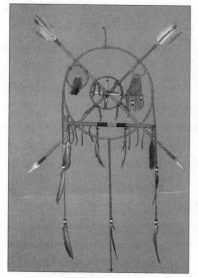 

23.5 and 23.6 **Navajo dream catcher and medicine wheel**

Figure 23.6 worn by tribal members to restore and protect their good health. In fact, he probably saw them countless times every day.

Given my father's lifelong fascination with dreams, I expect he was also familiar with the dream catcher seen in Figure 23.5. Dad, like his Dadaist contemporaries Man Ray, Marcel Duchamp, André Breton, Max Ernst, and others, believed in the efficacy of dreams. In the first Surrealist Manifesto, issued in 1924, the movement's spokesman, André Breton, placed the dream world at the center of their core beliefs:

> The mind of the man who dreams is fully satisfied by what happens to him. The agonizing question of possibility is no longer pertinent. Kill; fly faster, love to your heart's content. . . . I believe in the future resolution of these two states, dream and reality, which are seemingly so contradictory, into a kind of absolute reality, a *surreality,* if one may so speak.[20]

20 *Manifestos of Surrealism.* Ann Arbor: University of Michigan Press, 1972, pp. 13–14.

After his arrest for committing incest with his fourteen-year-old daughter in 1949, my father told LAPD detectives, "Everything is a dream to me, I believe someone is trying to hypnotize me. I want to consult my psychiatrist, but I don't trust him. He might find something wrong with me. If this is real and I am really here, then these other things [the incest, oral sex, and child molestation he had been accused of] must have happened." This statement is a powerful clue to his disassociation from the real world of emotion, love for others, and the pain that comes with unexpected death.

A Star Called "Dr. George Hill Hodel"

In our many talks during the final decade of his life (1990–99), my father dismissed astrology as quackery. In his opinion its only useful purpose was to pick the pockets of the gullible. The field that interested him was astronomy, especially as it related to Zuni and Hopi cultures.

In October 1998, seven months before his death, he diagnosed his own congestive heart disease. Shortly after his ninety-first birthday, knowing that his health was failing and fearing the real possibility of a major stroke that could leave him an invalid, he prepared to take his own life.

Still in possession of a valid medical license, he wrote out several prescriptions in his wife, June's, name for sleeping pills (barbiturates). After he'd accumulated enough pills to ensure a lethal dose, he wrote (in his block printing) "June Hodel conference notes," which were to be his final instructions.

But over the next several months, his strength rebounded. So he stashed the notes away in his desk, where they were found by June after his death.

Figure 23.7 is a copy of that note. Several   23.7

of his cryptic notations are relevant to this investigation. For example, the eighth line from the bottom reads:

LAST ACT OF LV DISP. ALL EFFECTS

Here my father is reminding himself to tell June that as a last act of love he wants her to dispose of all his personal effects. In what can be considered the most fateful ironies of all, she didn't carry this out. June didn't find my father's note until after she had given me his photo album of loved ones that contained the photograph of Elizabeth Short, which was one of the catalysts for my Black Dahlia Avenger investigation. What other "personal effects" did June also find and not show me?

The third line from the bottom reads:

L = CONC. ON EXCRETA

In a previous entry, my father had used "L" as an abbreviation for the word "life." In light of that, the phrase can be translated as, "Life is nothing but a concentration of excreta." Or, to be more profane, "Life is shit."

The most relevant notation is ten lines from the bottom:

RSRVD PL. IN CNST AQUILA

After my father's death, June explained that shortly after deciding to permanently relocate from Hong Kong to San Francisco in 1990, he had purchased a permanent memorial to himself in the heavens located in the 8-degree belt on the ecliptic known as Zodiac. In other words, he had bought a star and had it registered in his name.

The star—known as Dr. George Hill Hodel—can be found by pointing a telescope at the Zodiacal constellation Aquila (the eagle) and aligning the sight to RA (right ascension) 19hrs 56mins 53secs at declination 8'16 mins. The registration is placed in a vault in Switzerland and "is recorded in a book which will be registered in the copyright office of the United States of America." This practice is not recognized in the scientific community, but is more like buying a plot of land on the moon. Nevertheless, my father must have chuckled to himself at his private, heavenly memorial to his crimes.

It's another manifestation of his enormous ego, an immortal mocking of humanity fixed and registered in the Zodiac's constellation, Aquila.

Even after its namesake's death, star George Hill Hodel shines its sardonic, dark light on us, and will forever.

23.8 Constellation Aquila

Chapter Twenty-four

The next job I do I shall clip the ladys [sic] ears off and send to the police officers just for jolly. PS—They say I'm a doctor now. Ha-ha.

Jack the Ripper, 1888

After years of focused investigation, I've developed a better, albeit disturbing, understanding of my father. On the surface, he exuded supreme power and control. Every element of his public persona was carefully chosen to convey the highest sense of authority—from the cut of his expensive clothes to his carefully groomed appearance to his deeply modulated radio-announcer's voice.

Like Count Zaroff, he was a man of lofty tastes who reserved the best for himself—flying first class, marrying and bedding many beautiful women, drinking the finest wines, and sleeping in five-star hotels.

Tall, trim, and debonair, Father cut an impressive figure. People deferred to him, granting him license they would never confer on those they deemed lesser mortals. As part of his professional mystique and party-game repertoire, my father practiced hypnosis on beautiful young women. They always seemed to flutter around him like butterflies, attracted by his aura of authority.

In his worldview, humility was weakness. He reveled in the role of genius, doctor, surgeon, and man of science, and he believed he lived in a special realm, removed from the rabble. The rules of society didn't apply to him.

For example, my father never expressed the slightest remorse for schooling my half-sister Tamar to be his personal sex toy and introducing her to oral sex at the age of eleven. When he impregnated her at age fourteen, he urged her to see the pregnancy through and have their baby. He was upset with her when she refused.

This was a man who claimed the Marquis de Sade as one of his heroes. He believed as Sade did that, "It is only by enlarging the scope of one's tastes and one's fantasies, by sacrificing everything to pleasure, that that unfortunate individual called man, thrown despite himself into this sad world, can succeed in gathering a few roses."[21]

He agreed with Sade that "certain souls seem hard because they are capable of strong feelings, and they sometimes go to rather extreme lengths; their apparent unconcern and cruelty are but ways, known only to themselves, of feeling more strongly than others."[22]

My father used people, including his own children and wives, as if it were his right. His aversion to rules and convention attracted him to the philosophy of the surrealists that, in the words of founder André Breton, "proposed to express, either verbally, in writing, or by any other manner, the real functioning of thought in the absence of all control exercised by reason, outside of all aesthetic and moral preoccupation."

In other words, anything that interfered with one's desire to express oneself had to be pushed aside and squashed. My father took this revolutionary idea to its limits, unleashing sadistic urges that led to torture, bisection, and unthinkable murders.

He believed he was taking surrealism to a whole new level. He dared do what others only talked about. And thus was carrying out the bold design of another of his philosophical heroes, Thomas De Quincey.

De Quincey, like my father and Edgar Allan Poe, frequented opium dens as a young man. He's best remembered for the autobiographic *Confessions of an English Opium-Eater*, published in 1822. But it's a later essay of De Quincey's in *Blackwood's* magazine, entitled "MURDER, Considered as one of the Fine Arts," that seemed to have made the strongest impression on young George Hodel.

In it, De Quincey introduced his readers to the Society of Connoisseurs in Murder, who meet to critique homicides "as they would a picture, statue, or any other work of art."

With wit and irony, De Quincey wrote:

21 Marquis de Sade, "To Libertines," *Philosophy in the Bedroom*, 1795.
22 *Ibid.*

Design, gentlemen, grouping, light and shade, poetry, sentiment, are now deemed indispensable to attempts of this nature. Mr. Williams has exalted the ideal of murder to all of us; and to me, therefore, in particular, has deepened the arduousness of my task. Like Aeschylus or Milton in poetry, like Michael Angelo in painting, he has carried his art to a point of colossal sublimity; and as Mr. Wordsworth observes, has in a manner "created the taste by which he is to be enjoyed."

Eleven years later, *Blackwood's* readers were treated to a De Quincey story, "The Avenger," set in a small town in northern Germany. There, "with tiger passion," a madman commits a series of violent seemingly random murders for a full year and suddenly stops. Only at the end of the story do we learn the Avenger's identity and that he was acting with "the wrath of God." The murderer concludes:

Yet, if you complain of the bloodshed and the terror, think of the wrongs which created my rights; think of the sacrifice by which I gave a tenfold strength to those rights; think of the necessity for a dreadful concussion and shock to society....

In the 1940s, George Hodel announced himself to a terrified Southern California as a new manifestation of the Avenger—The Black Dahlia

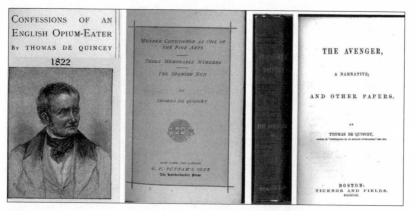

24.1

Avenger. In his notes to the press and police, he also explained his motives. Recall, for example:

> "Dahlia killing was justified."
> "Georgette Bauerdorf was Divine Retribution."

Two decades later following the Cheri Jo Bates murder, the Avenger continued to justify his vengeful wrath against those who had rejected him, this time signing his handwritten letters "Z." As mentioned earlier, he wrote:

> I LAY AWAKE NIGHTS THINKING ABOUT MY NEXT VICTIM. MAYBE SHE WILL BE THE BEAUTIFUL BLOND THAT BABYSITS NEAR THE LITTLE STORE AND WALKS DOWN THE DARK ALLEY EACH EVENING ABOUT SEVEN. OR MAYBE SHE WILL BE THE SHAPELY BLUE EYED **BROWNETT** THAT SAID NO WHEN I ASKED HER FOR A DATE IN HIGH SCHOOL. . . .
>
> BUT ONLY ONE THING WAS ON MY MIND. MAKING HER PAY FOR THE BRUSH OFFS THAT SHE HAD GIVEN ME DURING THE YEARS PRIOR. . . .
>
> BEWARE . . . I AM STALKING YOUR GIRLS NOW.
>
> BATES HAD TO DIE. THERE WILL BE MORE.

You see, my father didn't think of himself as a mere murderer. He considered himself an artist. And as an artist, he studied the history of his medium, and after determining the best practitioners, real and fictional, borrowed liberally from their techniques.

Perhaps his strongest influence was another serial killer known as Jack the Ripper. The number of crimes attributed to Jack, who is one of the most notorious murderers in history, vary from four to nine, depending on who is counting. All of his victims were believed to be prostitutes. He carried out his blood crimes in a tight geographical pattern in and around the Whitechapel district of London, between late August and early November 1888.

He strangled his victims and cut their throats. The victims' bodies were then mutilated and their organs removed (a kidney from one victim, and sexual organs from a second). Investigators at the time surmised that the suspect had some anatomical knowledge and probably was a doctor or surgeon.

Like his acolyte George Hodel, Jack mailed taunting postcards and letters (cursive, block-printed, and cut-and-paste) to the press and police, which appear to contain deliberate misspellings. In them, he threatened to expand his killing spree to include "men, and boys and girls." After slashing the throat of one prostitute, he mutilated her body, removed her kidney and uterus, then cut away a portion of her bloody apron and left it in a nearby doorway. Above it he wrote in chalk:

THE **JUWES** ARE THE MEN THAT WILL NOT BE **BLAAMED** FOR NOTHING.

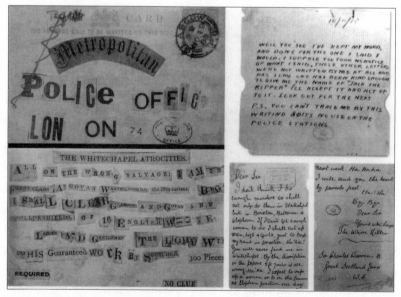

24.2 Jack the Ripper Letters/Postcards 1888

Below are excerpts from the original Ripper letters (with misspellings, and unusual and relevant words bolded):

"Dear Boss" letter sent to Central News Agency on September 27, 1888. . .[23]

You shall soon hear of me and my funny little games.

. . . Red ink is fit enough I hope ha-ha.

The next job I do I shall clip the **ladys** ears off and send to the police officers just for jolly.

PS—They say I'm a doctor now. Ha-ha.

Both Black Dahlia Avenger and Zodiac also used "ha ha" in their postings. Where the Ripper used red ink in 1888, George Hodel, the man of modern medicine, chose iodine to simulate blood and placed splotches of the red antiseptic on his 1944 Bauerdorf letter.

"From Hell" letter sent to press October 6, 1888

. . .

Sor

I send you half the **Kidne** I took from one woman and **prasarved** it for you **tother** piece I fried and ate it was very **nise**. I may send you the bloody **knif** that took it out if you only **wate** a **whil** longer

signed

Catch me when you can **Mishter** Lusk

The Black Dahlia Avenger essentially used the same taunt when he wrote, "We are going to Mexico City, Catch us if you can."

Letter sent to press on October 6, 1888

Now I **known** you know me and I see your little game, and I

---

23 On this same day eighty-one years later Dr. George Hodel as Zodiac savagely attacked Cecelia Shepard and Bryan Hartnell at Lake Berryessa *with a knife.*

mean to finish you and send your ears to your wife if you show this to the police or help them if you do I will finish you.

Yours truly Jack the Ripper

In the 1946 Degnan murder, George Hodel actually did what the Ripper threatened to do, mailing a man's severed human ear neatly wrapped inside a cardboard box to the Degnan residence and addressing it to Mrs. Degnan (the wife).

The "Whore Killer" Letter, sent October 6, 1888

Dear Sir

I don't think I do enough murders so shall not only do them in Whitechapel— . . . .

If I can't get enough women to do I shall cut up men, boys & girls, just to keep my hand in practice. Ha! Ha!

The Whore Killer

Zodiac had promised to shoot children as they exited a school bus. In his words, "pick off the kiddies as they come bouncing out."

Letter Undated

What fools the police are. I even give them the name of the street where I am living. Prince William Street.

The Black Dahlia Avenger and Zodiac notes are strikingly similar to Jack the Ripper's in terms of phraseology, tone, deliberate misspellings, and the use of cut-out letters.

Here are a few Avenger samples for comparison:

Here is Dahlia belongings.

Letter to Follow

Here is the photo of the werewolf killer. I saw him kill her. –A Friend

Zodiac also signed his 1974 SLA (Symbionese Liberation Army) letter "A Friend."

The person sending those other notes ought to be arrested for forgery. Ha Ha—BDA

Ask newsman at Fifth and Hill for Clue . . . BDA

We're going to Mexico City—catch us if you can

2K's

Some people develop their natural-born abilities to achieve greatness in music, science, and fine art. Dr. George Hodel used his cunning and intelligence to become a very successful and lethal serial killer. He created a hysterical terror from Manila to Chicago and left behind a legacy that includes not just one series of high-profile crimes, but at least three.

He did this by studying fictional and real criminal masterminds, including the infamous Jack the Ripper. He then planned his own crimes meticulously to outwit the police. He left his own unique signature by positioning his victims' bodies to create an intricate map of his ghastly work. As a self-proclaimed member of De Quincey's "Society of Connoisseurs in Murder," Dr. George Hodel elevated murder to a fine art.

Chapter Twenty-five

I hazard the guess that man will be ultimately known for a mere polity of multifarious, incongruous and independent denizens.

Dr. Jekyll

I'm neither a psychoanalyst nor a police profiler, and don't pretend to be either. But both as a veteran homicide detective and my father's son, I have a burning need to try to understand both my father's motives and pathology.

How do you explain a man who operated as a distinguished medical doctor and international businessman by day and a savage, vengeful killer by night?

The closest parallel I've found to my father's real-life story is author Robert Louis Stevenson's 1886 novella called *The Strange Case of Dr. Jekyll and Mr. Hyde.*

There's a reason that this story of a handsome, respectful London scientist who develops a potion that transforms him into a fiendish, lustful murderer has captivated readers and audiences for more than a hundred years. It's a brilliant dramatization of the pathology of a split personality and the good and evil sides of one man.

Like Dr. Jekyll, my father was a handsome, respectable man of science who had another, much more frightening side that murdered and bisected women, and seduced and impregnated his own teenage daughter. Women, including my mother, quickly fell in love with his "Dr. Jekyll" persona, but then soon discovered his "Mr. Hyde," which they loathed and feared. One evening when I was in my mid-teens, Mother, who was very intoxicated at the time, told me, "Your father pretends to be a doctor and a healer, but he's really insane. You don't know! He's a monster. Your father is a terrible man and he's done terrible things!"

Our twenty-first-century textbooks have a scientific term for this condition—Dissociative Identity Disorder (DID). The American Psychiatric Association's Diagnostic and Statistical Manual of Mental Disorders (DSM-IV) defines DID as a mental illness in which a single person displays multiple distinct identities or personalities, each with its own pattern of perceiving and interacting with the environment. According to the American Psychiatric Association, a diagnosis requires that at least two personalities routinely take control of the individual's behavior, with associated memory loss that goes beyond normal forgetfulness. These symptoms can't be caused by substance abuse or another medical condition.

My father meets all the above criteria. He did have at least two distinct identities, each with its own pattern of perceiving and interacting with the environment. And he did experience the dissociation known to accompany memory loss.

In fact, the one time he was caught, when he was arrested for incest in 1949, he told detectives, "these things must have happened," but the incident in his mind was "unclear, like a dream." He went on to say, "I can't figure out whether someone is hypnotizing me or I am hypnotizing someone."

I've always been struck by what seems to be a struggle between two sides of Zodiac's personality. The braggart and threatening murderer is given full voice in the early letters. But by the "little list," "Willow, Titwillow," Red Phantom, and the Belli letters, Zodiac seems to change. He becomes almost polite.

Another example of this is the "Badlands" letter (#23, from May 9, 1974). It is remarkable because it contains no spelling errors. Here Zodiac sounds like a cranky old gentleman writing a sarcastic letter to the editor. It reads:

Sir:

I would like to express my consternation concerning your poor taste & lack of sympathy for the public, as evidenced by your running of the ads for the movie Badlands, featuring the blurb—"In 1959 most people were killing time. Kit & Holly were killing people." In light of recent events, this kind of murder-glorification can only be deplorable at best (not that glorification of violence was ever justifiable). Why don't you show some concern for public sensibilities & cut the ad?

A citizen

Is this evidence that the more reasonable side of my father's mind had gained the upper hand? Perhaps.

Most compelling of all is the "Exorcist" letter (#21, from January 29, 1974) and its quote from *The Mikado*—"He plunged himself into the billowy wave and an echo rose from suicide's grave." It's the reference to suicide that I find remarkable. Is this an announcement of the impending disappearance of the Zodiac/High Executioner part of him beneath the "billowy wave" of his subconscious mind?

Maybe. Does it explain why Zodiac never struck again? I don't know.

What I do know is that most psychiatrists agree that Dissociative Identity Disorder often springs from early childhood physical, psychological, or sexual trauma. When a child is harmed by a trusted caregiver or parent, he or she sometimes splits off the awareness of and memory of that traumatic event in order to continue the relationship. These memories and feelings are then pushed into the child's subconscious, where they are experienced as a separate personality. Later in life dissociation becomes a coping mechanism for the individual when faced with further stressful situations.

Was my father a victim of incest? Does this explain why he trained his daughter Tamar to perform oral sex and got her pregnant at age fourteen? I don't know.

What I can repeat, however, is what my mother, Dorothy "Dorero" Hodel, often told me: "Your father absolutely hated his mother." As to the depth of his hatred and its cause, I can only sift through the clues and try to approximate the truth.

Certainly, my father left behind physical evidence that points to an active internal conflict. It pitted the powerful authority figure he presented in public against the emotionally arrested child demanding attention that comes through in some of his letters. In *Black Dahlia Avenger*, I pointed out his childish drawings and notes with their misspelled words that were mailed to the press and police.

Seething under the public persona of the forty-year-old doctor was an alter-personality of the childish man who wrote taunts such as, "We're going to Mexico City—catch us if you can" and "The person sending those other notes ought to be arrested for forgery! Ha Ha!"

Further evidence of the childish man within includes the arrow pointing to the photo of Armand Robles (in Figure 25.1), saying, "Next." And his stocking drawing over the face of Robles (in Figure 25.2) with: "Here is a picture of the werewolf killer's. I saw him kill her."

25.1

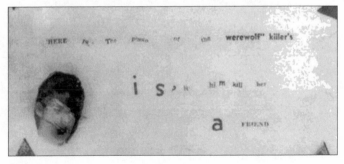

25.2

As a child, my father was highly pampered and tightly controlled by his mother, Esther, who before marrying my grandfather worked as a dentist in Paris. When George was five, his mother took him with her to France, where they resided together with Count and Countess Paul Troubetskoy for almost at year.

Throughout his childhood George Hodel was treated as a prodigy, studying piano, performing, and even having a separate residence built for him on his fifteenth birthday.

I never met my grandmother Esther. She died three years before I was born. According to my mother, when my father wanted to play baseball with his schoolmates after school, my grandmother would tell him, "No, Georgie, you're a pianist, not a baseball player, and you might hurt your hands."

25.3 Esther Lyov Hodel, circa 1912

25.4 George Hodel in Paris, circa 1912

Was he viewed as an intellectual freak by his classmates? Possibly. Was his child's spontaneity denied by his domineering mother? Sounds like it was. Did these denied feelings fester into something angrier and uglier locked inside his genius mind?

In my father's earlier biographical summary, I mentioned that as a sexually precocious teenager he had an affair with an older woman that resulted in the birth of his first child—a girl whom the mother named Folly.

For more than fifty years Folly's existence had been a whispered family rumor. My mother told me bits and pieces of the story when I was in my twenties: a vague reference to an early affair, which resulted in the birth of another Hodel, a half-sister, predating my father's acknowledged firstborn son, Duncan.

I broached the subject with him in the summer of 1997, when my father and June visited me in Bellingham, Washington, for a three-day tour of the San Juan Islands. One evening as the three of us sat watching the sun set, my father pointed out how time had seemed to pass so quickly now that he was just months away from his ninetieth birthday.

Seeing that he was uncharacteristically mellow, I asked, "Is it true, Father? Is there a Folly out there? A sister I've never met?"

As he paused, I could almost see him travel back in time. "The rumor is true," he answered. "I was very young, a boy of fifteen, and very much in love."

Then he filled in the details, telling me that while he was attending CalTech he had had an affair with a much older, married woman. Her husband discovered the infidelity and they separated. She moved to the East Coast and gave birth to the child, a girl whom she indeed christened Folly.

"I followed her east," my father continued, "found where she was living in a small town, and told her I wanted to marry her and raise the child. She wouldn't have it. She laughed at me and said, 'You're just a child yourself. Go away, George. This has all been a terrible mistake. Just go away from me. I never want to see you again.'"

Father said he remained on the East Coast and tried to convince his former lover that they should be together, but to no avail. Eventually he returned to Los Angeles and never again attempted to make contact with mother or daughter.

As a way of demonstrating the new computer software I'd recently purchased for searching and locating witnesses, I suggested we check to see if Folly was "in the system." He gave me the mother's last name and the name of the small town where she had been living seven decades earlier. I input the information and pressed Enter.

Incredibly, Folly's name popped up. Gazing at the screen in disbelief, my father turned pale. I suggested that maybe it was now time to make contact. In a firm voice that bordered on anger, he answered, "No! You must destroy this information. Destroy it now. She must never know. There must never be any contact. Do you understand?"

Those were the last words he ever spoke to me about his Folly.

Was this a possible trigger? Had he pursued his first love east and asked her to marry him only to be laughed at and rejected with those stinging words "you're just a child yourself"?

Did his hatred of women begin there? Would all future women who dared reject him pay the price? Elizabeth Short violated his trust by going to Chicago and investigating the Degnan murder. As a result, he tracked her down and killed her brutally. Georgette Bauerdorf also rejected him and was murdered.

Twenty years later, most of Zodiac's victims were teenage lovers in or just out of high school. Cheri Jo Bates was just eighteen, Betty Lou Jensen sixteen, David Faraday seventeen, Darlene Ferrin twenty-two, Michael Mageau nineteen, Bryan Hartnell twenty, and Cecelia Shepard twenty-two. Had young George Hodel, the intellectually superior but emotionally immature fourteen-year-old high-school senior, suffered other rejections in his socially awkward attempts at dating? In his Cheri Jo Bates confession letter, he referenced "the shapely blue eyed brownett that said no when I asked her for a date in high school" and threatened to kill more.

Are these the "blighted affections" he was referring to when he quoted from *The Mikado*? His rejection by women seems to have touched a deep-seated sense of inferiority that triggered a murderous, blinding rage personified by a variation of Mr. Hyde. The results were pure evil visited on the innocent, injuring and disrupting hundreds of lives.

In the Zodiac letters, he cast himself alternately as Ko-Ko the Lord

High Executioner and the tom-tit—the little sparrowlike songbird that threatens to commit suicide. The latter association is particularly interesting in light of a letter my father sent me in June 1980.

Five months earlier, I had mailed a highly personal letter to my father in the Philippines, in which I shared reflections in many areas of my life, including my deep love and respect for him despite the years of separation. I enclosed an article from the *Hollywood Independent* that said my partner, Rick Papke, and I had been chosen to receive the Inspector Clouseau Award for solving the murder of veteran film actor Charles Wagenheim.

Roughly four months later, I received the following very personal reply. It was by turns sad, cruel, tender, and fatalistic, and the clearest peek I know of into my father's complex, bifurcated mind.

Dr. George Hill Hodel

June 4, 1980

Dear Steve:

It was good to get your last letter, with its long perspectives. To communicate is such a mysterious process, at any level. And to truly communicate is rare. I am glad that you made the effort and that you succeeded. That you succeeded in beginning to make a breakthrough. One of these days, if time permits, let's try together, to push through further.

It is not easy to explain what I mean. But let me give you an example. A parable. But a true example. When you visit here in Manila again I'll show you the birds, and the glass, and the watchers (we), and we can try together to unlock the secrets of the three. Or is it four?

Safely hidden away from harm, in the overhead roof rafters of my penthouse in the Excelsior, are a tribe of small birds. Perhaps they are sparrows, house sparrows. They build their nests there, slip between the curves of the galvanized roofing into their separate havens, mate there, and raise their young.

Each season a generation of brave new little birds squeeze out through the curves of the roofing, and survey their cosmos. They practice hopping about, and pecking at each other, and winging along the balcony. They even discover a tiny swing which I have put up for them (birds love to play, you know) and they jump from the window frames to the metal swing, push back and forward, and hop back delightedly to their take-off place.

And then, somewhere along the line, and usually pretty soon, they make a discovery. A discovery based on advanced technology. A discovery which is totally incomprehensible, but which fills them with joy, and hope, and high excitement.

In Manila, as you may remember, my penthouse apartment faces out toward the west, onto Manila Bay. All through the afternoon, and until the sun sets behind the mountains of Bataan and the island of Corregidor, the sun's rays beat relentlessly on the glass west wall of my apartment. Air conditioners find it hard to compete with this heavenly barrage.

Therefore, in self-defense, we put up synthetic plastic coating— a mirror film—on all the western windows, to reflect the sun's rays and help to cool the rooms. It works quite well, and cuts down on heat and glare. Through the glass, we look out on the bay and the mountains and the sunset with slightly bluishly tinted glasses. And they look fine; they look all the better for this bit of blueness.

But to anyone on the outside (and we come back now to our brave young sparrows) the plastic-coated glass is a mirror. It is meant to be a mirror so as to turn away light and heat. It was not designed to deceive little birds. But they are deceived, and aroused, and delighted.

What do they see in the tinted mirror? They see beautiful young birds, amazingly like themselves, hopping about like they do, and full of life, and curiosity. Above all else, our little sparrows yearn to join their companions, and to sport with them, fly with them, even mate with them and continue their flight through eternities of love and time.

But there is a barrier to all these hopes. They do not know and cannot believe that the barrier, the wall of glass, can never be surmounted. There must be a way, they say, to break through somehow, into this paradise of beautiful young birds who await them, who tempt them, and who respond dancer-like to their every movement. How to enter this paradise which is right here, right at hand? How, they ask? Surely there must be a way, if they only persist. Surely they will somehow prevail, they say. Paradise will be theirs. Paradise awaits the brave, the strong, the pure in heart, they say.

And so, for hours on end, our little birds dash against the silent glass. Foray after foray, swooping from a vantage point (the Chinese lanterns near the roof) the little birds strike against the glass. The braver and more patient ones may go on all day, in their assault. The tinted glass is flecked with a thousand marks where little beaks have crashed against it, hour after hour after hour.

And then there is the third partner in this mystery. Ourselves. The tireless birds, the silent glass, and we. We stand wonderingly behind the glass, and contemplate the battle. We are like the gods, watching all and knowing all, knowing that the battle is foreordained. But how can we communicate our knowledge to the brave battalions of the birds? How can we warn them, console them? Send them off on other more hopeful missions?

Sadly, as we contemplate the glass and the determined little birds, we must settle with the truth. And the truth is that we cannot warn them, cannot tell them, and can only feel for them, and love them for their courage.

But are there only three of us? The birds, the glass, and we? Or is there a fourth? Who is standing behind our glass, invisible to us, incommunicable to us, gravely watching our brave attacks against the walls we cannot see? Is there a fifth presence, watching all the others? And a sixth, and others, hidden in mysteries beyond our dreams?

When you visit in Manila, I'll show the countless marks on the glass to you and to Dorero and Marsha, Michael Sean, and Matthew. If you come at the right season, you'll see the brave little birds themselves, and their efforts to break-through.

There are other ways, too, in which life's secrets are shadowed forth. Have you ever watched the insect who flies back and forth in the jetliner, seeking a tiny crumb, or wanting out? How can I inform him that he is flying from Amsterdam to Tokyo, and that his life is joined with the lives of us who see beyond the crumb. But not too far beyond. We know as little about our real voyage as the insect knows about the trans-polar flight.

It is good to know that you love me, for this is not easy to achieve, for you, for many reasons. Some of the reasons you have stated, and it is fine that you are able to begin to understand and overcome them. Some of the other reasons, for our love, may be harder to understand, for they may be shrouded in mysteries, like those of the birds and the glass.

I too love you, and this is easier, because you are the very by-product and testimonial of my love. There is an old Irish saying that "Ah, I knew you me boy, when you were only a gleam in your father's eye".

It is also easy (indeed, it is mandatory) for me to love you because I remember things that you do not. I remember the happy, well-controlled, serious, beautiful little boy whom we loved so much. And now love equally, but differently. Only a little difference.

I am enclosing a check for Dorero~ for the six-month period from July through December. Wish it could be more. Try to find ways to give to her—a bit of money, a bit of time, and love, much love. Remember—it was she who responded to the gleam. If she had not . . .

Dorero asked me to send her another enlargement (I brought one to her before in 1974) of her wonderful photo by Man Ray. I have had this copied, and will send it soon. If you want a print, I'll make one for you too. And for Mike and Kelv, if they do not have them and want them.

Congratulations on your work in the case of Charles Wagenheim and Stephanie Boone. There must be an enigma inside a mystery there, too.

Hope to be out your way one of these days soon. I am interested to know what you plan to do after three years. Your life may just be beginning then.

Give my love to all!

Always,

DAD

Conclusion

I relished the opportunity to work on the Zodiac case. . . .
I know that DNA technology will make the case progress
further if it is applied.

Homicide Inspector Michael Maloney,
San Francisco Police Department

In 2001, forensic psychiatrist Dr. Michael Stone of Columbia University developed a depravity scale from 1 to 22 to help courts rank heinous, atrocious, and cruel behavior. Category 1 includes those who kill in self-defense. At the bottom of the scale, Category 22 is reserved for the "most evil"—psychopathic torturer-murderers with torture as their primary motive.

In September 2007, on the Discovery Channel's program entitled *Most Evil*, Dr. Stone ranked my father, Dr. George Hodel, in Category 22.

I'm not surprised.

The Second Commandment handed down by Moses says, in part: "for I the Lord thou God am a jealous God, and visit the sins of the fathers upon the children unto the third and fourth generation." Even though I didn't grow up with my father past the age of eight, which is when he fled the United States, his sins weigh heavily on me.

As those of you who have read *Black Dahlia Avenger* know, I stumbled on the investigation into my father's criminal past by accident. Although it's been painful to learn what I have about the father I loved, I accept my fate. Perhaps he knew all along that my journey into his criminal past was preordained.

I sincerely hope that my investigation brings some closure to the friends and families of Suzanne Degnan, Josephine Alice Ross, Frances Brown, Cheri Jo Bates, Betty Jensen, David Faraday, Darlene Ferrin, Cecelia Shepard, Paul Stine, and Lucila Lalu y Tolentino. I also would like to bring peace of mind to survivors Michael Mageau, Bryan Hartnell, and the hundreds of policemen and investigators from Riverside, Vallejo, Napa, and San Francisco who spent hundreds of hours trying to discover the identity of Zodiac.

For the past five years I've been haunted by the fact that an innocent man named William Heirens is serving time for my father's crime. We can't give Bill Heirens back the sixty-some years of his life that he's spent behind bars. Zealous Chicago investigators and prosecutors took that away long ago. But we can grant him his freedom and help restore his reputation.

As a man who has dedicated his life to criminal investigation, I can't ignore the facts. In my opinion, the trail of evidence leads to one conclusion: My father, Dr. George Hodel, didn't stop killing women when he left Los Angeles in 1950. He reinvented himself as "Z" and, later, Zodiac, and extended his savage legacy into the San Francisco Bay Area and as far away as Manila. Prior to his reign of terror as the Black Dahlia Avenger, he murdered two women in Chicago and tortured and bisected a six-year-old girl.

I'm now convinced that it was Elizabeth Short's inquiries into the sensational Suzanne Degnan murder that got her killed. I'm also convinced that my father meant to dump Elizabeth's body on Degnan Boulevard, not Norton Street. And I believe that the pattern of dumping bodies on street names referring to other crimes is the signature link left by my father in Chicago, Los Angeles, Manila, and San Francisco.

His injured, needy, childish side needed to gloat. And in doing so, he left clues—like the fact that Elizabeth Short's gravesite lies on the radian provided on the Phillips 66 map sent by Zodiac. Had the SFPD ever seriously considered my father as a suspect, I believe he would have been caught.

They were looking for a younger man, not a sixty-two-year-old international marketing executive who traveled to San Francisco several times a year on business. And their Los Angeles–area counterparts, the LAPD, didn't do them any favors by expunging my father's name from their files.

As a homicide investigator who has been called upon to collect sufficient evidence to press formal charges and ultimately convince a jury,

I realize that the chain of evidence linking my father to Zodiac and the Chicago Lipstick murders is largely circumstantial. But as was found in the case of the Black Dahlia investigation, I believe that detectives possess and are still holding forensic evidence that links Dr. Hodel to the Zodiac killings and possibly even to one or more of the sixty-year-old Chicago "Lipstick Killer" murders.

It is likely that if we ever find ironclad, conclusive proof of the identity of Zodiac, it will come from the process of matching DNA samples. In 2002, SFPD's crime lab processed and developed what they believe may be a partial DNA profile of Zodiac. It's been reported that they have four loci markers available for comparison. A complete human chromosome contains thirteen markers, and four markers are not enough to positively identify a suspect. Further, despite claims to the contrary, neither can this four-marker sample be used to positively exclude any suspect. Why? On the October 17, 2002, episode of *Primetime Live: The Hunt for the Zodiac Killer* on ABC, San Francisco criminalist Dr. Cydne Holt revealed the source of this DNA: "I found a partial DNA fingerprint from a male individual who at some time has had contact with the stamp." The stamp she's referring was attached to one of Zodiac's letters.

Dr. Holt couldn't say for certain that the DNA sample belonged to Zodiac. In fact, the sample could have been deposited from the sweat on the hands of the postman or an employee of the *San Francisco Chronicle* who touched it, or a SFPD print man who dusted the envelope or any one of the many detectives who handled the letter over the past thirty-three years.

It's also my understanding that since 2002 law-enforcement agencies in Riverside, Vallejo, Napa, and maybe even California's Department of Justice have developed their own separate Zodiac DNA profiles. I've also heard that none of these profiles match one another, which raises major concerns.

I'm confident my father's DNA can be obtained from a number of sources, including his shoes, the wristband of his watch, and other personal items he left with me. I'm also in possession of the envelope of a letter mailed by my father to me in 1971. Not only did my father place a

26.1 George Hodel letter mailed to author 12/2/1971

dozen stamps on it, potentially including his saliva, but there also appears to be a hair strand stuck under the Scotch tape used as a seal.

An even more intriguing source of both my father's and Zodiac's DNA could be the pair of black leather gloves that were recovered from Paul

26.2

Stine's cab in San Francisco. The following is the DOJ special report filed by investigators. I direct your attention to the last line under the heading "evidence" two-thirds of the way down.

SFPD detectives determined that the gloves did not belong to the victim, and believe they belonged to Zodiac. Thirteen days earlier Zodiac was described as wearing a pair of leather gloves when he stabbed Cecelia Sheppard to death at Lake Berryessa. That means there's a good reason to believe that SFPD is correct and the gloves belonged to Zodiac and were

```
              **********

Date:  October 11th, 1969 - Saturday
Time:  9:55 PM
Victim:  Paul Stine, Male Caucasian, 29 years (Yellow Cab driver)
Location:  Washington & Cherry Streets, San Francisco
Victim picked up suspect at Mason and Geary Streets, proceeded to
Washington and Cherry where suspect shot victim once behind right ear
at contact range.  Suspect took victim's wallet, taxi keys and tore a
portion from the back of his shirt.  Witnesses observed suspect wipe
inside of cab with a cloth, then walk nonchalantly away from the cab
toward the Presidio, an army installation.

Witnesses described suspect as Male Caucasian, 35-45 years, 5'10",
190 pounds, crew cut reddish blonde hair, eye glasses with plastic
frames, wearing parka type jacket, navy blue or black, dark baggy
trousers and paunchy stomach.

Weapon:  9mm semi-automatic, possibly new model Browning.  (Not same
         9mm as used in Vallejo Police Department case.)
Ammunition:  9mm Winchester Western

Evidence:

Two portions of victim's shirt (white with black stripe)
Handprinting
Latents
9mm bullet and casing
Black leather men's gloves size 7
Subsequent to the homicide the suspect mailed a series of post cards
and letters, two which contained a portion of the cab driver's shirt.

San Francisco Police Department case #696314

Investigating officers:  Inspectors William Armstrong & Dave Toschi
                         850 Bryant St. - 94103
                         Phone 415-553-1145

              **********
```

26.3

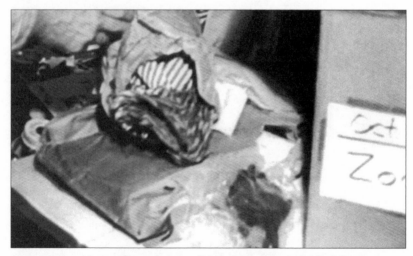

26.4 SFPD evidence photo showing Stine shirt and men's black leather gloves at the bottom of the frame in clear plastic evidence bag

left in the cab by mistake. Possibly they fell out of his pocket, or maybe he removed them before pulling the trigger.

I find the gloves to be an especially tantalizing piece of evidence. Why? Because my father regularly carried with him and frequently wore black leather gloves. I checked with a London glove expert and discovered that a man's size-7 glove is somewhat unusual. Unusual not because of the size, but because, in her words, "Size-seven gloves would be the type worn by a man with long, slender fingers—like those of a concert pianist." Pictured below is George with his characteristic pair of black leather gloves, his concert days long behind him, and his wife, June, captured on my home video recorder in November 1995, some four years before his death.

26.5 George and June Hodel, Rosario Retreat, Orcas Island, Washington, 1995

Are the Zodiac evidence gloves traceable? Possibly. Can DNA be obtained from inside the fingers of the gloves? I would assume so, because hands sweat. "Touch DNA" is now the state-of-the-art method of obtaining DNA on hard-to-examine surfaces.

I've reached the end of a very personal, difficult, and unexpected journey. Now that I present my findings to the public, this case will take on new life. The press will raise questions and demand answers. As with *Black Dahlia Avenger*, I expect new witnesses will come forward, new evidence will come to light, new links will be established.

And pressure will be put on law enforcement in California, Chicago, and Manila to be forthcoming. As an ex-cop myself, I understand their mind-set. I, too, have had to deal with annoying reporters prying into places they don't belong and the fact that some members of the public regard the police as "the enemy." I've seen the "circle the wagons" mentality that can develop and multijurisdictional feuds that sometimes arise when the klieg lights of publicity are turned on.

In the interest of honoring the victims of these crimes and their families, I hope that doesn't happen here.

From the law-enforcement point of view, the Zodiac case in particular has been complicated, immensely time-consuming, and frustrating. Some of the difficulty has been the result of different jurisdictions (Napa, Riverside, Solano, San Francisco) conducting their own investigations into what initially appeared to be separate crimes.

Since 1970 the California Department of Justice has assumed the role of coordinator of the Zodiac investigations by various local police and sheriff departments. That's why I suggest that California DOJ, headed by Attorney General Jerry Brown, conduct the follow-up investigation that results from this book.

Such a follow-up needn't be difficult or time-consuming. One or two state investigators will be required to collect the potential DNA evidence from Riverside, Napa, Solano, and San Francisco; ensure chain-of-custody on the samples; and compare them with one another. If the state forensic technicians find that any two samples match, we can be almost certain they represent Zodiac's DNA.

Once Zodiac's DNA is established, a comparison can be made with samples from Dr. George Hill Hodel in my possession. If they match, the case is *solved*. If not, the investigation goes on.

SFPD homicide inspector Michael Maloney, who was one of the last detectives actively assigned to Zodiac, died believing that DNA would one day solve the case. In an open letter to the public written in 2005, two years before his death, he said: "This case is so much about DNA that most police investigators' eyes would grow very large if given the chance and the means to work it."

I hope he's right.

As I end the current investigation and prepare for what's to come, I'm going to let my father have the last word. The following is a poem he wrote and published in his 1925 literary magazine *Fantasia* under the pseudonym Vernon Morel. Keep in mind as you read it that these are the earliest recorded words of the man who horrified Los Angeles in 1947 as the Black Dahlia Avenger, and may well be the same man who, two decades later, spread his evil through the San Francisco Bay Area as Zodiac.

Inference

I was conceived
In sin
On a mad night
Carnal
And incarnadin

Then was the incense rising
Poisonously
In the temple of Cybele curling
Dolorously
And in phantasmal wraiths writhing
Languorously

Then the night waned
Gloomily
And the thin spectral moon paled
Pallidly
And the lurid somber skies darkened
Dismally

And I was born

Image Acknowledgments

The author would like to gratefully acknowledge the kind assistance he has received from the following individuals: Librarian Pamela Quon and Curator Carolyn Cole of the Los Angeles Public Library. Brett Sharlow, The Criterion Collection/Janus Films. Also, my thanks to the Man Ray Trust, The Salvador Dalí, Gala-Salvador Dalí Foundation and the Artist Rights Society (ARS), New York.

Man Ray Trust/Artists Rights Society
Fig. 7.1 © 2009 Man Ray Trust/Artists Rights Society (ARS), NY/ADAGP, Paris Man Ray, *The Minotaur*

Salvador Dalí, Gala-Salvador Dalí Foundation
Fig. 17.2 © 2009 Salvador Dalí, Gala-Salvador Dalí Foundation/Artists Rights Society (ARS), New York, Salvador Dalí, *Persistence of Memory*

Time **Magazine**
Fig. 21.4 Cover edition, December 14, 1936

Criterion Collection/Janus Films
Fig. 21.2, 21.3, 21.6 Film stills, *The Most Dangerous Game*, RKO, 1932

Los Angeles Public Library
All LAPL images courtesy of the *Herald Examiner* Collection/Los Angeles Public Library
Fig. 2.5 Photograph of note "Want Terms"
Fig. 2.8 Photograph of note "Go Slow"
Fig. 2.9 Photograph of postcard from Avenger
Fig. 2.10 Photograph of two postcards from Avenger
Fig. 2.11 Photograph of envelope addressed to *Herald*
Fig. 2.12 Photograph of pasted envelope to *Herald*
Fig. 2.13 Photograph "Yes or No" letter to *Herald*
Fig. 2.14 Photograph pasted letters on sheet "a friend"
Fig. 2.15 Photograph of letter from Avenger
Fig. 15.14 Photograph of note "Werewolf Killer"
Fig. 25.1 Photograph of note "Black Dahlia"
Fig. 25.2 Photograph of note "Werewolf Killer"

Google Maps
Fig. 2.21, 4.4, 7.2, 8.4, 16.12, 18.7, 18.9

Author's Collection
Fig. 1.1–1.8, 2.1–2.4, 2.6, 2.7, 2.16–2.20, 2.22, 3.1–3.2, 4.1–4.3, 4.5–4.8, 5.1–5.3, 6.1–6.12, 7.1 (crime scene image), 7.3–7.5, 8.1–8.3, 9.1–9.7, 10.1–10.5, 11.1–11.8, 12.1–12.11, 13.1–13.10, 14.1–14.8, 15.1–15.13, 15.15–15.20, 16.1–16.11, 17.1, 17.3–17.5, 18.1–18.6, 18.8, 20.1, 21.1, 21.5, 22.1, 22.2, 23.1–23.8, 24.1, 24.2, 25.3, 25.4, 26.1–26.5

Every effort has been made to contact copyright holders, but if any have been inadvertently overlooked, the author would be happy to hear from them.

Bibliography

Borchard, Edwin M. *Convicting the Innocent.* Garden City, NY: Garden City Publishing Company, 1932.

Caen, Herb. *Herb Caen's Guide to San Francisco.* Garden City, NY: Doubleday & Company, 1957.

————. *Hills of San Francisco.* San Francisco: Chronicle Publishing Company, 1959.

Connell, Richard. *The Most Dangerous Game.* New York: Berkley Highland Books, 1957.

Conrad, Barnaby. *The World of Herb Caen.* San Francisco: Chronicle Books, 1997.

Davis, Howard. *The Zodiac Manson Connection.* Costa Mesa: Pen Power Publications, 1997.

deFord, Miriam Allen. *Murders Sane & Mad.* New York: Avon Books, 1965.

De Quincey, Thomas. *Murder Considered as One of the Fine Arts.* New York and London: 18__ (no date) (Nickerbocker Nuggets).

Dickensheet, Dean W. *Great Crimes of San Francisco.* New York: Ballantine Books, 1974.

Freeman, Lucy. *Before I Kill More . . .* New York: Crown Publishers Inc., 1955.

Graysmith, Robert. *Zodiac.* New York: Berkeley Books, 1987.

————. *Zodiac Unmasked.* New York: Berkeley Books, 2002.

Hodel, George Hill. *The New Far East: Seven Nations of Asia.* Hong Kong: Reader's Digest Far East, 1966.

Hodel, Steve. *Black Dahlia Avenger: A Genius for Murder.* New York: Arcade Publishers, 2003; HarperCollins 2004, 2006 rev.

Kelleher, Michael D. and David Van Nuys. *"This Is the Zodiac Speaking."* Westport, CT: Praeger Publisher, 2002.

Kennedy, Dolores. *William Heirens: His Day in Court.* Chicago: Bonus Books, 1999.

Krupp, Dr. E. C. *In Search of Ancient Astronomies.* New York: McGraw-Hill Book Company, 1978.

Penn, Gareth. *TIMES 17.* unknown city: Foxglove Press, 1987.

Poe, Edgar Allan. *Edgar Allan Poe Reader.* Philadelphia, IL: Running Press, 1993.

Reinhardt, Richard. *Treasure Island: San Francisco's Exposition Years.* San Francisco: Scrimshaw Press, 1973.

Richardson, James H. *For the Life of Me: Memoirs of a City Editor.* New York: G. P. Putnam's Sons, 1954.

Storm, Hyemeyohsts. *Seven Arrows.* New York: Ballantine Books, 1972.

Turvey, Brent. *Criminal Profiling: An Introduction to Behavioral Evidence Analysis.* San Diego: Academic Press, 1999.

Williamson, Ray A. *Living the Sky: The Cosmos of the American Indian.* Norman, OK: University of Oklahoma Press, 1987.

Miscellaneous:

Department of Justice, Zodiac Investigation: Case No. 1-15-311-F9-5861, 35 pages.

Department of Justice, Special Report: "Zodiac Homicides: Napa Co., San Francisco, Solano Co. Vallejo, Riverside," 10 pages.

F.B.I. FOIA Files on "Zodiac."

Los Angeles District Attorney, Bureau of Investigation: "Black Dahlia & Dr. George Hodel Files"; Electronic Surveillance Files on George Hodel.

Newspaper sources:

San Francisco Chronicle: 1969–1978
San Francisco Examiner: 1969–1970
Vallejo Times-Herald: 1969
Riverside Press-Enterprise: 1966–1971
Los Angeles Times: 1947–1972
Los Angeles Mirror: 1947
Los Angeles Herald-Express: 1947
Los Angeles Examiner: 1947
Chicago Daily Tribune: 1946–1947
The Manila Times: 1967

Magazine articles:

Front Page Detective, September 1975: "He Wants Slave Girls Waiting for Him in Paradise."
Detective Cases, April 1974: "Are They Closing In on Zodiac?"
Coronet, October 1973: "Is The Zodiac Killer Still at Large?"
True Detective, August 1971: "The Zodiac Killings—California's No. 1 Murder Mystery."
Argosy, September 1970: "Zodiac—California's Blood-Thirsty Phantom."
Startling Detective, March 1970: "Zodiac Casts a Stranger's Shadow."
Front Page Detective, February 1970: "Has the Zodiac Killer Trapped Himself?"
Inside Detective, January 1969: "Your Daughter May Be Next."
Real-Life Crimes, 1994, Vol. 5, Part 64: "The Zodiac Killer."
Real-Life Crimes, 1993, Vol. 3, Part 43: "Savage Rage of the 'Lipstick Killer.'"
National Geographic, January 1997, Vol. 151, No. 1: "Mystery of the Medicine Wheels."
Life Magazine, July 29, 1946: "The Case of William Heirens," page 30.
California Magazine, November 1981, "Portrait of the Artist as a Mass Murderer."

Film and video sources:

Charlie Chan at Treasure Island, 20th Century Fox, 1939
The Most Dangerous Game, RKO Pictures, 1932
American Justice: Who Is the Lipstick Killer?

Music sources:

The Mikado, Gilbert and Sullivan

Web sites:

Tom Voigt's www.Zodiackiller.com
Michael Butterfield's www.Zodiackillerfacts.com
Dr. Howard Davis's www.thezodiacmansonconnection.com

Acknowledgments

The investigation and writing of this second book has introduced me to many new friends. These individuals have enriched my life both personally and professionally, and a special few need to be acknowledged and thanked for their individual inspirations.

In Los Angeles:

First and foremost to be acknowledged is my friend and companion Roberta McCreary, who provided much of the vital field work and library research by day, and the encouragement, emotional support, and measured sanity by night.

Second is my good friend and collaborator, Ralph Pezzullo, who, fortunate for me, speaks fluent policese and knows how to translate "cop talk" into real English. Ralph's ability to restructure and organize my many scattered chapters into a coherent whole has been an absolute blessing.

Special thanks go to: my younger brother Kelvin and his wife, Sue, along with our Saturday morning breakfast moderator, Bob Alschuler. Also kudos to David Browning, Howard and Linda Sheldon, and my fellow cinephile, Steven Robinson Brigati, who passed over in 2005, may his soul R.I.P.

In Chicago, a true heroine and very special woman, author Dolores Kennedy (William Heirens: *His Day in Court*, Bonus Books Inc., 1991), who for decades has fought the good fight in her ongoing and untiring attempts to establish Bill Heirens's innocence. Also, Heirens's defense team, including Northwestern University professor and legal counselor Steve Drizen, and to all the unnamed heroes associated with the Innocence Project and their decades-old, against-all-odds, quixotic fight to try to help "Free Heirens."

In Bellingham, Washington, again my deep appreciation for the sound counsel, encouragement, and support from my friends and crack legal-eagles Dennis P. Murphy and Jill Bernstein.

In cyberspace, I would like to thank what I am calling the collective-detectives. A group-mind of "armchair detectives" from around the world that each individually contributed their time and focused thinking in an effort to try to help solve the Zodiac murders. Anonymous and known only by chat names like: Vallejo Dave, Johnny5, Greygost, Nachtsider, Dahlia, Vindog, and dozens more, their joint contributions as separate "message board" deductions, were critical in helping to piece together many of the splintered facts and mythstakes. Chief among those are Jake Wark and Tom Voigt, who maintain separate Zodiac Web sites. Tom's Web site (www.zodiackiller.com), which I refer to as Zodiac Central, has been the source for much of my investigative research, and his Zodiac online archive literally saved me hundreds of hours of what would have been old-fashioned gumshoeing.

Sincere thanks to my agent, Scott Miller at Trident Group, for finding the perfect fit with senior editor Ben Sevier at Dutton Books. Ben, a fellow Angeleno, with an impressive knowledge of true crime and an uncanny ability to separate the wheat from the chaff, made the harvesting process a pure delight.

Finally, my love to my two sons—Michael and Matthew. Know that you are my most cherished blessings.

Ralph Pezzullo would like to thank Steve; Scott Miller at Trident Media Group; Ben Sevier and Melissa Miller at Dutton; his wife, Jessica; and his children, John, Michael, Francesca, and Alessandra.

Index

NOTE: References in **bold** denote victims. These references relate to both the person and the case surrounding the crime. The generic use of "Hodel" refers to George Hill Hodel. Page numbers in *italics* denote photographs and illustrations.

About the Authors

Steve Hodel was born and brought up in Los Angeles. Now a private investigator, he spent almost twenty-four years with the LAPD, most of them as a homicide detective-supervisor. During his tenure, he worked on more than three hundred murder cases, and had one of the highest "solve rates" on the force. He currently resides in the Los Angeles area. His previous book, *Black Dahlia Avenger: A Genius for Murder,* published in 2003, became a *New York Times* bestseller. Visit his Web site at www.stevehodel.com.

Ralph Pezzullo is an award-winning author, playwright, screenwriter, and poet. His other books include the *New York Times* bestseller *Jawbreaker* with ex-CIA operative Gary Berntsen, *Plunging into Haiti* (winner of the 2006 Douglas Dillon Award for American Diplomacy), *At the Fall of Somoza*, and the novels *Eve Missing* and *The Walk-In*.